C.R.U.I.S.E

Can't Rest Until I've Sailed Everywhere

J. D Mo'orea

Copyright © 2018 by J. D Mo'orea

ISBN: 978-0-9872439-5-9

Cover photo by J. D Mo'orea

All rights reserved

Acknowledgments

In relation to this book, I simply want to thank each and every person that I met, while working on board some of the most luxurious cruise ships afloat. Whether it be a passenger, or a crew member, everyone that I met at sea, added something unique to my life and ultimately, this book. Just like a good movie, my life at sea had heroes, villains and extras; and I was the director. No matter how great or small your contribution, I thank you for inspiring me to share this journey with the world.

God Bless

J.D Moorea

(The author)

Table of Contents

Preface	6
Introduction	11
A Crash Course in Cruising	15
1. Welcome to Ship Life	28
2. Same - Same, But Different	53
3. The Ultimate Betrayal	97
4. Redemption	121
5. A New Beginning	154
6. Saga Saga Saga	193
7. Where to next?	216
8. A Couple of Random Stories	232
9. Conclusion	254

Preface

As a young child growing up on the Gold Coast of Australia, I lived a life surrounded by and fascinated with the ocean and boats. From about age three, I spent most of my weekends and school holidays, cruising around the beautiful waterways of the Gold Coast and Brisbane area, on one of my father's motor cruisers. Being the youngest child of a much older family, of which the other siblings had all grown up, I, along with Mum and Dad, spent most weekends on our boat.

While on the boat, I was left to entertain myself for the majority of the time. I remember thinking back then, how bored I was and wishing that my friends were with me, so I had someone to hang out with. What I didn't realize, was that all that time spent on the water, gave me an ingrained love, appreciation, and respect for the ocean and all its beauty. It also provided me with the "sea legs" that have, to this day, allowed me to only ever be sick at sea once; which I will explain later.

Because my father was older than most dads, kicking the football etc. weren't things we did together very often. We did however, fish, pump yabbies', set crab pots and tie knots for the boat. As I grew up, I often thought about how I didn't get to kick the ball often with dad and how

Preface

much I would have loved things to have been different. Only a few years ago though, I was sitting on my back deck preparing ropes and equipment for my own sixteen-foot boat, when it dawned on me. Even though dad may not have given me the things I thought I wanted as a child (in relation to sports), he did provide me with the unique knowledge, that I now use on most weekends, when I take my ski boat out and enjoy the water myself.

Those years growing up on the water with my parents, had planted a seed, that would later blossom into an insatiable desire to explore the ocean, far beyond the waters close to home. By the age of twenty-seven, I found myself longing to explore so much more, than what any episode of the Love Boat could show me.

Throughout my time at sea, the most common question people asked was: "How did you come to be working as an entertainer on a cruise ship?" Although most of the time I answer in a light, joking manner, occasionally, if they seemed truly interested; I would give them the following true story.

At age twenty-seven, I was working as a concierge at a five-star hotel on the Gold Coast for the world's largest hotel chain "Accor Hotels." I had worked at the hotel for seven years and had done almost every job the hotel had to offer; from waiter, bartender, pool bar manager, room service manager, to dish boy, and finally, concierge. After seven years in hospitality, I suddenly had an inexplicable urge to work on a cruise ship. I say "inexplicable" purely because the thought to make such a drastic career change, had not crossed my mind at any point up until then.

Besides working in hospitality, I was also a keen entertainer, and as a child, I had always wanted to be in a band, or be some sort of pop star. Throughout my teen years, I got involved with graffiti gangs, and as it turned out, we were much sought after to create murals all over the country, for various businesses. This not only allowed us to do what we loved, without breaking the law, but it also provided us with an endless supply of spray cans, to play with. We did murals for restaurants, clubs, and even famous touring rap artists, such as "Tone Loc."

Being a graffiti artist meant my mandatory participation in "rap culture," which included me rapping and being a DJ at every opportunity. I even worked on weekends as a DJ at a local nightclub at the age of sixteen. Back in those days, you could get away with being underage in clubs; but not anymore. When I was in my final year at high school, I chose to study music; even though I had not done so throughout high school at all. When it came time for the class to form a band for practical assessment, I suggested that I would be "The Rapper" of the group.

At this point, my teacher; Mr. Messer, came over to me and quietly spoke the words into my ear, that I will never forget. He said, "If you want to be a rapper, then why don't you fuck off to manual arts and build a DJ console?" I remember thinking to myself, *'fuck you',* but thought I'd be better off refraining from such a comment, as I already had a long list of detentions and punishments to my name. I didn't think much of his opinion anyway, so instead, I turned and said, "Okay, then, I'll be the singer." Looking back, that moment was probably the one that shaped my future more than any other, because my life changed direction immediately. I went from being a sports person, wanting to represent my country in cricket, to focusing on a completely different path.

The other band members and I set about learning and playing our first song for assessment, which was "Pride" by U2. We performed the song for Mr. Messer, and to my surprise, (and his too, I guess) he said to me afterwards, "You actually have a really nice voice. Why don't you audition for the school musical, Grease?" My reply to his comment was swift, "Musicals are for gays." "You get to kiss Justine." he rebutted. Justine was the hottest girl in school. She was blonde, had blue eyes, huge breasts (for any age, let alone sixteen), and she was an amazing singer. So, of course, I said yes.

> *I must make note, that I have many friends and close colleagues who are gay, so my comment about musicals being for gays, held no disrespect for anyone who is gay, but rather, given that the majority of male performers in the entertainment industry are gay, (or "flamboyant," as they call themselves), this was simply my perception at the age of sixteen; being totally naïve to the entertainment industry.*

Preface

At the time of being the star of Grease, I was still a virgin, so when the show finished, I was blown away, by the attention that I was receiving from girls, who had never previously given me the time of day, let alone wanted to shag me. In fact, when we went away on school camp the following Monday, my mate Kurt told me that two girls had a bet to see who could shag me first. A blonde and a brunette, were the candidates, so I had the ultimate choice. Needless to say, I didn't remain a virgin for very long. FYI: The brunette won. I soon discovered that singers get the girls, more than cricket players did (in 1990); especially if you're straight. In addition to my newfound attention from the girls, from that moment on, I also enjoyed a string of musicals, tribute shows, various concerts, and even performed as a support act for international touring artists such as Vanilla Ice.

Several years later, though, and after working in hospitality for so long and dating the wrong woman for six years, my dream of being an entertainer seemed to have died. One day, I saw a magazine in a doctor's surgery, that featured cruise ships and information about different cruise lines in it. As I read the contents of the magazine, a spark of curiosity started me thinking about cruise ship work, so I began to investigate how to get a job in the industry. Over the next few weeks, I spent hours on the internet (at a time when the internet was vastly different to today), researching cruise lines and looking for jobs. Page after page and day after day researching, had led to nothing. I could not find any information about where to audition, or where to send my resume or video show reel. Being in Australia made it even harder, because at the time, most of the cruise lines didn't travel outside of the USA or UK to audition. This meant that I had to find a way to get myself to them. I finally managed to find a website that had some information about the cruise lines, so I put together a package containing a video of me singing, along with some headshots.

I sent twenty copies off to twenty different cruise lines, to see if they wanted me. A few weeks had passed, and I received a package in the mail from one cruise line. I was so excited to receive the correspondence, but upon opening it, I realized it was simply my package being returned. I was mortified and so downtrodden. In the following week, I received package

C.R.U.I.S.E

after package, all returned from the cruise lines, and all with a similar letter accompanying them.

> "Dear Mr Mo'orea, Thank you for submitting your show reel for review with _____ cruises. This department does not handle auditions or recruitment for entertainers." (Or something to that affect).

This was so disheartening for two reasons. One, because I had wasted my money sending all those packages to the wrong people, and two, because they didn't actually tell me who I *should* send them to. Something that I learned many years later, was that all cruise lines cast for their ships in different ways. Some cast "in house," some cast externally, and others use a combination of both recruitment techniques. My dilemma was, that I had no idea who did what and where I needed to send my show reel to get a job.

Thankfully for entertainers these days, most cruise lines, travel all over the world to audition for singers and dancers. With the cruise industry being the fastest growing travel industry in the world, the cruise lines realize that the competition for good performers is intense. The cruise lines, advertise regularly on their websites and audition at least twice a year in the US, UK, Australia, New Zealand and Asia.

A few weeks after receiving my packages back, I had almost given up on the idea, when I was reading one of my company's magazines, in the staff canteen. In one article, it mentioned that the hotel chain owned boats that sailed on the Sydney Harbour, which had small shows on board. I contacted the lady who produced the shows on these small boats and arranged to audition for her a few weeks later. I recorded a demo video in my garage and auditioned in person for her as well. A few weeks later and after I had forgotten about it, she rang and offered me a job as a singer, on a ship in the UK. All hell broke loose as I scrambled to pack up my life and prepare to fly to the other side of the world.

I will leave this story there for the moment, as this is where the premise of this book begins.

Introduction

As I sit on the back deck of the world's largest cruise ship, taking in the myriad of things going on around me, I wonder how the hell the cruise ship industry had changed so much in the past two decades. When I first went to sea, cruise ships had one pool, one theatre and one restaurant. Phones were useless at sea and internet was non-existent. On this ship though, I was live video-streaming to my Facebook friends on my phone, with some of the fastest internet in the world, as I watched the ship sail away from Port Canaveral.

Five metres in front of me, sat two full-size flow-riders. Between them to the right, was the launching area for a zipline, which flew over more than one hundred balcony cabins, overlooking the Atlanta style "boardwalk" below. Past the zipline was a full-size sports court. To the right, beyond the other flow rider, was a nine-hole mini golf course and beyond the mini-golf and sports court, were two-story loft cabins. Two-story? WTF?

Behind me and six decks below, was the first aqua theatre at sea, in which performers dived from twenty-metre-high platforms, into a pool which had a retractable floor; turning it from a stage, into a pool, in less than thirty seconds. Oh, and I forgot to mention the full-size carousel, on the Boardwalk, which was hand carved and Johnny Rockets restaurant and cafés. This was just at the aft of the ship. I've not even started on the remainder of this mammoth floating beast.

I will elaborate more on this later in the book, but at this point of my December 2017 cruise, to say that I was in awe, was a huge understatement. As I sat with my iPad, contemplating what to write, questioning what was real, and searching for an explanation of how life had led me to being there, I remembered how blessed I was. In the preceding seventeen years, I had traveled the world, experienced the wonders of over 400 destinations and been paid to do what I loved doing; singing and travelling. I had gone from working on ships, to selling cruises, to just enjoying being a passenger on board, like everyone else.

Even after so many voyages, the thrill of walking up a ship's gangway, was still as awesome for me, as the very first time that I experienced that sensation.

As a professional entertainer, you become used to baring your soul and raw emotions to complete strangers, but to put it down on paper, for all to see, was a new experience for me. I can't say that I am in totally uncharted waters (pardon the pun), but nonetheless, this was more than challenging, and just a little bit daunting, to say the least. I've always been one to say what most people think, but are too afraid (or too smart) to say out loud, for fear of ridicule or condemnation.

My motto in life is that, "I'd rather be hated for my honesty, than loved for my lies." At this stage of my life, I use that as inspiration, as I pushed forward in the pursuit of a story that will surely entertain you, as much as it entertained me, throughout my time at sea.

Let me say, first and foremost, thank you for allowing me to share with you an insight into an industry that is not only the fastest growing travel industry in the world, but a way of life, that is so dear to my heart. In this book, I will take you deep inside the cruise ship industry and give you an inside look at the good, the bad, the funny, and the ugly parts, that are all unique to cruising. I will unveil life as it is on board these

Introduction

luxurious floating cities, which happen to be home to tens of thousands of men and women all around the world.

This book is not the *Love Boat*, or the *Titanic*, filled with romance and love. Well there is some, but it's not the main premise. I do however, give quite a detailed view of my own personal life while at sea, including intimate relationships, and maybe some sexual exploits. There is an old saying that goes, "A ship in the harbor is safe: but that is not what a ship is for." So, with that in mind, lets head out to sea and get covered in salt.

For me, life is not about being cautious. It's about living the life that I was destined to live and living it in the way that is right for me. It's about cramming as much as I can into the short amount of time that I have here on earth and treating every day, as if it could be my last. Sometimes, I stop, sit back and reminisce, about how much I have achieved in only forty-four years. Most people don't believe that someone could cram so much into life as I have. I'm by no means a world-beater. Just someone who has trouble sitting still.

Let me say from the outset, that the object of this book is not to defame, hurt, disgrace, insult, or upset any person, company, race, religion, or group. I am sure that all of those could very well occur, through the telling of this story; but it is not my intention. For anyone I met at sea, who has a problem with what is written in this book, may I suggest that perhaps you should have thought about your actions before partaking in them in the first place. This book is merely an honest recollection of events, witnessed during more than 2,000 days and 1,000,000 miles at sea, on board some of the most luxurious cruise ships afloat. It is a story of love, lust, betrayal, and lots of fun, frivolity, and debauchery along the way; with absolutely no regrets whatsoever.

The events in this book are all true and are being told exactly as they occurred. There is no fabrication (well not much) on my behalf, and at no stage will I portray myself as anything other than what I was during that time; despite strong legal advice from my lawyer. The names of some cruise lines, have been withheld (where possible), and crew member's names changed, to protect myself, from the not so innocent. While many people have been on a cruise ship at one time or another, very few have really "experienced" the true essence of what cruising is all about. To truly experience cruise ship life, you must live at sea for an extended period of time. I have been fortunate to have experienced so many wonderful moments at sea and to have met so many amazing people, from many walks of life. Not a day went by at sea, when I didn't give thanks, for everything I was experiencing at the time.

The idea for this book, came about after my second contract as a performer on a cruise ship. I have since completed several cruise ship contracts, and many more as a passenger or cruise agent. The cruise industry has given me, and many others, so many magical memories and it has opened my eyes to the world. It has taught me so much about life, love, and myself as a person. I hope this book opens your eyes too, as we take a look into this wonderful world that I simply adore.

My hope for you, is that after reading this book, you too will have an insatiable curiosity, that leads you out to sea to experience this largely unknown world.

So, sit back and relax as I take you on an incredible journey of love, lust, and betrayal.

"Let's C.R.U.I.S.E"

A Crash Course in Cruising

BEFORE ANYONE SETS foot on board a cruise ship as a crew member, they must have a valid passport, in many cases a C1/D visa for the USA, a Seafarers book, ENG1 Medical certificate, pass the SCTW Sea Survival course, first aid and advanced firefighting. They must also have any other relevant training for their position on board. All of this, is to ensure that no matter what is thrown at you at sea, you are fully prepared. After all, the crew are the only ones that can prevent an emergency at sea, from turning into a mass burial.

In January, 2012, the greatest cruise ship disaster, since the Titanic occurred, when the Costa Concordia cruise ship, ran aground off the coast of Italy. At the time, I read many comments on social media, by ill-informed journalists and the public, about how high the death toll was. Yes, any death at sea is too many, but I have to make this point very clear. If the crew on board the Costa Concordia, weren't as well trained as they were, the death toll would have been in the thousands; and not in the dozens, as it was.

The crew on that fateful night, off the coast of Italy, performed an incredible job, under the worst of circumstances. I am of course, not referring to the Captain, who was responsible for the crash, but rather, the rest of the crew on board. As it turned out, it was the entertainment team, that lead the way during this disaster. Even though the entertainers are usually the least trained on board, when it comes to an emergency, it was their confidence and ability to interact with passengers, that enabled them to calmly muster passengers, and get them onto lifeboats. This, along with the combined effort of all the crew, is what saved so many lives.

Imagine what it would be like, if your own life was at risk, on a sinking ship, that was listing at around 35 degrees. Instead of ensuring your own safety, you must put the lives of others, before your own. That is what the crew of the Concordia did, that night, despite probably being terrified themselves.

When you board all ships these days, before the ship casts its lines off, all passengers and crew much partake in the mandatory safety drill. This has been maritime law for many years, but it has become even more strict, since the Concordia disaster. The main reason that the Concordia didn't have a full safety drill that ill-fated day, was because they had already had a safety drill in their previous port, when the cruise began. Less than one-hundred passengers joined on the day of the accident, so it was not mandatory that another drill took place, until the following morning (For the new joiners).

Almost all passengers dislike having to attend drill and in most cases, the crew hate having to do them too. The difference is, that the crew know how important this exercise is, in ensuring the safety of all onboard. What passengers don't realize, is the level of ongoing training that crew do, to ensure that in the event of a disaster, the highest possible chance of survival, is available.

Next time you're on board a ship, take a look at your waiter, bar tender or cook. There is a very good chance, that in the case of a fire, that they one of the people, whose job it is to fight the fire. Your cabin steward, could be responsible for risking their own life, by checking all the cabins, to ensure that every passenger is safely out of their cabin. These people don't get picked at random for these tasks. There are designated and trained

A Crash Course in Cruising

thoroughly, so that in the case of an emergency, they are fully prepared to do their job.

This is why, while the media and some people focused on the lives lost, I was so full of praise, for the crew, who saved the lives of over 3,000 people on that fateful night in 2012; while only 32 soles perished. This is just the tip of the iceberg, (pardon the terrible maritime pun), when it comes to cruise ship life as a crew member. Therefore, it would be reckless of me, to allow you into the inner sanctum of the cruise ship world, without first offering you some sort of "cruise training."

To start with, let's look at some of the ship lingo, that I may use throughout the book.

Ship	A large vessel. (Don't call it a boat in front of the Captain)
Port	The left-hand side of the ship while facing forward.
Starboard	The left-hand side of the ship while facing backwards.
Bow	The front or "pointy end" of the ship.
Aft or Stern	The ass end of the ship.
Captain	The person whose ass, everyone on board must kiss.
Staff Captain	Second in charge. They only have to kiss the Captain's ass.
Chief Engineer	The person who drives the ship (The Captain doesn't drive).
Gangway	The means of getting on and off the ship.
Gangplank	Found on pirate ships; not cruise ships.
Crew bar	The only place that most crew members can drink or socialize.
Twirly	Derogatory term for dancers (They just twirl around, that's all).
Steiner	Salon girls, known for sleeping with several men on board.

C.R.U.I.S.E

Noro-virus	Possibly the worst illness you could catch; very contagious.
Snogged	Non-American term for kissing.
Chips 'n' Pie	Cockney slang for tits and pussy.
Puppies	Slim's favourite word for breasts (e.g., Nice puppies).
I-95 or M1	A hidden thoroughfare, that crew use on board.

Now that you've learnt the lingo, let's get started.

From the moment I set foot on board my first cruise ship, I knew that it was going to be like nothing I had ever experienced before. Almost instantly, I thought to myself, that it was a story and a way of life, that someone had to tell the world about. It was a world that you had to experience firsthand to believe that it existed. What I didn't realize at the time, was that the somebody who would tell that story; would be me.

Almost instantly, I realized that the world that you live in, inside a cruise ship, is more like being on another planet, rather than another city, or country. Simple things, such as days of the week and world events, vanish from your conscious mind, while morals and a sense of time, seem to morph into a way of life, that you have to live, to believe or understand. For example, when "9/11" was the focus of the world, we were sailing along, oblivious to the event that changed the world forever. It wasn't until several hours later, when we were close to land, that our phones all began going off, alerting us to the unfolding disaster. Not to mention, I didn't vote or even hear about any state or federal elections at home in Australia, for nearly ten years.

These days, cruise ships are far more connected than when I first went to sea. Back in those days, once you walked up the gangway, you really had no idea of what the rest of the world was doing, until you arrived in your next port. Trying to put into words what this bizarre existence is like, would be like trying to explain exactly how electricity works. Can you tell me exactly how electricity works? I can't, and this is the dilemma that I face, in trying to give you an exact explanation of the intricacies of cruising and what makes it such a different way of life.

A Crash Course in Cruising

Spend more than a month on board a cruise ship and I promise you, that you will begin referring to the days as "Bora Bora day" or "New York day" rather than Monday, Tuesday etc. What is even scarier, is when you begin referring to the days, by what day the menu rotation is up to, such as "Roast Beef day" or "Curry day." As for time, well, that seems to move at a pace that would make anyone question their own age, let alone how long they have been at sea. By that, I don't mean days go faster or slower. What I mean is that time seems to have a totally different way of existing.

To put it into understandable terms, let's compare it to the way we measure dog years, or the age of a dog in comparison to human years. For every year of a human life, they say that it equals seven dog years. So, in five human years, a dog would be thirty-five years old in dog years. Now let's take a similar equation and apply it to cruising, but instead of the formula being one equals seven, let's make it one equals three. For every month you spend on a cruise ship, it seems like three months. This is not to say that time moves slowly, or that time seems to drag on. What I'm saying, is that every emotion and feeling that you have, seems to be multiplied by three.

For example, if you're angry on a cruise ship, it seems to be three times more intense. A problem seems three times harder to deal with and likewise, if you're happy, or let's say in love, it also feels three times more special. Every emotion and every feeling, is multiplied beyond belief and certainly on a much more heightened level than on land. Why is this? Well, it is because of the "fishbowl effect" of being confided in such an environment, for a prolonged period.

Let's talk about intimate relationships at sea, for a moment. The funny thing about relationships on cruise ships, is that the rest of the crew know that you are dating someone, even before you're actually dating that person. How does this work? Well, it's quite simple. You may be sitting in the cabaret lounge of the ship, talking to someone of the opposite sex; or the same sex for those of you who are that way inclined. You could be having a drink together at one of the bars on board, when another crew member sees you together.

That person has dinner in the crew mess and sits with other crew members from their department and tell them, that they saw you having a drink with this person. At least three of those four or five people, go and tell another four or five people, that you were seen kissing. These fifteen or so people, each tell ten crew members that you were seen having sex in the spa at four in the morning and BINGO, you are now dating this person. It's as easy as that. And all this can occur in a matter of an hour. I've actually tried this out, by telling someone a rumour about who I was dating, and it got back to me within forty-five minutes; via fifty other crew members.

I've yet to find another situation in life, where you begin dating someone and find yourself seeing that person almost every minute of every day; instantly. Let's face it, you live together, work together, and in some cases, literally sleep together. You even eat at the same times in the same room. It is for this reason that *all* intimate relationships at sea, move *very* quickly.

Since retiring from cruise ships, I've struggled for some time with relationships. I found that I was still moving quickly, as per ship life, while the girl I was dating, who had never been at sea, was wondering why I was so full on. Often, they couldn't work out why I was in such a hurry to "get it on, get it up, get it in," and get to the altar, while they were only just planning where to have coffee, on our second date.

I've had many a girlfriend, well not that many, say to me since being back on land, that I move very quickly, or that I seem to be in a rush to make everything happen. I guess this is how I have been "wired" from being in this situation at sea, where relationships really do move so quickly. To me, it felt natural for a relationship to move so quickly, and I guess the upside of it, was that if they weren't the one for me, then it also ended quickly. That way, no one wasted too much of their time.

At sea, you find yourself spending so much time with the person you're dating, that you end up engaging in sex, before you even know their birth date, or their last name. Even worse, before you know it, the words "I love you" fly out of your mouth, without realizing that you've never actually been on a proper date with them, let alone, found out much more than their cabin number, or their favourite sexual position.

To the uninitiated at sea, there appears to be a serious lack of morals on

A Crash Course in Cruising

cruise ships. On the surface, cruise ships appear to be like a floating Las Vegas; and we all know the saying about what happens in Vegas. This lack of morals, is not because the people at sea are all raging nymphomaniacs or dirty whores. It is simply due to what I explained earlier regarding time and what I like to call the "fishbowl effect." This change of personal values when stepping on board, is also due in part, by the fantasy type ideals of cruise ships, created by many episodes of The Love Boat.

From the minute you set foot on board a cruise ship, you are being watched. Whether it be by one of the Filipino galley staff who barely see the light of day and therefore act like hungry hunting dogs at the sight of "fresh meat," or by many of the married bridge officers looking for a little on the side while they're away from their wife or husband. If not by crew members, then perhaps one of the hundreds of surveillance cameras around the ships, make you feel like you're instantly under the most incredible scrutiny you have ever experienced.

> Like "Sting & the Police" say: *"Every move you make, every breath you take, I'll be watching you."*

And on ships, they really are watching you. It is for this reason that the TV show "Big Brother" never had former cruise ship employees in their house. Once you have worked on a cruise ship, you are far too well attuned to the constant scrutiny, politics, and required alliances, needed to succeed in such an environment. It would not be a fair contest, if cruise ship crew were to enter the Big Brother competition. As I once wrote in a magazine article on cruise ships: "Think fast, speak slowly, and choose your allies very carefully. These are the rules of engagement for working on cruise ships," and it is so very true. If you do any of these things incorrectly, you could regret it for an entire contract, or even worse, your entire career at sea.

Add to this, a mythological bin, that is situated on the gangway as you enter the ship. On that bin, is the word "morals". When each crew member boards the ship, they are compelled to throw their morals in the bin, before assuming a totally different personality. With that in mind, it

C.R.U.I.S.E

was no wonder, that myself, along with so many others, ended up in all sorts of mischief on board. To be honest, even though it may not be what most would call "morally correct," it was rather liberating at its best, to be conducting your life in this way.

I see it in a similar way to how a child would see walking into a candy store for the first time. In front of you are endless opportunities to experiment with and to try. All in an environment, well away from the people who love you, and would judge you, and therefore restrict your level of experimentation. You can do, have, and be, all the things that society would see as wrong, and at the end of your time on board, you can walk away from the things you don't like, while embracing those that you do like.

Everyone on board a cruise ship, is there to enjoy themselves. Both the passengers and crew, are not away from their loved ones, as a form of punishment. They are there to experience the feeling of freedom, that only cruising provides. As Johnny Depp said in the movie, Pirates of the Caribbean, when explaining what a ship was. He said, "A ship is not just a keel and hull and a deck and sails. That's what a ship needs. But what a ship really is, is freedom."

A ship is the freedom, that allows you to explore more than just different cultures, or countries. It is the freedom to explore everything you are and everything you think you want to be. As anyone who has worked at sea will tell you, a life at sea is as close as a human can be to being totally free. When you're sailing across a vast piece of undisturbed water with the wind in your face and the feeling of the salt air on your skin, you can't help but feel totally and utterly alive. There is nothing on the horizon for as far as the eye can see, and nothing behind you, to remind you of all your troubles that you have left behind on land.

James Cameron captured the essence of this, in the movie *Titanic*, when Leonardo Decaprio stood on the front of the ship and proclaimed that he was king of the world. Out there, in the middle of the ocean, you really feel like there is nothing you could not be, have, or achieve; with the exception of pulling into a McDonald's drive thru. I too, have often stood on the bow of the ship and thought that I was the king of the world. It was at

A Crash Course in Cruising

that time, that there really was not a care in the world, or a dilemma that was unsolvable.

Since returning home from ships, I have found it harder to find that peace of mind and clear passage of thought, to be able to solve such dilemmas. It is no wonder that the cruise industry has fast gained the reputation, of being the most romantic type of travel, or holiday, anyone could ever experience. From the moment that you head away from land and out to sea, your cares simply wash away, like your hair gel in a torrential downpour, leaving you with no other option, than to let yourself go and to be totally at the mercy of the ocean and all of its splendor.

To sum up this chapter and to give you an idea of what cruising is really like for crew onboard, let me explain it like this. To a passenger, cruising is all about being pampered and waited on hand and foot. From turned down sheets at night, chocolates on your pillow, your toilet paper folded into a nice triangle at the end, to fresh towels twice a day, and an endless supply of amazing food and brilliant entertainment. They say that a passenger gains an average of ten pounds on a ten-day cruise or, as the crew say, "They come on as passengers and go home as cargo."

To the cruise line, cruising is about providing their passengers with an incredible experience and thus giving them a holiday that will bring them back to sea over and over. This will ensure the cruise lines ongoing success and therefore, provide the company and its shareholders with favourable returns, into the future. I have met many passengers, that have cruised more than one-hundred times and along the way provided the cruise line with a very handsome profit.

The title, and in particular the cover for this book, came about as a result of what I like to call the "polar opposites of cruising". Cruising has a wonderfully romantic reputation, but there is also a naughtier side to cruising, that for the most part; passengers don't witness. For passengers and some crew, cruising is about sailing to as many different destinations as possible. For others, it is about shagging anyone they can, while on board. For me, unintentionally; it turned out to be both. This is where I became conflicted, when naming the book, because cruising really is about both sides of the coin.

C.R.U.I.S.E

The name of the book was originally born out of a simple crew induction, that I attended, when I boarded one particular ship. Every crew member must attend their first induction, before commencing their duties on board. The induction, was a series of paperwork and a rundown of what was expected of them, while on board.

During the first induction, this particular cruise line, took the word "Cruise" and made their mission statement, based on an acronym of the word; as below.

C – Courtesy
R – Respect
U – Unfailing
I – In
S – Service
E – Excellence

This was the vision for how the cruise line wanted the crew to provide their passengers with an incredible cruising experience. Even though this was the case, and the crew more often than not, did an amazing job, pampering passengers, for the crew, life at sea, was about having as much fun as is legally; and sometimes illegally possible. On most ships, it is frowned upon for crew to "tamper with the ship's cargo" (passengers), but what the captain doesn't see, can't be frowned upon.

As we sat in our induction, and the staff captain, who was conducting the induction, was explaining the "C.R.U.I.S.E" mission statement to the group, a fellow crew member, leant over to me and whispered, "No. It stands for …"

C - Can't
R - Rest
U - Until
I - I've
S – Shagged
E – Everything

A Crash Course in Cruising

Trying not to laugh out loud, I chuckled under my breath and scribbled that acronym on the piece of paper in front of me, for future reference. Over my years on ships, I discovered a few different versions of this. One of which, became the second part of the title for this book.

C - Can't
R - Rest
U - Until
I – I've
S - Sailed
E – Everywhere

There is also "Can't Rest Until I've Snogged Everybody," or "Can't Really Understand Italians Speaking English".

To me, being at sea, was about both the "Sailed" and "Shagged". I wanted to sail to as many destinations as possible, while also enjoying the fun that a life as an entertainer at sea offered. As it turned out, this cruise line was not the only cruise line to use this approach, while creating mission statements. While researching another cruise line recently, for a job interview as Cruise Director, I discovered that they also use an acronym for their mission statement.

> *And on a footnote to this story, I have to make mention of my best mate and my brother who I would like to think of as intelligent men, but both had me doubled over with laughter, when I explained that I might be working for N.C.L (Norwegian Cruise Line). My best mate's response was, "Well, the Norwegian women are so hot," to which my brother said, "Damn, I bet it's cold in Norway."*

Now this may not seem funny, unless you know that Norwegian Cruise Line is not a cruise line that is in Norway, nor does it have heaps of Norwegian women working on board. I said to both my brother and my mate, after calling them a pair of dopey Muppets, "So by your reckoning, that would mean that Holland America Line, is full of Dutch people, Royal

C.R.U.I.S.E

Caribbean is full of Jamaicans, and P&O, which stands for Peninsular & Oriental; is run by Asians," at which point they both realized the stupidity of their previous comments.

My point in telling this side story, is that there really are so many misconceptions about cruise lines and cruising in general. Another huge misconception is that cruising is only for old people. An even crazier one, is that the crew fly in and fly out every night, once the passengers have gone to bed. Throughout the book, I hope to dispel more of these types of misconceptions about cruising, but for now, let's get back to the story.

The other cruise line's vision statement, that I discovered while researching the company, was as follows. Where the first cruise line used C.R.U.I.S.E for their vision, this next one, chose the word S.T.Y.L.E. This stood for:

S - Service
T - Teamwork and
Y - Yes
L - Leads to
E – Excellence

Upon reading this, my mind instantly went back to what we did with "C.R.U.I.S.E" and within ten seconds, the following version came out of mouth.

S - Shagging
T – 'Til
Y - You
L - Lose
E – Enthusiasm or (Energy or Empathy)

Needless to say, I did not recite my own version during my future job interview with this company. However, it is a constant source of laughter for me whenever anyone comes up to me and says, "You've got 'style."

Right about now, you're probably wondering why I even mentioned either of these acronyms and what they have to do with the premise of this

A Crash Course in Cruising

book. Well, as I said, I wanted to blow away any misconceptions that cruise ship life is just like "The Love Boat." For those of you not old enough to remember "The Love Boat," it was an Aaron Spelling-produced TV show, from 1977 to 1986, which depicted cruise ship life as being the most romantic place on Earth. It was where people always fell in love, everything was simply blissful, and they all lived happily ever after. Occasionally, this does happen, and cruising is very romantic and has probably re-ignited more marriages than any other form of holiday, but on all ships, there is a deeper, darker side that is never seen.

I'm not here to ruin anyone's image of cruising, or to destroy the industry in any way; far from it. I want to promote the industry and inspire you to go and experience it for yourself. Whether it is as a crew member, or if you're not able to do that, then at least experience cruise ship life as a passenger. I do want to make it clear right from the outset though, that cruise ship life is so much more than just the romantic, idyllic façade, that the general public perceive it to be. So, with that in mind, it's time for you to find out just what it's like, to live on board a luxury cruise ship. So strap yourself in and hold onto your underwear, as we go on a journey across the seven seas; crew style.

Welcome to Ship Life

"Nothing that I had done or had been up until now, could have prepared me for what I was about to embark on."

IT WAS THE 1st of June 2001, and I had just secured my first cruise ship contract as a singer and was busily preparing to embark on the journey of a lifetime. Imagine walking along the street one day, going about your everyday business, when you receive a phone call, that throws your entire world into total chaos; in a good way. That was exactly what had happened, only a week prior, when I received a call from the agent that I had auditioned for a month earlier, for a cruise ship contract.

As well as packing up my entire life, I had to make arrangements for while I was away. I had never travelled overseas, for more than a few weeks, so I had a lot to arrange. I still had car payments to make, bills to pay, and mail to be collected and dealt with, while I was away. Not being in the country for six months, meant that if something important had to be dealt with, then someone else had to take care of it for me. This is where I was very fortunate to have such a great mate and sister to deal

Welcome to Ship Life

with things on my behalf, which allowed me to focus on living the dream, that I was about to.

My mate, who was a lawyer, had drawn up a Power of Attorney for himself and Sue (my mother) to legally act on my behalf, should the need arise while I was away. This is not really necessary for people going away to work at sea, but it certainly makes life less stressful, not having to make international phone calls to banks while you're away, at hours that never really match up, given the time difference. At the time of my first contract, the internet was still quite new and it certainly wasn't as much a part of our lives as it is now, nor was it available on any cruise ship in the world. These days, I could go away on a ship for six months and have access to anything I needed, in order to conduct my life, back home. Back in those days, we weren't a "paperless" society, like we are now, so these days, mail would hardly be an issue either.

While I was super excited about going away, before I had even left the country, I found myself dealing with an unsavory situation. The agent, who got me the contract, Di, had (at the last minute), informed me that I owed her over AUD$500 in commission for getting me the contract. I have since learnt that paying commission is a standard procedure when it comes to agents finding work for entertainers, but regardless, the way she handled it at the time, was disappointing. I had not been informed of this transaction, at any point prior to this last-minute call. I had no problem paying a commission for the work that she had done, but at no stage during meeting her, auditioning for her, or in the lead up to, or after being offered the contract, did she mention anything about commissions. Prior to that day, I was very naive as to how the industry worked, so I presumed she must get paid by the cruise line, for securing me as a singer for them.

Di called me on the day before I was to leave and asked me to acquire the exchange rate from British pounds to Australian dollars, as I was being paid in British pounds on board. This was so she could calculate her commission. Of course, I asked her, "What commission?" to which she told me that I owed her commission for getting me the contract. She informed me she would be posting the invoice to me, and that I was to pay her as soon as possible.

Over the course of the next few weeks, I basically told her to shove her commission up her ass, but after consulting my lawyer mate, I decided to give her half the amount of her requested commission. Several people I have met in the industry since, have said that she is known for this type of behavior and she also likes to threaten performers with "never working in the industry again," as she claims to have a strangle hold over all of the cruise lines. This is something I have since found not to be true, as I myself have been an agent, recruiting for cruise lines. She now only has one cruise ship that will deal with her, and as the story plays out, you will realize, that her threats did nothing, because I ended up working on ships for quite some time.

Of course, Di huffed and ranted for several weeks after I told her I would only pay part of her requested commission. The funny thing was, that at the completion of my first contract, she wrote me the most wonderful letter, thanking me for doing such a great job and commented on how happy the cruise line was with me. She went on to say that because of me (I was the first singer she had placed with that cruise line), she was now placing more than eight singers each year with the same company; all of whom pay her $500ish in commission. "There's your fucking commission, Di," I thought to myself, but hey, despite this unsavory situation, I will always be extremely grateful to Di for giving me my first opportunity in the cruise industry.

Let the journey begin.

So, after much preparation, there I was, nervously waiting at the Brisbane International airport, ready to board my flight to London, where I would be joining my first cruise ship, a few weeks later; in Portsmouth. I had packed up my entire life, said goodbye to my "semi-serious" girlfriend and was ready to embark on my first real adventure. As the announcement came over the PA system to board my flight, I jumped to my feet, kissed my

Welcome to Ship Life

friends and family goodbye, and with my hand luggage, I proceeded to the gate. As I walked to the gate, I punched the air, as a sign of achievement, at having made the leap to conquer the world, in my own small way. It was at that moment, that I knew my life was about to change forever. Nothing that I had done or had been, up until now, could have prepared me for what I was about to embark on, but I was, for some reason, not bothered by this at all. In fact, I was totally pumped and ready to meet it head on.

After a long and exhausting twenty-four-hour flight, followed by a further two hours dragging a suitcase, tech case, laptop, and guitar through London's entire rail network (I have learnt to travel much lighter these days), I finally arrived at the rehearsal studio, Plantation Wharf, Battersea, that would double as my home for the next three weeks. I met Mark, who was the account manager for the company, and a few of the other office staff, that I had spoken to over the phone, in the weeks leading up to my arrival.

The following day, I met Simone and Layla (my fellow cast members), as well as Debbie, our director, and Gayle, our choreographer. This particular cast changeover was not a normal one though. There were five of the current cast who were staying on board for a further six months, while the three of us joined them. This meant that rehearsals were extremely challenging, to say the least, with only three people out of eight, present. It's hard enough trying to learn three one-hours shows in three weeks when you have the full complement of cast members around you. It's even more difficult trying to do it with huge gaps all around the stage and people you are supposed to be interacting with, simply not being there.

The three shows we were learning were "Legends at Sea," which was a tribute to famous pop and rock stars such as Frank Sinatra, Ricky Martin, Robbie Williams, Elvis, and so on, "Hooray for Hollywood," which consisted of tunes from movies, and the last show was "Grease On," which was a cut-down version of the hit musical, "Grease." I had played Danny Zuko in two previous seasons of Grease in Australia, so I was familiar with the songs and the style of choreography, which helped. Layla, Simone, and I did manage to learn these three shows on our own, and with those under our belt, we trudged off to the sea survival training academy in Southampton for our "Sea Survival" course.

The sea survival training, basically involved learning all of the things that are common sense if faced with an emergency at sea. Things like how to right an overturned life raft in the water, entering the water with a lifejacket on, etc. The one thing I really did enjoy was the practical side of things, which happened later in the day, after we had sat through hours of boring theory.

Once we had completed the theory part of the day, we made our way to a huge warehouse type building, that became a simulated ship and ocean, in a fierce storm. Inside, we had to jump off a three-meter diving board, fully clothed, with a life jacket on, into a wave pool that we couldn't see, because we were in total darkness. All of this occurred, as freezing cold water rained down on us, from sprinklers in the roof, while the sound of sirens and thunder from the PA system, rang in our ears. As scary as this was, it was such a rush, to simulate what it would be like, in a similar emergency at sea. Once we were in the water, we then had to swim to an overturned life raft, which we had to right and then board, in order to pass the course.

We had one poor girl, who was planning to work at sea, on smaller charter boats. By small I mean in comparison to 300-metre-long cruise ships. The problem for her, was that she could not swim at all. In my opinion, this was slightly crazy, but good on her for facing her fears. When it came time to jump into the pool from the high platform, she took so long to step off, that one of the instructors gave her a little helping push. At that point, the girl panicked and uncrossed her arms; which was the opposite of the instructions that she was given, to enter the water wearing a lifejacket.

When she hit water from that height, the opposing forces of her body weight going down, against the buoyancy or her lifejacket, meant that she went straight through her life jacket and sank to the bottom of the pool. This pool was several metres deep, so as a non-swimmer, she wasn't coming back up in a hurry. Realizing that the girl could not swim, the instructors both jumped in and rescued her from drowning. Needless to say, she failed the course and was considerably embarrassed; as we were all watching. As for the rest of us, we all passed with flying colors, and with all the rehearsals and sea training completed, Layla, Simone, and I, headed off to join the ship, feeling that we were totally prepared for anything ship life could throw at us....

Oh, how we were so wrong!

A whole new world.

New surroundings, new people, new food, and a home that now constantly moved, was only the beginning of the total chaos that began to reign supreme in my life. My entire sleeping patterns were turned upside down, as we had to begin rehearsing at 1:00 a.m. with vocal practice for two hours, after which, we were able to use the main show lounge, which doubled as a nightclub. From 3:00 a.m. 'til 7:00 a.m., while trying to stand upright on stage, we would slowly begin mapping out the shows in the theatre, with our five new cast members. The rest of the cast were so fantastic and made Simone, Layla and myself feel so welcome. Clare, our dance captain, even went out and bought us all new quilt covers, chips, and chocolate to make us feel more relaxed as we settled in.

Seven in the morning was bedtime, and we got as much sleep as we could, before being woken up by passenger announcements and cabin stewards, trying to clean our cabins throughout the day. This went on for a week, and as fatigue set in, tempers began to fray. Not toward each other, but towards ourselves. Choreography that we had previously learnt, was seemingly disappearing from our minds, as our bodies began to break down, through a lack of rest, along with added frustration.

The old cast members showed us around and helped us wherever they could. One of the first things that I noticed about cruising, was the overabundance of beautiful women, that either worked at sea, or travelled as passengers. Females, seem more enthusiastic that men, when it comes to cruising. Even my own cast was full of hot women. Both Layla and Simone were cute, and Katie, who was to be my "Sandy" in "Grease On," was breathtaking. I found it quite difficult staying focused, with such beautiful women around me, but somehow, I managed to; at least for the first week. Despite all of the turmoil and distractions, I was still very excited at the thought of being paid to do what I loved doing, while also travelling the world.

Even though my career in the entertainment industry up until this point, had been somewhat successful, I knew that this was only the beginning of it. My mother had always preferred that I had a "real job" when I left school; as most parents wish for their children. Even though this was the case, she had always been supportive of my talent and encouraged me to follow my dreams. Unfortunately, she passed away eighteen months prior to my entertainment career taking off. I guess subconsciously, I wanted to achieve greatness in my chosen field, as a way of repaying her, for many years of encouragement.

My only regret looking back, was that I didn't pursue this path earlier, so she could have seen me on stage more. Due to the timing of her death in relation to my career, she was only able to see me in two shows. She was a keen music lover and loved live shows and theatre, so I know she would have loved to see her youngest son in this arena. Everything happens for a reason though, and if I had have gone to sea before I did, I may have been away for her last few months of her life and not have been there to say goodbye when she passed, which I would have regretted, much more.

The show must go on.

It was now 5:00 a.m. on Friday morning, five days into rehearsals on board, and we were preparing for our first dress rehearsal. We were getting dressed for our first full run of "Hooray for Hollywood," and the ship was getting absolutely pounded by six-metre waves, as it sailed through the Bay of Biscay, off the west coast of France. The hideously rough weather was making it extremely difficult to stand; let alone dance or perform. Knowing the tight schedule that we had to keep, Debbie was staying as hard as nails with us, to make sure that the shows would be

Welcome to Ship Life

ready within the next few days. Now, let me say, that Debbie was by no means a bitch or a nasty woman. She simply had a deadline to get us ready by, and no sized waves were going to stop her from reaching her target. And let's face it, she knew it would not be the last time that we would have to perform in rough seas, so she knew this would be the best training we could possibly get.

Debbie was once a performer in London's West End herself, so she knew just how much to push us and when to back off. Her husband, Blain, was a Canadian gentleman, who made a name for himself as the doctor in the movie "Alien," as well as being the voice of the children's cartoon hero, "He-Man." Yes, that's right, I worked for "He-Man." I found this to be quite exciting, having been a child of the 80's. I recall finding this information out one day and asking Blain to do his "He-man" voice for me. Blain and I stood in the studio, which was lined with mirrors, a high roof and timber floors, so the acoustics were perfect. He said, "Close your eyes," which I did, and with that, he belted out the words, "By the power of Grey-skull....I have the power." To this day I can still recall, giggling like a kid again hearing "He-man" right there in front of me.

Back on board the ship, I took my place sitting behind wooden cut-outs of various Hollywood actors, placed on stage, as I waited for the music to begin for our dress run. I was still getting used to the costume I was wearing and especially the dance jock, I was wearing for the very first time in my life. For those of you who don't know what a "dance jock" is, it's a G-string, males wear on stage to keep everything in place (if you know what I mean), or, as Debbie said, "So no one can see what you're packing." It's design keeps your "tackle" packed in tightly, and has a wide enough waistband that no lines can be seen, no mater what costumes you have over the top.

As I sat there, adjusting my uncomfortable jock that was fair up my ass, I noticed Simone sitting beside me, holding a large, black garbage bag, for Layla to throw up in. This was happening as Simone attached Layla's beautiful head dress, with one hand. Yes, as they say, "The show must go on." While Layla may never laugh about this moment, I have to say I have never seen a young woman look so elegant, wearing a stunning white ball gown, while projectile vomiting into a garbage bag.

All this chaos was going on, as the orchestra began the overture to the show. Before we knew it, the garbage bag was hurled side stage (God knows what happened when it landed), the curtain opened, and the dress rehearsal went on, with barely a hitch. While it may not have been our best ever performance of the contract; it was certainly one to be proud of.

After packing up our costumes, we left the show lounge that morning, at 7:00 a.m., very satisfied with our efforts. We had not only performed a near-perfect dress run, but none of us had fallen over, or thrown up on stage during the performance. As we walked to our cabins, I kissed Layla and Simone good night (or good morning, actually) and proceeded to my cabin, down on deck two. As I approached the bottom of the stairs, I noticed two of the ship's engineers doing some work on what appeared to be some sort of sewage holding tank.

As I walked past, where the men were working, I caught a whiff of this ungodly smell. Instantly, I felt every bit of adrenalin and food from the last five hours, attempting to reinvent itself right there in the corridor. I quickly scrambled for my cabin key and somehow made it inside, just in time to "redecorate" the shower recess in my cabin. I am very proud to say that this remains, to this day, as the only time I have ever been sick at sea. I refuse to put it down as "sea sickness," even though we had endured six hours of the roughest weather I had experienced, at the time. I would like to mark it off as a matter of someone else's "motions" that made me sick and not the "motion of the ocean."

So, there we were, one week into a six-month contract, and already we had endured probably the roughest seas imaginable, massive amounts of sleep deprivation, countless safety training, a totally new environment with, shall we say, "interesting food," and all these new faces. Many of these new faces, were quite a distraction, given that they were of the opposite sex, very attractive, and seemingly keen to get to know me. As there was only one other straight male member of the cast, I was receiving quite a bit of attention from the female crew members. This excessive amount of attention was not something that I was used to, and given this new territory for me, I was literally in unchartered waters.

Nothing can be finer...

It took some time, for me to find my way around my new environment. Anyone who has been on a ship will tell you that you end up lost for the best part of the cruise. One place that I did find myself visiting frequently, was the beauty salon on board. I'm not one of these "metro sexual" men, who have to have their nails done or bikini line waxed. I had much more masculine reasons for frequenting the salon. I found myself being interested in a cute, young, English beauty therapist, by the name of Colleen. As we got to know each other, it seemed apparent that Coleen was as keen to get to know me, as I was to get to know her. She was twenty years old, very petite, with long dark brown hair and was of very slight Asian appearance. She was from the U.K and on first impressions, she seemed like a very sweet girl.

Like myself, it was Coleen's first contract, and she too had only joined the ship a few weeks prior to me. We hit it off quite well and somehow found ourselves in what would soon be one of those shipboard relationships, that I mentioned earlier. A few weeks had passed, and I was settling in quite well to ship life, when one of the ladies from the production company's office in London, came on board with her husband, for a few days. After the show one night, I stood at the bar with Fran and David, chatting about various things. Fran was also Australian, so we had much to talk about.

David, not to mess around, asked me, if I had met anyone on board yet; meaning had I shagged anyone. I told him of this nice salon girl, Colleen, that I had met. David smiled and said, "Oh you've got yourself a *Steiner.*" I was puzzled as to what he meant. He explained to me, that the company that provided the staff for the salon on board most cruise ships around the world, was called "Steiner." He continued to inform me, that there is a saying in the cruise industry that goes, (to the tune of "Chattanooga

Choo Choo"), "Nothing could be finer than to wake up with a Steiner in the mor-or-or-or-ning."

David and I both had a laugh at this. Fran was far less amused and slapped David on the arm, for making such a distasteful comment in public. Fran then excused herself to go to the bathroom, at which time David leaned toward me and said, "Steiner girls are like Barbie dolls; just push their belly button and their legs fly open." I found myself laughing quite hysterically, while at the same time, wondering if Colleen was like that, with all the guys. Either way, my relationship with Coleen, continued for the entire six-month contract, with very few problems, other than the ones I will mention later in this chapter.

My name is… Steve Pulford… Sorry…. Slim.

The thing I love the most about cruise ships, is the incredible diversity of personalities that you meet on board, whether it be passengers or crew members. Nowhere else in the world, is there such a diverse range of nationalities, religions, and social backgrounds, all in one confined space. Of all the thousands of people I have met on cruise ships, there is one person, who stands head and shoulders above the rest, so far as being unique. His name is Steve Pulford, or as I and anyone else on ships refer to him, "Slim."

If you're wondering why I have used Slim's real full name, instead of changing his identity, like everyone else in this book, it's quite simple. Slim wanted me to. Slim is a larrikin, who loves the limelight and he is not ashamed of anything he had done at sea. He had read previous versions of these stories and he is proud to have his name attached to them.

Slim came aboard the ship, about a month after I did, and from the moment I met him in the show lounge one afternoon, I knew that we would have a laugh together. I walked into the lounge about 4:00 p.m. that day, and I spotted this really large guy with short, bleached-blond hair, standing in the sound booth. He was casing out the lounge, and had spotted a group of girls, who he was admiring.

Welcome to Ship Life

I went over to him and said, "You must be Steve, our new sound guy."

"Steve, who the fuck is Steve? I hate that fucking name. My mother doesn't even call me that." He laughed. "They call me Slim."

"Nice to meet you, Slim; I'm J.D," I said, extending my right hand to shake his.

Slim shook my hand, then pointed to a group of girls sitting near the bar. "Have you seen the 'pie' over there?"

I looked to see a group of cute girls dressed rather provocatively and in particular one girl with rather large breasts.

"Geez, you don't get many of them to the pound," Slim remarked (referring to her breasts). "Fuck, you don't get many of them to the bucket."

We both laughed, and from that moment on, Slim and I were best mates on board. Whenever there was some sort of mischief to get up to, you could be assured, that Slim and I were somehow involved.

As the story unfolds, you will hear me mention Slim quite a bit, so I guess I should tell you a little about him. I think I am one of the only people who actually know his real name, but from that day on, everyone referred to him as Slim. Even the Captain addressed him as Slim. Now, Slim did not get his name as a piss take of him being a very overweight guy. Slim got his nickname because, with his really short, bleached-blond hair, he looked like American rap star, Eminem, a.k.a. "Slim Shady."

Slim is one of these guys who absolutely hates authority and will do everything he can, to piss anyone off, who has such authority. He's a great guy and really is quite sweet deep down, but let me say, that very few people ever get close enough, to see that side of him. He keeps most people at arm's length, with his vulgar and tasteless behavior and comments.

To give you a quick idea of how disgusting Slim can be, it was later that night, that I, along with the entire entertainment team, worked out what sort of a creature Slim was. The entire team sat eating dinner in the crew mess, when Slim sat down at the end of the long trestle style table and shouted at the top of his voice, "Can someone pass me the period juice," (referring to the tomato sauce). Half the table gagged on their dinner, while the other half looked at him in shock. Someone handed the tomato sauce to Slim, at which time he proceeded to empty almost the entire contents of the bottle onto his food, while shouting the words, "Oh look, its heavy flow." From that moment on, we all knew that we were in the presence of a truly unique individual.

Eye Eye Chips & Pie.

During my numerous, six-month contracts on ships, I worked with several cruise directors, all of which I learnt so much from. I have to say, though, the one who stands out the most is probably "Stevie C," who took over as cruise director about two months after I joined my first ship. Steve is 6'4", of African-ethnic background, and hails from Yorkshire, in the UK. He's an awesome guy, but as Steve tells me, he was part of the Leeds United group of fans, that ran riot in the 1990s, starting all sorts of problems at football matches across England. Steve influenced me to support the same team that year, because, at the time, Leeds had nine Australians playing for them. With that in common, we instantly got along like a house on fire.

Whenever a nice-looking girl walked past us, as a group, Steve would say to us or them, "Eye Eye," or "Eye Eye, Chips and Pie." One night, Steve decided to tell a little story to the audience. He told them, that he was a little homesick and to remind him of home, he would think about his favourite food, which was chips and pie. He said that whenever he came on stage throughout the cruise and yelled out, "Eye Eye," the audience had to reply with, "Chips and Pie." So for the entire cruise, whenever Steve would come on stage, he would say, "Eye Eye," and the crowd would all reply, "Chips and Pie."

This may not seem too unusual, unless you understand that the crowd didn't know that "Chips and Pie" was a kind of slang for "tits and pussy." If you put that all together and think that it is being screamed out by 1500 people of all ages, it is quite amusing to witness. What made it funnier was when I was walking through the ship two days later and passed an eight-year-old boy holding his mum and dad's hands yelling at the top of his voice, "Eye Eye Chips and Pie, Mummy, I really want some Chips and

Welcome to Ship Life

Pie." As you can imagine, I nearly pissed myself as I walked past. Okay, so some of you may not find it funny, but trust me, if you saw it actually happen, you would laugh.

So, between me, Steve, and Slim, we got up to some crazy shit throughout the next few months. Traditionally, this particular ship would do three-day mini cruises from Portsmouth, England to Bilbao, Spain and back; twice a week. Then on Friday nights, we would cruise across to Cherbourg, France for a wild "party night cruise." The three of us would get up to all sorts of mischief on the regular cruises, but even more so on, the Friday night cruises, because the ship was full of drunk women, looking for trouble themselves. Steve C, promoted me very quickly to Assistant Cruise Director on my first contract. I guess he saw my potential, not only in the job, but also as a "deputy" to him, in all things mischievous. It was my job to cover his backside, when need be and also to help him out, on the various scams that were going on. I don't think a single cruise went by, when the three of us were not up to trouble of some sort.

The first four months of the contract went by without too many dramas though and certainly nothing really worth putting in this book. The itinerary we did, was what some crew would call the "bus run." The same itinerary week in, week out, so, while we had a routine to be settled in, nothing exciting really happened. Every Monday and Thursday, we'd get to Spain early in the morning, go straight to the internet café to check emails, and then off to the nearest bar, to get totally trashed before returning to the ship to sleep it off, before the show that night. This particular ship was supposed to be a "dry ship." By dry ship, I mean that crew members were *not* permitted to drink alcohol at all, hence why we would drink so much on land.

There had been several issues with other ships in the fleet, with collisions and a reported rape, due to officers drinking on duty in the months prior. It was for these reasons, that the company decided to take this course of action, to prevent further incidents. While this seemed like a good idea, it really didn't stop crew from drinking. It only made them get smarter, with how they bought and drank their alcohol.

C. R. U. I. S. E

For example, because the ship doubled as a ferry, we had several Lorries travel across to Spain or England each week. The engineers, in particular, knew these drivers very well, because it was the engineering team, who would secure the trucks on the cargo deck. The engineers would arrange for the drivers to bring on dozens of cartons of beer, which were unloaded once the ship was at sea. The engineers would put a random unoccupied cabin "out of order" for maintenance purposes. This cabin would be the place where the truck drivers would deliver the alcohol to be stored. The cartons of beer, or bottles of alcohol were then distributed (at a price) to the crew and officers.

The other trick was to get one of the truck drivers to buy alcohol at the duty-free shop for you; for a small fee. In the cruise director's case, he could swap a voucher for a free cruise, for several bottles of alcohol. This free cruise certificate could then be sold by the driver at a premium during summer when cruise fares were at their highest. Even though people hardly ever saw the crew drunk in public, if you were to wander the crew corridors late at night, you would easily find extremely drunk crew, having cabin parties.

This was not always the case, though, as sometimes, it was a good thing that we weren't meant to drink. The Bay of Biscay that we sailed through each week, was known as one of the worst stretches of water in the world. Even Sir Robin Knox-Johnston, who was the first solo sailor to sail around the world, told me over a beer, one day on a cruise ship, that the Bay of Biscay was the worse stretch of sea he had ever encountered. It was almost always really rough and in my opinion, you really don't want to be drunk and sea sick at the same time. If you think it is bad when you lie down after a big night out and the room is spinning, then you should try it when the room is spinning and going up and down; at the same time.

Speaking of rough weather, one of the biggest challenges for the entertainment team at sea, was having to deal with rough weather, during the shows. Even though, I have only experienced a few occasions, where we had to cancel a show, I have lost count of how many times, I have performed, under less than ideal conditions. Even though it is disappointing for the passengers when a show is cancelled, due to rough weather, the cruise director has to take into account the safety of the performers. If a show was to go ahead and the ship hit a big wave in the middle of the show, a dancer could get seriously hurt, or suffer a career-ending injury.

From time to time, I watch some of the shows that I had performed in and wonder why I wasn't able to pull off a pirouette or a particular move. Then I remember that I was dancing on a ship. Even though on the camera, it doesn't seem like the ship is moving, or if you're in the audience on board, you don't feel it too much, but if the ship is moving a lot, it becomes a huge challenge for the cast to stay upright; let alone be brilliant.

One funny moment, that wasn't anything to do with weather but rather just stupidity, happened on my first contract. On that ship, we had a stage, that was on a hydraulic system. The entire stage could be raised or lowered if needed. The stage could only be raised about thirty centimeters, but that made a big difference during certain shows. On one occasion, it made a huge impact on all the cast, as well as the audience. The stage had not been raised during this particular contract, due to the belief that if it was, Keiron, who was quite tall, would hit the roof with his hands during certain numbers. Despite this, on one particular occasion, for "Grease On," we decided to raise the stage to see how it went.

The stage surface itself, was brass, so it tended to be more slippery that most stages at the best of times. The entire cast talked about the fact the stage was being raised during our preparations and we reminded each other of the raised lip that we had to step up onto, to enter the actual stage area. It was now show time, and my new "Sandy" (Natalie) and I, were in the middle of the stage, waiting for the show to begin. The curtains opened, and we began with the traditional dialogue, which is seen at the beginning of the movie "Grease."

My final line, which was, "Of course not, it's just the beginning," was the cue for the band to play "Grease is the Word" and for the cast to run onto the stage for the opening scene. I completed my line, the band played, and the cast came running down the ramps onto the stage; three from either side of the stage. As they got to the lip of the raised stage, both Keiron and

C.R.U.I.S.E

Darren, who were in the front of each line, forgot to take the step up and tripped and slid face first, onto the stage.

Following close behind, were the other four dancers, who also tripped and slid into the others, who were lying on the stage laughing. There I was, trying to act cool and kiss my beautiful Sandy, while the rest of the cast were piled up on the floor, like a heap of rubble; laughing hysterically. The audience also found this extremely funny, and it took the entire first number of the show, for both the cast and the audience to regain their composure. Needless to say, we never raised the stage up again.

It was a few weeks later, during the same show, when I had split my lip, in the days prior somehow. My bottom lip had mostly healed, but as the show started, as a result of my mouth movements from singing, my lip must have split again and was bleeding. I was singing "Summer Nights" and it was the part of the song where, the boys and I were crouched down as I was singing. Glen, who was one of the dancers was looking at me, licking his lips as I sang. I noticed him doing this and thought he was being filthy by suggesting that I "licked" Sandy. I continued singing, trying not to laugh at Glenn constantly licking his lips at me, until I tasted a drop of blood and realized that he was trying to signal for me to lick my lip to wipe away the blood, and not signaling to perform oral sex on Sandy.

The Grease show was probably the show that we had the most fun in, because it was a pretty easy show to maintain the quality of performances. As a result, someone was always up to mischief during that show. On one occasion, Kieran had found a Barbie doll, in a corridor, that had no arms and no legs. It only had a torso and a head full of blonde hair. In the opening number, Kieran ran over to me to High-five me, but as he did, instead of giving me a high-five, he smacked my hand and cupped it as he let go of the Barbie-doll, leaving it in my hand. He must have been carrying this stupid doll for the entire number. Now I had the doll and the object was to offload it to some unsuspecting cast member. I managed to put it in the pocket of Glenn and as the show progressed, Barbie made her way around the entire cast several times. The object of the game though, was

Welcome to Ship Life

for this to take place without the audience seeing or suspecting anything was going on.

We got to the final number and even though I had handled and offloaded Barbie a few times, I was not in possession of it, so I figured that I was safe. Whoever was left holding the doll at the end of the show, had to buy the rest of the cast a drink. We were busily singing "we go together" and all was looking good for me avoiding a large bar bill, when we all crouched down as a group, before jumping back up as part of the choreography. I crouched down, with my hands behind my back, then felt something being placed in my hands. A split-second later, I had to jump up, with my arms outstretched and my palms facing forward and fingers pointing upwards.

I jumped up from the crouching position, knowing that I had something in my hand, but not sure how it was positioned. I outstretched my fingers on my left hand, but kept my right fist clenched. As I looked up at my right hand, all I could see was my closed fist and a mop of blonde hair hanging out the top. Kieran was laughing behind me, as I scrambled to hide the hair, while not missing lyrics or choreography. With less than thirty seconds to go, I broke with my routine choreography and shimmied over to Kieran, who was facing the audience at the front of the stage. I pulled out the back of his pants and shoved Barbie as far down his pants as I could, before shimmying back to my position for my final bow. With only twenty seconds remaining now, there was no way, he would be able to retrieve the doll from the depths of his pants. "Yes." I thought to myself. I had avoided buying the round of drinks and I thought that it was appropriate that the person responsible for starting this game, was the one left holding the baby…I mean Barbie.

Another story that comes to mind, was during my second contract (on the same ship), when the cast was performing "Hooray for Hollywood." Ricky, Lauren, and Lee were on stage performing a "Star Wars" section, where Ricky was Darth Vader and Lee was Luke Skywalker. The typical fight with light sabers began, and at the climax, Lee sliced Ricky's Darth Vader helmet off. As Lee sliced Ricky's helmet off, Ricky covered his real

C.R.U.I.S.E

head with his cape, so the audience could not see it. Ricky was then supposed to run off into the wings, with his head covered.

On this particular occasion, though, Ricky became disorientated with the cape over his head and misjudged which direction he needed to run. Instead, he ran straight off the stage, head first onto a couple's table, in the front row, sending them and their cocktails flying. What was even funnier was, all you could see were Ricky's legs and cape flapping around, as he tried to get himself out, from being wedged upside down, in between the chairs and table. To make matters worse for Ricky, we were filming that show, so afterwards, we sat around for hours, watching it over and over and over.

Probably the most memorable on-stage incident on that ship, was an occasion during my second contract, when the cast were performing a "good bye band set" for the passengers. This occurred on the last day of the cruise, as we sailed up the English Channel, into Portsmouth. Several members of the cast would sing a number each with the resident band. One of the dancers, named Charlotte, was not a great singer, but as was the case of this show, everyone had a turn to sing.

When it was Charlotte's turn to sing, she somehow managed to miss the key that she was supposed to sing in, and she sang so out of tune, that I thought my ears were going to bleed. At the time, I was with Slim, in the sound booth watching; with my ears covered. Slim reached into his pocket and removed a bunch of keys. He began waving the keys around in the air, jiggling them, to get Charlotte's attention. Charlotte finally looked in our direction and seemed totally puzzled at what Slim was doing, waving his keys in the air.

To Charlotte's surprise, she was mortified to hear Slim yelling at the top of his voice, "Pick a key Charlotte, any fucking key will do." Charlotte, myself and the audience, could not believe what had just come out of Slim's mouth. At the same time, I could not stop laughing, at how relevant and funny his comment was. Needless to say, Charlotte was not impressed with Slim, and I don't recall her talking to him, for the rest of the contract, after that event.

Welcome to Ship Life

Anita G…ood shag.

It was four months into the contract and things were going along nicely. I was enjoying my job, doing what I loved, and travelling while getting paid. I had Colleen on board, and two great mates in Steve & Slim. The shows were going well, and I was enjoying a life at sea, although I was beginning to miss home a little. As the contract progressed, I was starting to get a little anxious, about what would happen with Colleen and I, after this contract ended. It's one thing to let go and love someone, but when you also have the thought, that at the end of the contract, you may never see each other again, you really start to question the process.

You wonder if the feelings you are feeling at that moment, will be worth the pain, that will possibly come in a few months' time, through no fault of your own. In many cases, couples, live on opposite sides of the world, so this has to be taken into consideration when getting emotionally attached to someone at sea. If it's just casual sex, then no problem, but when there are emotions involved, it becomes a whole new ball game.

Time is of the essence on board a ship, and especially when it comes to building a solid foundation for a relationship, that will hopefully hold strong when the time comes to spend a considerable amount of time apart. Colleen and I were making the most of every moment, but on one particular cruise, she had to take a backseat, as my job had to be my main focus; even though it ended up being something else, that consumed most of my time that week.

WThis particular cruise, was more important than any other, because the managing director from another cruise line was on board, to watch the shows. He was there to finalize a deal for our production company, to put our shows, on the other cruise line's ships. Debbie was on board and was taking no chances that something could go wrong. Duncan, the regular band singer, was not one hundred percent healthy, so Debbie wanted him to rest before the final show. Duncan played a major role in the last show, so I filled in for him that afternoon, by doing the band set.

During the set, I noticed a very attractive blonde woman, in her mid-thirties, staring at me for the entire set. I didn't take too much notice, but I did notice that she was also there in the front row, for the evening band set as well. After the show that night, I went down to my cabin to see what Colleen was doing. She was in her PJs, watching a movie and told me she was about to go around to my cabin and go to bed. I told her I was going back upstairs to the bar, and I would be back soon. I went upstairs for a sneaky drink, that the bartender gave me, in a soft-drink glass, so no-one knew it was alcohol. As assistant cruise director, it was my job, along with Steve's, to socialize and make sure passengers were having a good time. Soon after I arrived at the bar, the woman from earlier, came up to me at the bar. We spoke for a while, and I noticed she was getting rather close and a little "touchy feely" with me. This would have been fine if I was single, because she was blonde, attractive and very busty; which is my weakness. However, I was pretty content with my current girlfriend; or so I thought.

We had been talking for about ten minutes when I heard Steve, my cruise director, yell over the microphone from the DJ box, "Eye Eye," which, as you are now aware, is our "call sign" for female talent in the room. I looked toward him, to see which direction he was looking. I nearly crapped myself, when I saw that he was pointing towards the back of the room and mouthing, *Colleen* to me. I turned to look, and sure enough, there was Layla, Keiron, and Colleen, standing in the corner, looking a little suspicious. I said to the woman (Anita) that I had a "situation" downstairs with my staff, and I would be back in a few minutes.

As I approached the cast, I heard Layla say to Colleen, "Here he comes," as Colleen tried to scurry around the corner out of sight. I asked Colleen what she was doing, to which she said that she was just getting some smokes. Now it was only ten minutes earlier that Colleen was in her pajamas ready for bed, and now she was fully dressed, getting cigarettes, so I knew something was not right. I suddenly realized I was being investigated, and even though I had done nothing wrong, at that stage, I felt like I needed to come up with a good excuse. Colleen seemed a bit upset, so I went back downstairs with her, to smooth over the situation.

Welcome to Ship Life

It took me around ten minutes to get it out of her, but she finally told me that Layla and Keiron had seen me talking to Anita, and they went down and got her, so she could see for herself. Do you see what I mean about always being watched? With a little quick thinking, I said I was simply talking to this woman, who was very interested in the shows. Why did I feel the need to defend myself, when I was not doing anything wrong? Well, it must have been the fact that this woman was very hot. I would probably find it difficult to say no, if she wanted me, so perhaps, I felt guilty, in case I did do something. Either way, Colleen believed my story, and with that, I kissed her goodnight, told her I wouldn't be too late, and went back upstairs.

When I got back to Anita, I explained to her that the situation downstairs was all dealt with. One thing I have learnt, is that you never mix "crew business" with "passenger business." I have seen too many people come unstuck by discussing personal business of crew members, to passengers and then have it come back and bite them on the arse.

I continued talking with Anita, and she continued get closer and closer to me, until she was more or less all over me. I was beginning to feel a little uncomfortable with this, not only because I had a girlfriend, but because I was worried that Colleen may reappear at any moment. I suggested that we went somewhere else to chat, to which she suggested we go to her cabin.

As soon as we arrived in her cabin, she threw me on the bed and tried to rip my suit off. I tried to stop her, but she seemed determined to have her way. This situation would normally be every man's wildest dream, but I didn't want to go back down to Colleen smelling of sex; not to mention the fact that I would have been doing the wrong thing. I tried to convince Anita that I had to leave. I told her that I was tired and had heaps of work to do in the morning. Despite my best efforts, Anita wasn't buying it and continued to pull at my clothes.

She ripped my shirt buttons off my shirt and began scratching me all over. She finally agreed to let me go on the condition that I came and saw her in the morning when I got a chance. I agreed, however, she then changed her mind and would not let me leave without giving me a blowjob first. Despite my concern about my morals, I let her do what she wanted and then went back downstairs to Colleen, feeling very relaxed, but very guilty at the same time.

When I arrived at my cabin, Colleen was asleep, so I had a quick shower and jumped into bed, presumably undetected. As I was about to go to sleep, Colleen started touching me and making it obvious she was not only awake all this time, but that she was also quite horny. The pressure was well and truly on, given that it was less than ten minutes since I had "arrived" with Anita, and now Colleen also wanted me to pleasure her. So, with the immortal words of my best mate's dad ringing in my ears—"The one you knock back is the one you never catch up on"—I did what I had to do and not surprisingly, slept very well that night.

I woke up the next morning and as promised, went and saw Anita. Once again, as soon as I walked into her cabin, she grabbed me and ripped my clothes off. This time, I was a little more willing to go ahead with it, so there was no messing around. I mean, shit, I had already broken every moral bone in my body, so what was the point in stopping. I know! Two wrongs don't make a right, but they sure as hell make it feel much better.

Later that day, the ship docked, and Anita had to leave. We said our goodbyes, exchanged phone numbers, and made plans to see each other, at the end of my contract. Why? I hear you ask. Well, surely three wrongs could at least make half a right.

Several weeks later, the end of my first contract finally arrived. I had survived for six months on board, in what was often a crazy "floating house of ill repute." I had somehow survived both my totally immoral behavior, as well as a shipboard relationship. I had a week before I was due to fly back to Australia, so I agreed to go and visit Anita in Birmingham for the weekend, before visiting my mate's past host family, who lived in Denmark.

I know what you're thinking. What happened to my relationship with Colleen? Well, as I mentioned in the introduction, I must have placed my morals in that bin on the gangway, and I guess I forgot to pick them up on the way out. Colleen was still on board for another month, and we were going to see how we both felt after that time. There were no promises, as there never can be on ships, but we both hoped that something might come of it. I guess I figured that if I got all of this kind of behaviour out of my system and Colleen and I decided to get serious, then I would be more likely to be 100% devoted to her for a very long time. It sounds good in theory, right?

It really is difficult holding out for something, that might never eventuate; especially when I was twenty-nine and Colleen was only nineteen. I know I wasn't helping the situation, by visiting another woman on the side. I'm not really sure why I was doing this, but at a guess, I would say it was probably my way of boosting my ego, that had not previously had much female attention. I had always enjoyed a steady flow of female attention, but nothing to the level of what I was experiencing as a lead singer on a cruise ship. Nothing had changed, so far as my looks, or personality, but I guess girls like someone with status or notoriety as well as a man who can sing to them.

After leaving the ship, I spent a couple of days in London debriefing with the office, then caught the train up to Birmingham. I met Anita in the train station, at which point we went to the hotel she had booked for us. I don't think I even got to put my bag down before she jumped me. This lady was certainly one hot-blooded woman. After we got past our "one on one horizontal greeting," we got cleaned up and went out for a drink and something to eat at a local pub. We started chatting, and I began to tell her how I was going to write a book about my time on the ship. She said to me, "I hope you're not writing a story about me." To which I laughed and told her I had been thinking about it.

She paused for a moment and said to me, that I couldn't write a story about her. I asked her why she didn't want me to write about her, but she wouldn't tell me. Now, at forty-four years of age, I know of many reasons, why someone wouldn't want a story written about them, but at twenty-nine, I was a little more naïve. I said to her, "There are only two reasons why you wouldn't want me to involve you in a story." Looking back, there are more than two, such as respect, morals and not airing dirty laundry in public are valid, but in the moment, I failed to think of them, so said to her, "Either you're a hooker or you're married." She laughed and said it wasn't so much that she was married, but more the fact, of whom she was married *to*. Besides being a little shocked, I was now extremely curious. Whose wife had I slept with?

After quite a few drinks, I managed to get it out of her, that her husband was a recently retired professional football player, in the English Premier League. According to her, he was very well known, and that the public knew who she was. Geez! Talk about a saucy episode of the TV show Footballer's Wives—and I was right in the middle of it. So, even though, I still went ahead and told this story, I have chosen not to put her husband's name in the book, or her full name, simply because I don't feel that it would fair to their children. Anita was planning on divorcing him soon after, but regardless, it's not my place to cause more trouble, than is necessary.

Anita and I had a great time just hanging out together for the weekend. On the day that I was heading for Heathrow (after visiting Denmark) a week later, Anita rang and said that her husband had found my number in her phone and was probably going to call me. She told me that he knew nothing about us, so not to give too much information away. About ten minutes later, I received a phone call from a guy claiming to be Anita's friend. He said he was organizing a surprise party for her that weekend, and he saw my name in her phone and thought he would see if I wanted to come along. *How stupid does this guy think I am?* He sounded like he was a few beers short of a six pack, so I played along for a while and told him I would love to come to the party. He was obviously trying to get me to admit that I had slept with his wife, as he was asking me how well I knew her.

My guess was that he would give me a fake time and address, to lure me somewhere, at which point, he'd probably jump me with a few of his mates. Like I said, I'm not that fucking stupid. I said nothing, and he told me he would ring me in a few days to tell me the address of the party. Unfortunately for him, I left the country that afternoon, and my mobile phone was switched off, until I returned two months later, so that was the last I heard of him. I kept in contact with Anita for a while, but I have somehow lost contact with her these days. I hope wherever she is, that she is happy and in love with someone better now.

Same - Same, But Different

"I mean after all, isn't that what every girl wants? Something that's 12 inches long, hard and very satisfying?"

No, this chapter doesn't take us to the fast-paced, crazy city of Bangkok, or anywhere in Thailand. That comes later in the book—although I did get the title of this chapter from my time in Thailand and in particular from those t-shirts, that we're all familiar with.

After six months away from home, in the generally cold and bitter English weather, I was back on the Gold Coast for a glorious Australian summer. The sun was shining, the beach breaks all along the coast were going off, and I was taking time to catch up with friends and family, after a long six months, on the other side of the world. I knew that I only had two months off, so I was determined to make the most of it. I was due to fly back to the UK, for another contract on the same ship, after Christmas, so sun and the beach were my priorities for now.

I'd been home for a about a week, and I was expecting a phone call from the office in London to advise me of the exact dates, to get back on the ship, so when the phone rang with a "withheld number," I presumed it was them. When I answered, the voice on the other end was not Mark from the office, but rather Colleen. She was calling to tell me, that she had booked and paid for a ticket, to come and see me in Australia for a month. Totally unexpected, but nonetheless, very exciting! After the initial shock, I arranged for her to stay with me, at my best friend's parents' place, with whom I was staying while I was home.

A few days later, I received another call from a withheld number. This time, I thought it was Colleen and proceeded to answer the phone with my usual greeting to her.

"Hi, bub," I said.

To which, a masculine voice, on the other end of the phone replied, "Gee, thanks sweetie." Laughter filled the phone line. "It's Mark from the Live Business in London, J.D. Expecting someone else?" he said. We both had a laugh, then Mark proceeded to tell me they didn't need me to return to the ship, as a singer and assistant cruise director the following year.

I'm sure my heart stopped for a moment before Mark said, "We want you to come back as the cruise director."

"You bastard," I shouted down the phone. "I'll kill you when I see you."

Amongst his laughter, Mark stuttered, "It will be worth it, for the sake of hearing the silence down the phone just then."

I *could* have killed the cheeky bugger. I was ecstatic to be given this opportunity, but I wished that he had broken the good news to me, in a different way. We continued the conversation, chatting about the details of the job and pay, etc., and as I hung up the phone, I found myself extremely excited about the prospect of being cruise director on only my second contract. At the same time being quite daunted by the job at hand.

This was a big jump, to go from assistant cruise director, to being in charge of more than twenty entertainers and the entire entertainment program on a cruise ship. In most cases, to get to the position of cruise director, you must start off as cruise staff, or junior assistant cruise director. You then work your way up to assistant cruise director, deputy

Same - Same, But Different

cruise director and then cruise director. I'd always wanted to be Julie, from the *Love Boat* as a kid, and now I was about to be exactly that (minus that short skirt and killer smile that Lauren Tews, the original Julie, wore in the TV show.

The next few weeks flew by, and before I knew it, Colleen arrived, and we had a great time for a month with no thought of the prior misbehavior with Anita, on my behalf, crossing my mind. That's the beauty of cruise ship life. You can do what you want on a ship, and it hardly ever comes back to catch up with you on land. Did I say that? I think I may have spoken too soon.

Colleen and I did a small amount of travelling around in the little time we had but for the most part, we really just ended up relaxing on the beach, during her time in Australia. The month came and went pretty quickly, and before we knew it, Coleen and I were sat in the Brisbane International airport, waiting to board our flight to London. Colleen had to return home, and I was flying straight into rehearsals, with a new cast; but this time as the boss.

It was a comfortable trip with all the usual meals and movies, etc. as well as the part I love the most; the free alcohol. I had a few drinks in the hope that it would help me sleep, as I knew that as soon as I arrived in London, I would be going straight to meet my cast, who had already begun rehearsals a few days earlier. Just like my cast the previous year, they had three shows to learn in three weeks. My part in the shows this year, would be much smaller than the previous year, even though I would be more heavily involved, than most cruise directors would be in the production shows. Debbie was going to make the most of the fact that I had only recently completed these shows myself and was going to use me as much as possible.

One of the three shows would be a new seventies show called "Boogie Romance". Deb had written the show herself and given that I was Australian, had created a character just for me. The show was set in a nightclub in the 70's and I was the leader of a leather-clad gang, called "Dodgy Dan and the dangerous dingoes from down under." Thanks Deb. Given the success of the Australian Movie Crocodile Dundee, Deb also stole the "That's not a knife" scene and added it to the show as well.

Speaking of using my Australian heritage. On many occasions on my first contract, British passengers would come and ask what Australia was like and if I knew anyone from the television show Neighbours, which was produced in Australia, but much more successful in the UK, than back home. On one occasion a young girl came up to me and asked for an autograph and asked if it was true that I was Kylie Minogue's cousin. Before I could reply and set the young girl straight, she also said it was so cool that she was meeting Jason Donovan's step brother in person. Apparently Slim had been telling passengers this type of thing, so now it made sense, why passengers were always taking photos of me around the ship. For anyone outside of Australia, I am pretty sure you have heard of singer Kylie Minogue, but Jason Donovan was just as famous in the 1990's as he played Kylie's boyfriend on the television show and they also dated in real life. In England, both of them were huge celebrities as a result of the show's success.

Back to London.

After an exhausting twenty-four hours in the air, Colleen and I arrived at Heathrow airport. I was getting quite excited about meeting my new cast, but sad to say goodbye to my girlfriend. Colleen and I collected our luggage and made our way through customs, before saying our temporary goodbyes. Colleen had a connecting bus that was taking her to her home town a few hours away, while I on the other hand, had to catch two tube trains, an over-ground train, and then a taxi to the office; the same as the previous year. Thankfully, other companies send a private car for me these days, so once I land, I sleep in the limousine until we get to the ship.

Coleen and I reminded each other, that it was only going to be six weeks, before we would see each other again. I then began dragging my mountain of luggage down to the tube station. Although I was going to be busy, I knew that it was going to be difficult for me, being away from

Same - Same, But Different

Colleen. We'd become pretty close, having spent so much time together in recent weeks and I had hoped that this, would be enough, to get through the next six weeks apart.

Most people, who have recently finished a contract on a cruise ship, spend the first week saying they will never do another contract and the next month missing it so much, that they end up going straight back to sea. It's an extremely addictive lifestyle. I mean, after all, you get all of your meals cooked for you, your cabin cleaned, your laundry done, and each day, you wake up and have breakfast in a new city. Not to mention the fact that you get paid much better than on land, and it is also tax free in most situations; legally. It's no wonder some people do this their whole life.

On the point of cruise ship work being "tax free". The reason for this, is quite simple. Most cruise ship staff, work either six-months on board at a time, or they work three-months on; two-months off, as an example. This means that in many cases, they can be deemed as a non-resident, for tax purposes, because they live and work outside their country of residence, for more than one-hundred and eighty days per year. Add to this, the fact that you get paid in cash on board. Plus, most cruise ships are registered in a country, different to where they sail, and the crew onboard, are from a different country again. This all leads to a very confusing, and messy taxation situation, that most countries, have not been able to work out. This means, that the crew member pays tax to no one.

So, after negotiating trains and taxis in London, I pulled up out front of the office at about 3:00 p.m. on what was a bitterly cold February day. It was certainly a shock to the system, coming straight from summer back home in Australia, to this. I unloaded my luggage from the taxi and rang the front bell for the office. Mark came running down the internal staircase to open the door.

"Hello, Squire, how are you." he said.

"Glad to be back." I replied.

He helped me bring my luggage into the office and asked if I would like to unpack, or go and meet the new cast, who were rehearsing in the back room of a little pub around the road. I told him, that I would love to go and meet the cast, but would like to freshen up a little first. After all, I had been traveling for over twenty-four hours and was pretty much wearing the same clothes as when I left, so I would have certainly smelled a little. Mark helped me carry my things up into Debbie and Blain's apartment (where I would be staying), which was in the same complex as the office.

Deb's place was amazing. I had stayed there a few months earlier, before I returned home to Australia for Christmas, so I knew what to expect, but nonetheless, it was breathtaking to see again. It was four stories up and consisted of three different levels inside. It was absolutely amazing. Two large master bedrooms overlooked the Thames, each with an en-suite and spa, and then an additional four very large double bedrooms, all on the lower level of the apartment. Up one flight of stairs and to the main entrance was a massive entertainment area with a double-sided fireplace and grand piano; all with a spectacular view, overlooking The River Thames.

Past the lounge room, was the dining area and separate kitchen area. The dining table seated fourteen people, and the kitchen was in proportion to catering to these numbers. Also on this level were two guest bathrooms, as well as an amazing balcony, that spanned the entire length, of twenty meters, at least, of this amazing apartment. The same level had an open plan ceiling, which opened up to the next level where the TV room and sitting area was situated. Oh, and I forgot to mention Blain's office, which was up a forth level, via a ladder, leading to a crow's-nest style office, with 360-degree views of London. All in all, the place was breathtaking. It was only Debbie and Blain and their son Dan, who lived there. With Blain away quite often for work and Debbie and Dan being social butterflies, I knew that I would pretty much have the place to myself, so it was certainly more than comfortable for my needs. Mark helped me with my things, and I quickly got changed into some warmer clothes and washed my face then made my way back down to the office.

Same - Same, But Different

Not what I was expecting.

Mark and I made our way around to the pub, where the cast were rehearsing and walked into the back room to join them. We sat for a minute, watching them as they rehearsed, and at first glance, they all seemed like your average singers and dancers; although two of the males were quite fat for dancers. Mark and I sat and watched for a while as Gayle (the choreographer) and Debbie, put the cast through their paces.

After a few minutes, Debbie stopped the rehearsal and came over to say hello to me. "Bunnies, come over here and meet your cruise director," Debbie said. A few of the cast looked shocked to see that I was not as old as most would be as cruise director. Deb turned to me and gave me a huge hug and said, "Welcome back, Lovely; it's good to see you." Debbie then grabbed my hand and introduced me to the cast, as she pointed to them one by one. "This is Dom, Regan, Ricky, Lee, Hannah, Kirsty, Cassie, and Lauren," she said. "Lauren," I thought to myself. Of all the girls in the cast, she was the one that really stood out. She wasn't particularly stunning in her rehearsal gear, but she had a cute smile, hair like it should be in a shampoo commercial, and the biggest breasts I had ever seen on a dancer in my life. I had no idea what she was like as a dancer, but one thing was for certain; she was going to need some extra strong bras and costume tops, to contain those puppies.

The more I watched Lauren, the more attractive I found her. Even though she was in rehearsal gear and wasn't wearing any make up, there was something about her; other than her breasts. I know this really sounds bad, given that I had only said goodbye to Colleen two hours earlier, but there was a certain something about Lauren. At the end of the day, they all packed up their things, and we sat around having a few drinks with Debbie, Mark, and Gayle. It was good to have a drink with the cast and get to know them a little.

They told me that I was totally not what they were expecting as a cruise director. They said that they were expecting someone a lot older than me. They also didn't realize, that I had been the lead singer the year before. I also discovered that Lee and Ricky were both gay, and Ricky was the boyfriend of Rob, who I had worked with on the ship the year before. We had quite a diverse range of nationalities in the cast. Regan and Kirsty were both from Australia (yes, two more people who my agent got commission from, due to my effort the year before). Dom was from France and spoke very little English. Ricky was from Wales. Lauren was from Scotland, and Lee, Cassie, and Hannah were from England. They all seemed nice, and from what I saw of them rehearsing earlier, they were reasonably talented.

The big news that I found out during our chat, was that Lauren was staying at Debbie's place in the room next door to me. Unfortunately, in almost the same breath, she mentioned that she was in a long-term relationship with a guy named Barry, who lived back in Scotland. This was a good thing, as I knew it would stop me from even thinking about trying to chat her up, because I knew she was attached. Although she said she was very much in love with her boyfriend and said that she wanted to marry him, I knew the effects of being on a cruise ship for a long period of time and how it either makes or breaks relationships.

The following day, I knew Debbie was in no rush for me to join the cast, so I cleaned myself up and had a very healthy McDonalds McMuffin and coffee (I am being sarcastic of course), before going to rehearsals. As soon as I arrived, my eyes were again instantly drawn to Lauren. She was looking decidedly more gorgeous today, than yesterday. I'm not sure whether it was that she had made more of an effort with makeup and clothes or because I was more awake than the day before.

I sat and observed for a while, as they performed and did notice that Lauren was glancing at me quite frequently. After admiring her for a few minutes, I began to think to myself, that I should not be thinking like that and that I should keep it totally professional. I was already in a relationship, but even more importantly, I was her boss. This was totally not what I was expecting, but nonetheless, quite interesting. Lauren was twenty-one, which for me was not too young to go out with; seeing as Colleen was only nineteen. The age also meant, that just like Colleen, she was young, and there was more chance of it "turning to custard" easily. I sat there and told myself, that I was going to be a good boss and would lead by example. To gain the cast's respect, I had to keep things totally professional, while also being approachable. With this in mind, I got myself ready and got stuck into a busy three weeks of rehearsals.

About five days into rehearsals, I woke up early and realized that it was Valentine's Day. I rolled over and grabbed my mobile phone and rang Colleen to wish her a Happy Valentine's Day. I had sent her a small teddy bear a few days earlier, which she had received and was sleeping with in her bed when I rang. Later in the day (12:30 p.m.), I was working in the office, preparing entertainment programs for the ship, when I heard the doorbell ring. Upon arriving at the front door, I saw a man standing there, with a huge bunch of flowers. He said to me, "Do you have a Miss Lauren _____ here at all?"

After thinking for a second, I realized that it must be Lauren from the cast. I grabbed the flowers and took them inside. There was a card amongst the flowers which read, "Happy Valentine's Day, my little weesaks. Love Barry." A little strange, but nonetheless, I presumed that "weesaks" must be some sort of Scottish slang for sweetheart or baby. Seeing as it was now after lunch, I thought Gayle and Debbie would need me to rehearse shortly, so I should make my way around to see what was going on. I packed up my work and grabbed Lauren's flowers and made my way around to the pub.

That night, Lauren and I were watching TV at Debbie's place, but given that there wasn't much on, we were chatting, more than watching any specific program. Throughout the conversation, Lauren made a few flirtatious comments, that made me wonder, just how serious she was about her boyfriend back home. I didn't think a lot of it, but over the course of the next few days, these types of flirtatious remarks became more frequent.

A few days later, I woke at the usual time, but instead of getting ready for rehearsals, I was getting ready to go down to the ship in Portsmouth. I was going for a handover cruise with Steve (cruise director). I was looking forward to catching up with him after three months, while also "learning the ropes." I spent most of the morning packing and getting organized for the trip. I went over to rehearsals at lunch with my suitcase to say goodbye to everyone, but they were all on lunch when I arrived. I bumped into Lauren at the entrance of the pub as I was leaving.

"Where are you off to?" she asked; noticing my suitcase.

"I'm on my way to get on the ship for a cruise," I said. I explained to her that I was spending a few days with Steve to go through the hand over process.

"Debbie's place will be so quiet with both you and Blain away for the weekend," she said (Blain was also away on business).

"Will you miss me?" I asked in a cheeky way.

Lauren looked at me with an equally cheeky little school-girl grin. "Maybe," she said.

"Do you want my mobile number so you can text me while I'm away?" I asked.

She smiled and looked at me with those gorgeous eyes, then replied, "Maybe."

We exchanged numbers. She smiled at me and said, "Don't miss me too much. Have a safe trip."

I smiled at her, then turned and left the pub. Again, while I was flattered that she was flirting with me in this way, I was wondering if that was simply her nature, or if she had other plans for her and me, while we were at sea together.

Home away from home.

I made my way to Clapham Junction Station, bought my ticket, and waited for the next train headed for Portsmouth, where the ship docked each week. As I was waiting for the train, I began flicking through my phone, out of boredom. As I went through the numbers in my address book, I saw Lauren's name. I looked at the number for a few seconds and thought about sending her a text message, but then decided against it.

About twenty minutes into the journey, just as I was drifting off to sleep, my phone beeped with a message. I looked to see who the message was from. As I opened it, I saw that it was from Lauren. I found myself getting a little excited. I couldn't believe she sent me a message so soon. The message read: *Hi it's Lauren. How r u. R u missin me yet? Luv Lauren.* I pressed reply on my phone and simply wrote back: "*Maybe,*" then laughed to myself, as I sent it.

I smiled, as I put my phone back on the table in front of me and closed my eyes again. Not even two minutes later, my phone rang. At first, I thought that it was Lauren ringing. I picked up my phone to see it was the office calling. I answered the phone, to hear Mark's voice on the other end of the line.

"Hi, J. D, its Mark," he said. "How are you, Squire?"

"Fine, thanks, Mark," I replied.

"We have a little problem," he said. "Steve has gone to hospital and might not make it back to the ship before it sails tonight."

Mark continued to explain the situation to me and told me, that I would have to take charge of the entertainment program for the cruise.

"You will be fine. Craig, your assistant, has Steve's keys, and he knows how the ship runs. I have spoken to him, and he is ready to assist you, should you need anything," he explained. "We wouldn't do this to you, if we didn't think you were capable of doing the job."

The phone call wrapped up, with Mark giving me a few more details of the on-board Entertainment fund and the banking for the bingo, etc.

As I hung up, I thought to myself, *holy shit. I'm now the cruise director.* I knew it would be okay, as it was the off season, and there was no cast on board yet. There was only a house band, DJ, and Craig, my light entertainer, who did the game shows and bingo on board, so the entertainment program was pretty straightforward. I was ready for the challenge and also excited about being the cruise director, a little sooner than I expected.

I arrived in Portsmouth at around 4:30 p.m. and met Craig and Gareth (DJ) in the terminal. I had never met Craig before, but had worked with Gareth the previous year, when I was in the cast. Craig helped me onto the ship, gave me the cruise director's keys, and gave me the rundown of what was happening that evening. After helping me on board, Craig ran

C.R.U.I.S.E

into town, as he had to get a few things, while I re-acquainted myself with the old tin can, that I once again called home.

The first thing I noticed while I was walking around, was that nothing at all had changed. There were the same familiar faces in the bars and at the purser's desk (the pursers are the equivalent to receptionists in a hotel). The pursers were going about their usual business, taking care of passengers' passports, currency exchange, wake-up calls, immigration, and clearance of the ship. Everyone was a bit surprised that I had returned as cruise director, but they were all glad that someone who knew the ship and the shows, was taking over. One of the first places I visited was the Galax Bar, where most of the entertainment takes place.

As I was walking around the ship, my phone rang, and it was Slim. He was ringing to tell me that he too was coming back to the ship in a few weeks. He said that he only agreed to another contract, because he had heard that I was cruise director. He told me how excited he was to be coming back to work with me again. He assured me that he would behave, if I asked him to, but that he and I were going to get up to all sorts of mischief that contract, which I didn't mind, as long as we were able to cover our backsides.

Later that night, the house band and I, kicked off with a few tunes in the usual band set. Nothing out of the ordinary—just some Tom Jones, Bee Gees, and the usual easy-listening stuff. We got to the last song of the half-hour set, which was a tune called "Because I got high" by "Afro man." Now, I'm not quite sure why the band leader chose to do this song, but I was not about to pull rank on him, on my first night filling in, so I sang it.

Anyone who is familiar with the song, will know it contains some quite funny and also quite explicit lyrics. I *wasn't* all that familiar with the song, so I had the lyrics in front of me, for reference in case I forgot the words. As I got toward the end, I hesitated on some lyrics, so I looked at the words and read the next line as I sang it. This wouldn't normally be a problem, except the version I had in front of me, was the full version and not the one with expletives bleeped out or substituted.

I continued to sing the line as I read it, *"And now I'm jacking off and I know why."* As you could just imagine, the band cracked up laughing when they heard me sing those lyrics. At first, I didn't realize what I had sung, until I heard Gary, the drummer, yell out, "I ca-ca-ca-can't believe y-y-you just su-su-sung that, J.D." Well, at least that's what I thought he said. It was a bit hard to decipher what he was saying, amongst his laughing. Besides, Gary has quite a stutter, so he is sometimes hard to understand anyway. Gary is a lovely guy, who I had a lot of respect for as a musician, and I am by no means making fun of people who have a stutter. It was just a very funny situation at the time, made worse by his stutter. Thankfully, the rest of the evening (and the rest of the cruise) went much smoother.

Back to rehearsals.

My fill-in cruise flew by, and before I knew it, I was on a train, headed back to London, to finish off rehearsals. We only had a few more days, before the entire cast and I, were due to join the ship, so it was going to be busy. On our last day of rehearsals, we were to perform one of the shows, for all the people at the office to see. Debbie had hired out a room, so they could watch us perform, because the office staff, very rarely got to see that side of the business. This is something that most cruise lines do during rehearsals. It is a great way for the creative team, production team, office staff and cast to get together and for everyone to see what their hard work equates to on stage, before it gets put on the ship. The day went along without too many dramas, and the show that night also went great. Afterwards, Debbie put on drinks for everyone, and of course the cast and I took full advantage of the opportunity to get totally wrecked.

When the venue closed at the end of the night, we decided that Debbie's place would be the best place to continue partying. The cast and I grabbed our belongs and began walking to Debbie's. It was only about a ten-minute walk, but at the pace we were going, it seemed to take forever. Along the way, Ricky and Lee got themselves into an argument over which one of them was the best kisser. They decided to enlist the services of Lauren and Hannah to decide.

Lee and Ricky each kissed both the girls, but then proceeded to also kiss Kirsty and Cassie, as well. Then Lauren kissed Regan and Dom, while Hannah kissed Cassie and Dom. As we walked along, I remember thinking to myself; *What a cozy cast I have here. This lot will do great on ships.* Before I knew it, Cassie had grabbed me and had pulled me into a "lip lock." Then Hannah spotted it and ran over and planted one on my lips.

When Hannah had finished having her tongue down my throat, she turned to Lauren and said, "Hey, Lauren, you and CD haven't kissed yet." CD is the name that Hannah called me. It's simply short for Cruise Director. So, with that, Lauren "slinked" over to me and ever so gently pressed her lips against mine, before engaging me, in a full-blown tongue kiss, while the entire cast stood around, watching and cheering. All of this, mind you, unfolded in the middle of a dark street in London. Looking back, if this was happening in 2017, I am certain that the rest of the cast would have their smart phones taking pictures and video of this whole debaucherous episode on the London street, so it could be posted all over social media. Thankfully, in those days, phones were only phones.

D'ya like that?

We finally got back to Debbie's place and made our way upstairs, where we discovered that Debbie had arranged a banquet of food and drink for us. It was just magic. The lights were dim, there were several bottles of fine champagne on the table, gorgeous food as well, and both sides of the fireplace were burning brightly. Our musical director, James, had joined us and made his way to the stunning, white baby grand piano in the corner and began playing some old musical theatre tunes, as we got totally smashed and tried to sing along.

After having been drinking for a good few hours, I needed to excuse myself and head to the bathroom to "break the seal." I looked around and noticed that Lauren was not in the room, and in fact, I didn't recall having seen her, for quite some time. I didn't think a great deal of it, so I trotted off to the toilet, which was up the corridor. As I approached the toilet, I heard someone violent coughing, followed by what sounded like someone vomiting. The door was slightly ajar, so I opened it a little more, to find Lauren on her knees, wiping her mouth with toilet paper. I helped her up and asked if she was okay. She said she was fine and that she was going to bed. She stood up and took two steps before stumbling into me, so I picked her up and carried her downstairs.

We entered her room, and as I tried to put her down gently on her bed, I lost my balance, and we both fell on the bed with me falling on top of her. In the position we were laying, we looked at each other, and with only an inch to move to touch lips, we kissed. The thought never even crossed my mind, that this was the girl, who had just finished throwing up. We continued to kiss for quite a while, after which time we somehow ended up totally naked. I say "somehow", because neither of us really remembered how we got that way.

Before we knew it, we were deep in the throes of drunken sex. Meanwhile, Paul, who was one of the cast members from another ship, that was rehearsing at the same time, had also noticed that Lauren was missing from the party and had decided to come down to see if he could score. The next part of the story, is in Paul's words, as I was far too drunk to remember much of what I was doing, let alone what he was doing, or what he heard.

Paul claims that he arrived at Lauren's door and was about to knock, when he heard moaning from the two of us inside. He stood at the door for a moment and (in his words) heard an "Aussie voice" say, "D'ya like that?" at which time he thought, *no point in staying here*, and he headed back up to the party. I say, "no point in staying," because he was looking to score with Lauren, but knew he was too late. Now, I must say that even though I may have in the past been known to say some pretty stupid things in bed, the words "Do you like that" or "D'ya like that," are not something I would say.

Meanwhile, back in the bedroom, Lauren and I were doing our best to make the experience pleasurable for each other, but unfortunately, neither of us were succeeding, and in fact, Lauren passed out, within a few minutes, so that was the end of that. I thought it best to leave her to sleep it off and wake up in peace, rather than roll over, still half drunk in the morning and think, *oh my god, what did I do?* so I went off to my own bed.

In the morning, I turned up in Lauren's room, with two cups of coffee; one for each of us. I knocked and entered her room. Lauren was awake but still in bed. I handed her the coffee, and she looked at me and simply said, "We did, didn't we?"

To which I replied, with a sheepish grin, "Yes."

"Gee, thanks for leaving then." She laughed.

"I thought it was the best thing to do." I said.

We both agreed, that it was best for this to stay as our secret for the meantime, as it would only make the next week on board more stressful, if everyone was gossiping about us. Besides, we bot had partners, so each of us had to think about what we wanted to do, given the situation. No sooner had we agreed on it, Lauren's phone rang. It was Hannah, and Hannah's first words were, "Debbie just found out that you and CD, had sex last night."

"Oh my god!" Lauren screamed, and then said to me, "Debbie knows."

Apparently, Paul went straight into rehearsals that morning and told all the cast and Debbie what he had supposedly heard. Word got around the office so fast, that by this time, the entire office was running around saying, "D'ya like that?" (do you like that) in an Australian accent. Lauren was gutted, and I too was a bit embarrassed about the situation. According to Hannah, Debbie just laughed when she found out and said, "They could have at least waited until they got on the bloody ship." So there was our personal life on show for everyone to see, and this was even before we got on board.

The Cruise Director's code.

It was later that same day, that Debbie, the cast, and myself all arrived at the ship for "Hell week." This was the same as the first week on board the previous year, except I also had to learn all the cruise director duties, on

Same - Same, But Different

top of rehearsals, given that Steve was in hospital the week before when I was supposed to learn everything with him. Fortunately for me, I wasn't required at all the midnight rehearsals with the cast, because I knew two of the three shows, from the year before.

On most ships, the cruise director does not perform in the production shows. The cruise director's job is to manage the entertainment team, liaise between the production company and the cruise line on any issues, and create and implement the cruise planner or entertainment schedule for each cruise. In my case, though, I had the extra challenge of having cameos in each show, as well as providing the links between numbers, while the cast got changed throughout the show. This was quite a challenge for me, as even though I was used to being on stage, it is very difficult. As any compère or comedian will tell you, to stand on stage and be witty, funny, and informative, while also making the link seem natural, free flowing, and seamless; is not as easy as it may look. There are a lot of little details and critical timing, that make it look as polished as it does.

With a little bit of spare time, Steve and I went through the business side of the job. Because Steve and I were quite good mates, one of the first things we discussed, was what anyone who has been cruise director on this ship, considers the most important thing you can learn. Put simply, it was almost like having a license to print money.

The way it worked, was that the day you board as cruise director, your predecessor sits down with you and explains various methods of making a lot of extra money on the side, through various means. Now, I know almost every ship afloat had similar scams going on, but this particular ship was by far the most lucrative. It was up to you, as to whether or not you wanted to partake in these money-making schemes. I will leave it up to your imagination, as to whether or not, you think I did, or if I am just telling you a good story. Either way, what was compulsory, was that you passed this information on, to the next cruise director, regardless of whether or not you used this information yourself, during your time on board.

The ship would hold two games of bingo, each day, in the afternoon and evening. The bingo tickets were sold for one pound per ticket, or a strip of six tickets for five pounds. Once you collected all of the money, you would go back to the cruise director's office, count it, and then enter the amount into a spreadsheet on the computer. The computer would then calculate it and tell you how much a house was worth and how much a line was worth. We only played one line and one house each session. The computer would also calculate ten percent for the onboard entertainment fund, which paid for tickets and markers, etc.

I know that nothing so far seems out of the ordinary, however, what would happen, as part of the scam, was that once you would count the money, let's say the total was £1,000, before you would enter the amount into the computer, you might pocket £100, or £150. This meant, that the amount that you actually enter into the computer, would be £900 or £850. The computer would give you an amount of roughly £205 for a line and £560 for a house (after the 10% for entertainment fund was subtracted).

Next, before you put the prize money into separate envelopes for the winners, you would remove another, let's say, £50 from the line prize money and £100 from the house prize money. This leaves a line paying £155, the house paying £460, and you with around £300 - £350 in your pocket. Like I said, bingo was played twice a day, six days a week, leaving your "bingo profits" at somewhere around £3,500 - £4,000 per week—and that's just the bingo.

The thing that made this situation fool proof and unlike any other ship, was that firstly, the passengers paid in cash. Most cruise ships are "cash free", and secondly, the passengers never knew exactly how much you would enter into the computer and the office, never knew how much you gave to the passengers. This meant, that there was no way of tracking any of it and no way of anyone proving whether or not anything untoward was happening.

In addition to bingo, there was another great money spinner that took place, on this ship. Each and every month, head office would send on thirty-six large envelopes, which all contained a certificate for one free, three-day cruise. Each of these cruises were valued at £400+ and even more, during the summer months. The cruise director's job was to give

Same - Same, But Different

them away as prizes for our major game shows, or to raffle them off, for various charities or organizations. As long as you could account for all thirty-six each month, then no questions were ever asked.

There is nothing wrong with any of that, but where it became fun, was, if you could put a few away each month, then you could profit from the spare certificates. Sometimes, the weather would be too rough, and we would cancel a game show, which meant the prize for that night, was put to one side, and could be used however you liked. We would also hold raffles each month, but sometimes, the raffles would get cancelled due to rough weather also. On average, you could have up to ten free cruise certificates spare each month, for various reasons.

Because the ship also doubled as a ferry, we had lots of truck drivers frequent the ship, who knew that the cruise director might have a spare mini cruise, that could be purchased for £150. Some of them would then sell it for £200+ for a profit. Selling the mini cruises was not the most profitable way for the cruise director to off load the free cruises. The raffles were by far the best way. On average, each raffle would fetch £600, so once again, you'd be looking at another £1,500 per week profit—on average—from this side of the operation. As long as we filled our quota for charities, like the "Biscay dolphin society", or some other charity that we were obligated to have raffles for, then no one cared.

All in all, as cruise director, you might be looking at £5,000 - £6,000 per week in extra cash in your pocket for very little effort. When you also add to the equation, that in 2002 the Australian dollar was on 33c to the British pound, that meant a profit of somewhere in the vicinity of $15,000 - $18,000 per week you could be earning as an Aussie Cruise Director on board. This of course, was on top of the cruise director's wage, which was paid in cash as well.

There was of course some risk involved, if anyone else found out about this operation, so therefore, it was best to act alone. Sometimes, Craig would help me sell tickets for bingo, or raffle tickets and I'd buy him drinks or give him a lazy £50 here and there. He didn't ask, and I don't think he cared too much either, as long as he was getting something out of it.

I remember the first time I had the opportunity to fiddle with the bingo money. I got back to the office and counted the money. I sat in my chair for a few moments, contemplating whether or not to actually do it. I think I was only game enough to take £20 pounds out before entering the amount into the computer. I wasn't game enough to fiddle with the amounts for a line or house that first time. After a few times though, I found myself getting more daring, until on some occasions, there may have been more than £400 vanish before the computer entry and £300 after (if the original pot was over £2000).

Needless to say, most of the cruise directors on board this particular ship, did use this system and would even add more ways of making money to it. The other rule to this situation, was that before your contract ended, you had to purchase something substantial, for the cruise director's cabin, to make it a little bit better for each person following on. So, with a problem of trying to work out where I would keep all my newfound savings, I thought, my purchase for the cabin, would be a safe. While out shopping one day, I purchased a great, solid safe and installed it in my cabin. It was not huge, but it certainly was big enough to keep that much money in. By the time I handed the cabin over to the next cruise director, it had a plasma TV, DVD player, 5.1 Surround sound system, PS2, remote control cars, and many other boy toys to play with.

Tits for Toblerone.

Another perk of the job on board this particular ship, was the endless supply of chocolate at my disposal. I wasn't the biggest chocolate fan, but nonetheless, I realized quick smart, that with most women, and in particular, with Lauren, nothing soothes period pain, like a huge block of "Toblerone." Even though I always joked about it, I've since discovered that cocoa is actually a natural muscle relaxant and antioxidant, which in fact means that it *does* soothe period pain. So, men, go and get shares in Cadbury and your life will be much more peaceful.

Each week, at least five or six boxes of Toberlone's would be delivered

Same - Same, But Different

from head office, and they were supposed to be given away to the children during kid's discos, etc. Most of the time, though, they were forgotten, and the pile of boxes in my office would simply keep piling up. There was a point where I think there must have been at least thirty boxes, and I noticed that they were all nearing their expiry date. Each of these thirty boxes, contained twelve, twelve-inch Toblerone's. That's at least three hundred and sixty huge blocks of chocolate in my office, about to go to waste.

It was one Friday night and our usual "Friday night party cruise," when I finally got around to doing something about the mountain of chocolate piling up in my office and blocking my way in. On these particular nights, the ship was basically a floating night club with approximately two-thousand passengers, most of which were on Hens' nights or bucks' nights. The object of attending these nights, was for the passengers to get as smashed as possible and shag as many people as possible; it seriously was. I kid you not, when I say it was nothing less than a rampant orgy at sea. I can honestly say that even though this was the case, and I often struggled with my morals whilst at sea, I never once shagged anyone or misbehaved in any way, on these nights. I did however, spend most of the nights, staring at the endless traffic of British women, getting their tits out.

My cabin was up at the front of the ship, near the bridge, and outside my window, on the outside deck, was a bench seat where, on most Friday nights, you would find at least two or three couples having sex (not all at the same time). On more than one occasion, I had to bang on the window to scare them off, so I could get some sleep.

On this particular night though, I was not having an early night, and at about 10:00 p.m., I made my way down to the nightclub, to see how things were going. Slim was in the sound booth playing DJ, as he usually did on these nights. As I entered the booth, Slim excitedly greeted me.

"Have you seen all the fucking pie here tonight?"

Well, who couldn't see it, I thought to myself. It was everywhere. The place was crawling with really drunk English women, who were not afraid to wear tops, that didn't cover up their tits at all. I said to Slim, "Hey, I don't suppose you know how I can get rid of thirty boxes of Toblerone, do you?"

C.R.U.I.S.E

"Are you fucking kidding," was his reply. "Bring them down here, and I'll get rid of it in five minutes flat."

At first, I thought he was joking, but when I later saw how he did it, I was not surprised at all. I arranged for some of the bar staff to bring it all down to the sound booth. They piled it up at the back of the booth, and let me tell you, you've never seen a bigger pile of chocolate.

Here's the funny part. Slim grabs the microphone and addresses the audience. He says, "Right you girls, I've got something that's twelve inches long, hard, and extremely satisfying, so if you want to get a bit, come and see me in the DJ Box. That's right, girls, it's time to play Tits out for Toblerone."

I mean, after all, isn't that what every girl wants? Something that's twelve inches long, hard, and very satisfying? With that, three very cute, and rather well-endowed young women, ran over to the DJ box and asked, "So what do we have to do?" To which Slim replied, "Well, it's Tits for Toblerone, love, so get em' out if you want some."

Without a moment to think, all three of them lifted up their tops and bras to give both Slim and I an eye full of the best tits I'd seen, since Lauren's 32E sized puppies.

"*Whehey?*" Slim yelled. "That's the way, girls!" as he handed each of them a Toblerone.

Before we knew it, we were inundated with hot women, with breasts of all shapes and sizes, giving us a look at their finest assets. Let's face it, their brains were certainly not what they were most blessed with, given that they were happy to flash two total strangers; all for a block of chocolate. Some women were even taking it further, by licking their nipples and asking Slim and I to play with them. As Slim predicted, in less than five minutes, he had managed to give away over three-hundred chocolate bars and I had seen more breasts, than I think I had seen either prior to, or since that night.

Same - Same, But Different

Lauren or Colleen.

Lauren and I had been on board for a few weeks by this stage and had gotten a little closer than either of us had expected. Besides the last night of rehearsals, we had been intimate on a few occasions since, and the topic of "what to do" had come up in conversation. Lauren had not told her boyfriend, Barry anything, and I was of the opinion that I wanted to tell Colleen in person, rather than on the phone. The dilemma I faced was that Colleen was only coming back to the ship, to be with me, but now Lauren and I were trying to work out if there was anything serious between us. This was only the beginning of my total confusion, when it came to what I really wanted.

Talk about "looking for love in all the wrong places." I had no clue at all, so I kept putting off the problem and trying not to think about it, in the hope that the situation would miraculously take care of itself. Colleen was such a sweet and innocent girl. She was cute, funny, petite, and very devoted, whereas Lauren was sexy, voluptuous, raunchy and obviously a bit of a bad girl, so I really was torn as to what I wanted. I mean, couldn't I have it all? Definitely not, it seemed.

I was trying to work out how to handle this situation. Do I call Colleen to break it off and risk losing her altogether, even though I'm not sure if there is anything worthwhile between Lauren and I? Or do I stop what is going on with Lauren and try to make it work with Colleen? Lauren said, that she didn't want to tell Barry over the phone either. She also had feelings for me, but wasn't sure how serious they were, at that stage. I don't think either of us was particularly happy, that the other had a partner on land, but at the same time, it didn't exactly stop us either.

This is what I was talking about, when it came to relationships on a ship being so different. It's not that you as a person change. It's kind of like, there is another power, that has control of your emotional state and guides you into situations you would not normally get involved in on land. It could be the fact, that ship life can be very lonely, or perhaps the feeling of being trapped on board and isolated from the rest of the world, makes you cling to anyone, in a similar situation. In the end, both Lauren and I, blocked out the fact, that we had other partners, until we had to face it. That day came, just before Colleen was due to come back on the ship.

The day before Colleen was due to return, Lauren and I had a lengthy chat and decided we both wanted to make a go of things, and we were both going to end our other relationships. Lauren knew that when Colleen first got on board, she would expect me to be normal, and as soon as I wasn't, she would realize something had happened. I decided that the best thing for me to do, was to have a good chat to Colleen the moment she boarded. Lauren agreed to give me space that day and night, to sort things out with Colleen.

The following afternoon, when Colleen arrived, I met her in the terminal and gave her a kiss and a hug, then helped her with her luggage up the gangway and into her cabin. The moment we arrived in her cabin, I sat her down and explained to her that I needed some time alone, and that I thought it was for the best if we were friends rather than lovers. Of course, the first question she asked was, whether or not I had been with anyone; to which I lied and said no. I totally understand this was not the right thing to do, however, as most of us know, when it comes to situations like this, it's never easy to be totally honest, even when we know it is for the best.

I've never been one to intentionally hurt people, even though I realize that my actions in this case, were quite weak. I knew Colleen was hurting enough by the situation, and I didn't want to add to this by telling her that the reason for my not wanting to be with her, was because I had been with Lauren. The only problem with this approach, was that now Lauren and I had to somehow, keep our relationship a secret from Coleen. Well, let's be honest, we had to keep it a secret from everyone, because if anyone knew, then everyone would know.

Unfortunately, this didn't last too long, as word started to spread around the ship (and to Colleen) that Lauren and I were quite close and may be more than just friends. In fact, it was only a few days later, when Coleen found out. It was late one night, when I went to the soft drink vending machine, not too far from my cabin, to get Lauren and I some drinks, when I

Same - Same, But Different

ran into Colleen. I'm not too sure why she was up on that deck, given that my cabin was on deck nine and hers was on deck two. I think she may have actually been coming to see me, even though she didn't mention it.

I grabbed the two drinks that had been dispensed, at which point, Coleen questioned why I had two drinks and not one. I'm sure I was not all that convincing when I told her that I was saving the other one for later. She didn't question my answer, but asked if she could come and spend some time with me. Now, normally, this would not be a problem, as I cared about Colleen and really enjoyed our time together, except Lauren was in my cabin at this stage; in lingerie. I told Colleen I was tired and wanted to go straight to bed, and with that, I left, and she returned to her cabin to go to bed; or so I thought.

Within the next half an hour, Lauren and I were being intimate, but within minutes of us getting naked, my cabin door flew open (yes, I stupidly left it unlocked), and there was Colleen, standing in the doorway, with a handful of pictures of her and I, which she had torn up. She screamed at me, "You lying fucking arsehole," (which was true), threw the pictures everywhere, and slammed the door shut again. This was the last I saw of Colleen for quite a while, and it was quite some time before we even spoke to each other.

As for Lauren and I, this was only the beginning of what became a very interesting contract, to say the least. As the relationship developed, it became apparent that Lauren wanted to make sure that I was devoted to her. Unfortunately, this situation was a little one sided. Despite my attempts to convince her that she should end things with Barry, she often told me she would, but that she was waiting for the right time and she didn't want to do it over the phone. At the time, I was very trusting of Lauren and honestly thought she was telling me the truth. However, as the story unfolded, I may have been a little naïve.

...To be continued.

C.R.U.I.S.E

Aussie style.

One of the hardest things about working on cruise ships for long periods of time, is the fact that you're so far away from your family and friends. You end up meeting some fabulous people, and those around you, all become like family, but sometimes it's the smallest things, that mean the most while you're away from home. In this case, it was quite a big thing. It was our usual "Friday Night Shite," as we called it. The Friday night party cruise across to France, where everyone gets wasted and has as much sex as possible.

I arrived back on board, this particular Friday afternoon, after a few beers at the local pub and headed straight to talk to the chief purser, to see if there was anything special planned for the night. The chief purser is like the hotel director of the ship, so he or she, along with the cruise director, is in charge of the day-to-day running of the entire ship and all of its activities. On some ships, they are called the hotel director.

I sat down with Bruce, and he informed me that Foster's Brewing had supplied the ship with a huge amount of beer, promotional material, and merchandise to stage a "Foster's Party Night." Since I'm an Australian and Foster's is an Australian company, Bruce asked me what a typical "Aussie party" would involve; to which my immediate response was, "Wet t-shirt competition."

"You're kidding me, right," replied Bruce, as he shook his head, in disbelief, at my response.

At first, he flatly refused to let me host such an event, but I managed to convince him to discuss the various pros and cons of it on a cruise ship. After much debate, he agreed to let me to stage the wet t-shirt competition that night. I can't remember what kind of bullshit theories I came up with as "pros," but they must have been damn good, to outweigh the many cons and the potential issues we could face. I'm pretty sure, that at this point, there had never been a wet t-shirt competition on any ship in the world; however, this was the first of two, that I got away with at sea.

It was a logical idea, in my eyes, to provide maximum promotion for

Same - Same, But Different

Foster's and also a perfect opportunity to give away the massive amount of merchandise, that Fosters had provided us with. After all, aren't beer companies like Foster's trying to portray that drinking their beer, leads to good times and sex with big-breasted women? Or was that just what I got out of their TV commercials as a teenage boy in the 1980s? Fosters had provided us with dozens of white t-shirts, that were quite tacky, but perfect for a wet t-shirt competition, so I was not about to waste such a perfect opportunity.

With that, I headed straight up to the nightclub, to get things sorted. I opened the door to the sound booth, to find Slim with his arm around a six-foot-tall, cardboard cutout of "Skippy the bush kangaroo," who was holding a can of Foster's lager. Slim had placed his headphones over Skippy's head and was making kangaroo noises, like he was imitating the television show, "Skippy."

Slim said, "What's that, Skip? It's time to get pissed on Foster's. Good idea, Skip. What's that, Skip? JD's gonna get his dick sucked tonight?" Slim laughed at himself, as I shook my head, at his comment.

"Where the hell did he come from"? I asked Slim.

"He came with the Foster's stuff, boss," Slim said (imitating Steve Irwin). "Isn't he a *beauty*?"

We both pissed around for a while, playing with Skippy and all the other Foster's stuff before formulating a game plan for the evening. Craig; my game show host arrived, and between the three of us, we had the entire night sorted.

Later that night, the room was packed, and it was time to get the wet t-shirt competition going. Craig found ten of the most well-endowed women we could find. English women are certainly well stacked, from my experience, so it wasn't too hard for him to find enough busty contestants. I generously offered to help the women get changed backstage into their Foster's t-shirts, which they were all accepting of my assistance. Not one of these girls had any problems with me being there, as they got their clothes off.

We took the ladies on stage and had them line up, facing the raucous

C.R.U.I.S.E

crowd. As the boss, I made sure that it was my job to wet their shirts, so with great pleasure, and to the crowd's delight, I began spraying water out of a spray bottle onto their tits. For my liking, and the liking of the crowd, this way of wetting the women, was too slow, so I grabbed the buckets of water, nearby and started pouring jugs of water, over their tits instead.

You're probably thinking, "what's the big deal? It's just a wet t-shirt comp." The unique thing about this, was that you would not find another cruise ship anywhere in the world, that would have allowed this to happen. Add to this the fact that most of them rubbed their breasts up against me and then took their tops off on stage, and it was no wonder it was the highlight of the evening's entertainment.

The rest of the evening was also a brilliant success. We had various games and competitions, including having to drink two pints of Foster's through a straw, while on their hands and knees, to give away all of the prizes we had. After all the excitement of the evening, I decided to go back to my cabin for a while to "cool off." Lauren and the cast were off the ship for the night and out on the town in England. I decided to give her a quick call to see how she was doing. I spoke to her for a while, and upon hanging up, I thought it best to have a reasonably early night.

For some reason, though, I thought that I should go back down to the party, to make sure everything was fine, before going to bed. I arrived downstairs in the nightclub, to see that the party was still in full swing. I opened the sound booth door to find Slim, my musical director; Andrew, and the bass player, all groping at a skanky-looking blonde woman. Andrew had latched onto the girl's left breast like a sucker fish, while the bass player had his tongue down the girl's throat. Meanwhile, Slim had my microphone, improperly positioned between her legs and had inserted inside her.

"Slim!! That's my microphone," I said.

Slim just laughed and said, "I know, boss; that's why I grabbed this one."

I watched in disbelief for a moment, then reached into my pocket, grabbed a handful of cocktail vouchers, and handed them to Slim. "Here, give her some of these, for keeping my team entertained," I said.

Same - Same, But Different

"I already have. How did you think we got her to do this, boss?" replied Slim.

With that, I closed the door and left them to it. As much as they looked to be having a good time, and I am sure I would have been more than welcome to join in, for more than one reason, I declined to do so and went back to my cabin. Part of being a good boss on a cruise ship, is allowing your team to let off steam sometimes, while not being seen to be a part of it. If I don't see it, I can't act upon it, is my theory and therefore, I can't be held responsible by the Captain, if the shit hits the fan. Even though what they were doing may not have been morally right, they were not hurting anyone, and the woman involved, was a willing participant. Besides, I learned that by giving them all some slack from time to time, when I *did* need to pull the reins in, they always responded favourably, out of respect for me.

Themed cruises

I mentioned in the previous story, that things like wet t-shirt competitions, never happened on cruise ships. That is not entirely true. While these types of things, don't happen on most regular cruises, some cruise lines, take it even further, by having themed cruises. Themed cruises, attract a particular type of passengers, with specific interests in the subject. The cruise lines go all out in making sure that the theme is provided, in every facet of the voyage.

Most themed cruises are harmless, such as "food and wine cruises", or "comedy cruises", where the ship brings on various comedians, or has a sole focus on special food and wine. There are also some rather interesting themed cruises as well, that have proven to be quite popular. Some of the more common themed cruises, are "country and western music", "Star-trek", psychic cruises", "spiritual cruises", or in Australia, we have "Melbourne Cup cruises" and "state of origin cruises" catering to sporting fanatics.

For the more adventurous, there are even "gay and lesbian cruises", "nudist cruises" and "swinger's cruises". I bunched these three together, because, for the most part, all three, end up resembling the other two at some point. I've not been on any of these three themed cruises, but from all accounts, they are extremely wild. I have, on occasions, been known as a part time nudist / swinger, but I'm not sure that even I, would be comfortable, with 2,500 naked / horny people, all in the one place. I know that Slim, on the other hand, would be in his element on one of these cruises.

One of the dancers that I worked with, later in my career, was a dancer on one of the nudist cruises. She said that it was the most bizarre experience, she had ever experienced. She said that there were literally, thousands of naked passengers, everywhere she went on the ship. As a dancer, like all the crew, she was clothed, which probably made it even more bizarre. Maybe, I would I enjoy it. I know that it would be something that I would never forget. Maybe one day, I will give one of these themed cruises a try, for a laugh.

Although, it was never an official "themed swingers or nudist cruise", on board, it almost felt like it, on many occasions, with the crew. It was well known, by the crew, that what happens below passenger decks, in crew areas, is unrestricted, providing, no one gets hurt and no one is violated, or made to do something, against their will.

You can't do that in public.

Speaking of people being violated…As you've probably worked out by now, my not-so-little mate, Slim, was quite a handful. Slim had no respect for authority whatsoever, so it was very lucky, that I had our friendship to draw on, if I needed Slim to toe the line. The thing with Slim, was that when he got one of these urges to misbehave, quite often, it erupted like a volcano or an earthquake. It was usually out of the blue, without warning, and it usually caused tremors throughout the entire ship. This next incident was no exception. In fact, this incident sums up that analogy perfectly.

It was during one of our production shows titled "Legends at Sea," right in the middle of the "Rock Brit Awards" section, where I was on stage

Same - Same, But Different

as a reporter talking to the crowd. The other cast members were busily running around the stage with fake cameras and microphones, acting like paparazzi. I addressed the crowd as follows: *"We're here at the Rock Brit Awards, and the paparazzi are anxiously jostling for a front row position. It looks as though Mister Robbie Williams has just arrived! Yes, the wild man of rock and pop has just stepped onto the red carpet. Oh, and arriving at exactly the same time is Liam Gallagher! This is indeed an exciting moment in the world of Rock and Roll, anything could happen here."*

Ricky, dressed as Liam Gallagher from the band Oasis, walked up onto stage from the audience and stood front and centre. The other cast members gathered around Ricky, as I continued: *"Oh my god! Some bird from the news of the world has just leaped onto the red carpet and jumped in front of Mr Gallagher. He's pushed her and the crowd is plunged into silence."* This line was a cue for the band to begin playing the song "Roll with It," by Oasis.

At this precise moment, and in the 2-3 seconds of silence, between my cue and the band starting, Slim put a microphone to his arse and ripped off one of the biggest farts, I had ever heard. His "gastro-nomical" movement, went thundering through the entire sound system, in a way that sounded like it would have equalled the noise levels of Hiroshima, on the day they dropped the bomb there. I totally lost it on stage and so did the other cast members. I ran backstage to take a breath and to wipe the tears of laughter, from my face. As I arrived backstage, I heard Slim's voice come across the intercom system.

"Boss, Boss, are you there," he said.

I walked over to the intercom and spoke (well, tried to, as I laughed). "Yes, Slim."

"Oh my god, boss, did you hear that? I almost shit my pants," he said.

Having trouble speaking, I managed to mutter back, "Yes I heard it. And I think the rest of the world heard it too." Through all of this, the audience, were still laughing, and poor Ricky, was doing his best to sing the rest of his solo number, on stage.

The interesting thing about Slim, was that even though he was totally vulgar and had no sense of morals whatsoever, he really was quite harmless. I've never seen him go out of his way to hurt anyone. He's always the one to step in and break up a fight and is always so laid back. It's just that he likes to have a laugh, at the expense of himself or anyone else and he manages to get himself into more strife, than anyone I have ever met. How that boy has not got himself sacked, is beyond me.

Biker trouble.

A classic example of why I, along with most people, learned to tolerate Slim and his indiscretions, was when we had a group of one hundred and four Hell's Angels bikers get on board this one day in Spain. They were travelling back to England, and from the moment they got on board, all the crew were on edge. Not because they were menacing towards us, but because they hooked into the beer as soon as they boarded at 10:00 a.m. Needless to say, that by late afternoon, with a gutful of booze, they were beginning to get a little rowdy.

I managed to locate their Sargent at arms (the big boss) early on, and he was awesome at sorting any of them out, if they started to play up. I had no problem with them having a laugh, or getting a bit rowdy, as long as they understood, that we had women and children on board, so a little bit of respect for other passengers was appreciated. It was about 2130 that evening, when I got word that we had a medical disembarkation that needed to take place immediately. A passenger had fallen ill and needed to be airlifted to France by helicopter. With that being in progress on the upper decks of the ship, security and all the senior officers and bridge officers were all tied up while they completed the airlift.

That was fine, as the show was about to start, and it didn't affect us at all. That was until one of the Hell's Angels had a disagreement with another guy in the show lounge. Me, Slim, Fletch (the bar manager), and Dom (my lighting technician), all went over to smooth things over before it erupted. Just as we approached the two arguing, they started throwing punches at each other. The instant those two started throwing punches, four or

Same - Same, But Different

five of the Hell's Angels boys stepped in and began kicking the shit out of this other lone guy, right in front of his girlfriend. I instantly went for the phone to call the bridge. Meanwhile, Fletch turned and ran like a girl. Dom grabbed the closest fire extinguisher and started spraying them with foam, while Slim jumped right in the middle of the fight to break it up.

Of course, when I called the bridge, the response I got was, "We can't help you." A lot of fucking good they were. We're holding off a full-scale war with nothing more than a crazy fat sound tech (Slim) with no thought for his own safety and a gay guy (Dom) with a fucking fire extinguisher, and they're too busy on the bridge. Gee, thanks. Thankfully, some of the other Hell's Angels had enough sense to break it up. They sat back down, and I jumped up on stage, shaking like a leaf and addressed the audience. Now, I'm no big guy and certainly no match for over a hundred Hell's Angels, but for a moment in time, even though I was shitting my pants, I somehow appeared to be ten-foot-tall and bulletproof as I spoke to the crowd.

"Look!" I said. "I know you're all having a good time, and I know you guys have all had a gutful of booze, and I also know you might want to beat the crap out of each other, but if you do, then I don't think it's too much to ask, that you go out on deck and beat the crap out of each other away from the women and children. Does that sound fair?"

For a split second, my heart was in my mouth as I awaited their response. Then, instantaneously, the crowd all erupted into spontaneous cheers of agreement with me.

Thank god for that, I thought to myself. I thought I was dead meat for a second, for telling them to pull their heads in. I jumped off stage and made my way to the bar for a well-earned drink. Fletch snuck me a quick one, seeing as all the officers were assisting with the evacuation. As I stood at the bar, one of the Hell's Angels came up to me.

"You've got some big fucking balls. But you're an Aussie, so that's to be expected." He laughed. "You think we have a bad reputation. We're nothing compared to your Aussie Hell's Angels. Complete respect, fella." He smiled and shook my hand, and that was the last of the trouble for that night.

C.R.U.I.S.E

That bloody "moral" bin on the gangway.

I mentioned in the introduction, that on all ships, there seemed to be a mythical bin on the gangway, where most crew members seem to throw their morals, upon boarding a cruise ship. Well, I am no exception to this. I had been extremely guilty of acting inappropriately when it came to being faithful to my girlfriend(s) at sea. As you already know, I failed when put under pressure by beautiful women, on more than one occasion, and unfortunately, for those of you who disapprove of this sort of behavior, there is more of it to come in this book.

I look back now on these instances, and while I do not necessarily agree with this type of behavior, I do believe that every single thing we do in our lives is somehow part of the big picture, and that there is always a lesson for us in these situations. To say that Lauren and I had a perfect relationship at any stage of our time together, would be a complete lie. Lauren and I had great passion and were extremely attracted to each other, however, we failed in all the other crucial areas of a relationship. When it came to trust, honesty, loyalty, you name it, we sucked, so it was no surprise to know that as soon as someone of the opposite sex showed a keen interest in me, I took the bait.

There was this one girl, who took a liking to me during a cruise. Her name was Stephanie. She was very cute and quite young; nineteen, according to her. At the time, I was twenty-eight, and my last girlfriend (Colleen) was nineteen, and hey, Lauren was only twenty-one, so nineteen wasn't too young for me to be chatting to. Besides, that's all I had on my mind; at that stage. Stephanie told me that she wanted to do work experience as cruise director on a ship. She asked me how she could go about it and if I minded if she followed me around, as I went about my business. I had no problem with this, so that evening, I sat down with her and her friend and had a drink and discussed various things about being a cruise director.

We chatted until about 1:00 a.m. in the nightclub, and everything was innocent; from my side. What I didn't know, though, was that I was being watched by Ricky and Lee, from the other side of the room. As it turned

Same - Same, But Different

out, they were keeping an eye on me on Lauren's behalf. You see, Lauren and I had several arguments over the course of the contract, about me talking with female passengers. My job as cruise director, was to make sure that everyone was having a good time on board. Unfortunately, Lauren was extremely jealous; as I mentioned. This was probably due to the fact, that she still had a boyfriend in Scotland. Lauren would get very upset, if she ever saw me talking to a female passenger. I could talk to male passengers for hours at a time, however, if she saw me look at a female; we would have a big issue.

So, Ricky and Lee had noticed me talking with Stephanie and her friend, and over the course of the evening, Ricky and Lee had made their way closer to us, so they could listen in on our conversation. I told you the politics on ships were crazy. At 1:00 a.m., I excused myself from the two young ladies and went to the observation deck at the front of the ship where I would quite often sit and watch the ship plow through the waves. It was indoors and had nice lounges, so it was a very nice place to sit and reflect.

Only a moment after I sat down, Stephanie appeared around the corner and asked if I minded if she sat with me. I didn't say anything at the time, but it seemed obvious, that she had followed me there, in the hope of being alone with me. We chatted for a few minutes, and then she leaned over and began kissing me and rubbing her hand over my crotch. At that point in time, my mind was saying I should stop her...for many reasons, but the heat of the moment somehow overrode that feeling, and I simply let her carry on. Suddenly, a dozen thoughts ran through my mind, primarily, *what about Lauren? What if someone should see us? Should I be doing this?* But before I could work out the answers to these questions or work out what I should do, she had undone my fly and began performing oral sex on me, right in the middle of a public area.

After a very brief moment, I did manage to gather some morals and stopped her from doing what she was doing. I re-gathered myself—along with my fly—and told her that I thought it was best that I went to bed. The following morning, I arrived in the Galax bar and stood at the back of the room watching Craig as he did one of his game shows. Just as I arrived,

C.R.U.I.S.E

Stephanie's friend stormed over to me and said, "You are so disgusting. I can't believe you would take advantage of a sixteen-year-old girl like that."

Of course, I was totally stunned at her comment, given that Stephanie had said she was nineteen and also that at no time did I try to do anything to Stephanie. I guess I'm not the first guy in the world who has had something like this happen to them, and I'm sure I won't be the last. Needless to say, anyone I meet these days, gets asked to provide some sort of photographic identification, before I even *think* about getting intimate with them, no matter how old they look.

> *The fifty-year-old woman I dated many years later got a real thrill out of me asking her for I.D. (well, her fake boobs were underage, even if she wasn't. LOL!)*

A footnote to this story: It was only a few years ago, when I received a random facebook request, from a gorgeous woman, from Essex in England. Here name was Stephanie (Yes, that Stephanie) and she had found some old photos of when she was onboard, fourteen years earlier. We became friends and got to know each other in a more civilized manor. I must say, I was very impressed how Stephanie turned out. She was not only very attractive, but had become quite successful in her life. She is now even married and is very happy. One thing that didn't change, as she told me, was her crush on me and her memories of her cruise, all those years before.

That's one thing that is so special about what I did on cruise ships. Even to this day, I still get people message me, or run into me on different ships, or even in the street, around the world. They all remember me and how I made their cruise a memorable one, which is so nice to hear, so many years later.

Later that day, after the grilling by Stephanie's friend, I went back stage into the fire escape and noticed that Lauren was typing a text message on her phone. As soon as she saw me, she quickly shut her phone and tried to hide it. I asked her who she was texting and why she was acting so suspiciously, to which she replied that she was texting a friend. I asked her if she was texting Barry, and she said she wasn't, but when I asked her to prove it, she refused. I reached for her phone to have a look at it. As I did so, she pulled her hand away. I tried to grab her hand, and in the ensuing struggle, the phone flew out of her hand and down the stairs of the fire escape, that we were standing in. As it landed, it smashed into several pieces.

"You fucking arsehole. It's over," Lauren screamed as she ran off, leaving her phone behind.

I didn't want someone else to find her phone, so I picked up the pieces and attempted to put it back together. Surprisingly, it all fitted back together and turned on like nothing had happened. Of course, curiosity got the better of me, and I had a look at the messages she had sent. Sure enough, there were several sent messages to Barry, saying how much she loved him and how she couldn't wait to see him in a month, etc. I was upset about this, but given that I had acted inappropriately in the relationship, there really wasn't much I could say.

While I was putting her phone back together and seeing if my jealousy was justified, Lauren had run downstairs and into her cabin, crying hysterically. Ricky lived in the cabin next door and heard her and went in to see if she was alright. Lauren told him I grabbed her phone and threw it against the wall to smash it. She told Ricky, that she had broken up with me. At that stage, because it looked like there was no chance for Lauren and me, Ricky told her, that he and Lee had seen me leave the Galax bar with a girl, who they were told was fifteen. Now, I'm not sure where fifteen came from (possibly to make the story seem juicier), but that's ship gossip for you. Either way, Lauren bought Ricky's story, which added more fuel to her reason to end our relationship. Looking back now, though, it was pretty obvious that Lauren had been looking for an excuse to end it all anyway.

Cast change over.

That same afternoon I had to run into the terminal to meet the new cast that was coming on for a cruise, to watch the shows. Deb used to send the new cast on, before they started rehearsals, so they could see what the shows look like. I didn't have time to worry about anything that had happened the night before or earlier that afternoon. I had a cast to get settled, before heading into town myself, to buy some things. I ran into the terminal and greeted them all. They seemed like a nice enough cast. Leanne, the dance captain, introduced me to all of them.

"This is Greg, Phil, Kara, Paula, Andy, Lee and Charlotte."

Charlotte squeezed through the group, grabbed my hand, and said, "Hi, just call me Charlie," as she winked at me.

"Okay, Charlie," I said. "Well let's get you all on board and get settled."

Just as we were about to head off, Lauren came up to me from behind and whispered in my ear, "I know about the fifteen-year-old."

Looking somewhat shocked and not knowing if anyone else had heard what she said, I sarcastically replied, "Okay, love you too," and laughed, trying to cover my shock, as Lauren ran off. I took the new cast on board and showed them to their cabins, before heading into town, still reasonably shaken by the events of the last twenty-four hours. I met up with Ricky in a pub in Portsmouth and explained the situation with Stephanie and that what Lauren was telling him was not totally correct. Ricky was a pretty reasonable guy. He was Lauren's friend, but we had history too, as I knew him from the year before as Rob's boyfriend, so there was a mutual respect there between us.

Later that night, the new cast came to watch the show. At the end of the show, both casts and myself, stood around chatting and getting to know each other. It was obvious that Charlie had taken an instant liking to me, and although she was very cute and I was now apparently single again, I was not about to jump into anything, before thinking carefully about it this time; especially with a cast member. It was also quite obvious that Lauren had also noticed Charlie's advances and didn't like it. This was despite Lauren not wanting a bar of me, herself. A few of the new cast, decided that they were going for a late-night spa and asked if the others and I wanted to join them.

"Come on, it will be fun," said Charlotte (who I will refer to as "Charlie" from now on).

"I'll think about it," I replied. "You go ahead and I'll see." I left the group and headed up to my cabin. On my way upstairs, Lauren approached me from behind and started abusing me for Charlie's obvious affection toward me.

"I can't help it if someone is interested in me," I said. "Besides, it's none of your business now, anyway. You're only shitty because someone else is interested."

What she said next almost floored me, given the circumstances. She said, "I still love you and think I want to try to make it work."

I said, "You're just saying that, so no one else can have me. Sort yourself out, then come and see me." I turned and continued up the stairs.

A little later on, I decided to go and see how everyone was down in the spa. As I arrived, I saw that pretty much both casts were in the spa; it's a big spa. They were all trying to persuade me into joining them; especially Charlie. After a little thought, I decided to go and get my board shorts and join them. I thought that it would be a good opportunity to get to know the new cast, in a casual setting.

A few moments later, I arrived back down at the spa, and as I approached the spa, the only gap in the group appeared between Charlie and Ricky; who had Lauren on the other side of him. I sat down, and in no less than thirty seconds, I felt a hand on my leg. I looked to make sure it wasn't Ricky's (after all, he is that way inclined) and just as I noticed that it was Charlie's, the hand moved up my leg and got a good handful of my manhood. My sudden reflex reaction almost caused me to leap out of the water, but I somehow managed to sit still, as I carefully worked out what to do.

I didn't want to make a scene in front of everyone, as I hardly knew most of them, while at the same time, I really didn't want Lauren to find out either; despite the fact, we were no longer together. Thankfully, the bubbles from the spa created enough of a wash, that no one could see what was going on under water. I left things as they were for ten minutes, before saying, "Hey, I'm off to have a sauna across from my cabin. Anyone care to join me?" I didn't think that anyone would be interested, but of course, in an instant, Charlie said, "I'd love to."

C.R.U.I.S.E

"That sounds great," said Lauren as well.

Oh shit! I thought to myself. *This is exactly what I was trying to avoid.* I quickly got dressed in the hope that both would change their minds, or not find their way to the sauna. Both girls simply wrapped their towels around themselves and picked up their things, as they briskly followed me.

The three of us headed upstairs and entered the changing room, which was adjacent to my cabin. We dropped our things, and opened the sauna door. The light seemed to be blown in the sauna, but that didn't matter, as the sauna itself still worked. As we entered, I did get quite an eye full of Charlie's body. She was certainly fit. She had such an amazing slim figure and a tiny little bum. This was in stark contrast to Lauren's curvy bum, which was somehow in proportion with those massive tits of hers. The three of us sat there, in total darkness for a few moments chatting, when suddenly I felt a hand on my leg again. Again, I was stuck as to how to stop this from happening, as I really felt quite uncomfortable, given that Lauren was also there. I still wanted to be with Lauren, so this situation wasn't helping.

We sat for a while and things didn't seem to progress any further, which was good, so I left things as they were, until maybe ten minutes later, when Charlie started rubbing her hand all over my crotch. She really was trying to arouse me, and to be totally honest; it was working. I was quite aroused, and she knew it. The girl was determined to get some action that night, and nothing was going to stop her. I thought I'd better get out before something else happened, so I headed for the door and grabbed my towel while trying to disguise my obvious bulge from Lauren. The truth of the matter, was that if Lauren wasn't there, I have no doubt, Charlie and I would have fucked in the sauna; which is a pretty hot (pardon the pun) fantasy.

After drying off, the three of us went to the crew mess for something to eat. We all sat for nearly two hours, hoping someone else would leave. Lauren was hoping Charlie would leave. Charlie was hoping Lauren would leave, and I really didn't care who left, as long as one of them did. I was the meat in the sandwich, so to speak, so if I left, I had no doubt, they would both follow; again. Eventually, Lauren decided it was her bed time and left

Charlie and I in the crew mess. After a few moments, I also went to leave, but Charlie said that she didn't know how to get back to her cabin and asked if I could show her where it was. I didn't want her to be wandering around the ship at all hours of the morning, so I helped her find her cabin.

As we arrived at her cabin, Charlie forcefully pushed me against the wall and began kissing me passionately. Once again, who am I to deny a very cute young woman of this kind of fun, if she wants it? I did, however, think it was not a good start to our professional relationship, to go getting involved like this, especially seeing as my last relationship with a cast member had gone totally "tits up." I guess this is where most men, with morals, would have stopped Charlie, but I guess deep down, a big part of my ego was loving the power of knowing that women wanted me. Who knew if this "purple patch" of meeting women was going to last, or if it was just a "lucky streak."

After enjoying her soft lips and passionate advances for a few moments, I suggested to Charlie that we keep this to ourselves, for professional reasons and wished her a goodnight, before going back to my cabin for a good night's rest, after what was an eventful and exhausting twenty-four hours.

The bunny boiler returns.

A few days later, the new cast was heading back to London, to commence their three-week rehearsal period, before returning to the ship, to take over from Lauren's cast. I sat down and had a quick chat with the new cast, prior to them disembarking and gave them all one of my business cards. I let them know that if they had any questions regarding anything to do with the ship, they could call or text me and I would help them out. They all left, and to be honest, I thought it would be the last I would hear from any of them until they came to join the ship three weeks later; I was so wrong.

Not even an hour after they left, I received a text message from Charlie, which read: *Hey, CD, thanks for a great cruise. I'm so excited about seeing you again in a few weeks. Love, Charlie xx.* I thought nothing of it and went about my usual turnaround day business, which involved preparing for the following cruise. A little while later, I got another text from her, saying she missed me, and then another one, later that night, saying that she hoped that we could get to know each other better, when she came back. These messages were very flattering; however, my heart was still getting over Lauren, and I wasn't sure I wanted to get involved with anyone else.

Later that night, there was a knock at my door, and Lauren entered and said she wanted to talk. She wanted to give things another try between us. We talked for a while and agreed we'd get back together. I kind of felt that her main motivation was because she had seen Charlie's interest in me, and she wanted to make sure that Charlie was not getting me. Either way, I was happy we were back together. Perhaps, I was just happy to not be alone on board.

When you're alone at sea, you really are alone. You can't just call your mates up, or pop over for a beer and talk shit with them, to get your mind off not having a partner. You only have a few options; one is to go to the crew bar to drown your sorrows, and the other is, well, jump into bed with anyone else, who is at the crew bar; and clearly alone and drunk too.

The ship arrived in Spain two days later, and at about 5:00 a.m., as the ship came within sight of land, my mobile phone started beeping with one text message after another, which woke both Lauren and I up. I checked to see who they were all from, in case they were urgent messages from the office and surprise, surprise, they were all from Charlie. They all said pretty much the same thing—that she was missing me and she was so excited about seeing me again.

Of course, Lauren's jealousy caused her to ask me who sent them all, and I told her they were from Charlie. I didn't, however, tell her the content of the messages, nor did Lauren know anything had happened with Charlie on the previous cruise. I mean, did I really need to aggravate the situation by telling Lauren that Charlie kissed me when Lauren and I were not together? Things with Lauren and I were still fragile, so I did not want to add any more tension to an already sensitive relationship. I guess I could have just been honest, but I figured nothing would come of it all, so it was best left with Lauren not knowing anything at all.

Same - Same, But Different

Unfortunately, these kinds of text messages continued for the following week, to the point where Lauren was getting so annoyed, that she would wait until I went to the bathroom, then go through my phone to see what Charlie had written. There was even one occasion where Lauren had taken Charlie's number out of my phone and sent Charlie a text from her phone saying "stay the fuck away from my boyfriend," but she didn't tell Charlie who it was from. This was the point where I needed to do one of two things: I either needed to tell Lauren that something had happened when Charlie was on board, or I needed to talk to Charlie and sort it out.

Still not wanting to upset the apple cart with Lauren, I took the second option and went to London to visit the new cast, on a Friday night after their rehearsals. I had told Lauren that I was going to talk to Charlie, and she was fine with that. Lauren wanted Charlie to leave me alone, so Lauren and I could get on with our relationship.

I left Craig (my assistant) in charge of the party cruise overnight and made my way up to London by train, to meet Debbie and the cast for a few drinks after rehearsals. After a few drinks, Charlie and I went out for dinner. We had a bit of a talk about things, but I don't think she really understood what I was trying to say; or maybe she didn't care. After dinner, we went back to my hotel room, where once again I explained to Charlie, that Lauren and I were together and that what happened on the ship between Charlie and I was not going to happen again.

What came next was a total shock to me, as Charlie and I both did something that was quite unbelievable. She walked over to me and said, "If you don't fuck me now, I will tell Lauren about everything that happened on the ship, and I will also make up some stuff too." She also said that she would do anything she could to break us up, so she could have me.

That was her contribution to this situation, but wait, then I (in an absolute moment of weakness), I actually did what she asked.

Still to this day, I am baffled, at how I could have been so weak as to not say, "No, I won't do that," and go back and tell Lauren about what was really only a kiss, when we weren't together anyway. I'm not sure if it was the alcohol from dinner talking, or maybe deep down, I actually wanted Charlie. Perhaps I was just living out every man's fantasy of having beautiful women throw themselves at me.

Charlie was a bit loopy, but extremely sexy. Needless to say, Charlie got her way, and I got myself deeper into shit, than I could ever imagine, prior to my trip to London. What was I going to do? For anyone who has been unfaithful or had an affair with two people at the same time, you know exactly how hard it can be to not get caught out, when you're all in the same city; well, try achieving that, when you're all on the same goddamn fucking ship. As I fell asleep that night, I couldn't help but think, *how on Earth am I going to come out of this one alive*?

The following morning, I made my way back to Portsmouth and waited until the ship came in. I spent the whole day wandering around thinking, *what the hell did I do that for*? *How could I be so weak*? While also thinking, *I can't wait to tell my best mate about this one, If I get out of it alive*. Lauren and the other cast arrived in town later in the day and joined me for a drink, and of course, the first thing Lauren asked was if I had sorted things out and put Charlie straight.

"Yes, baby." I said. Meanwhile, I was thinking that the only thing I had put Charlie straight on, was when I put her straight on her back. So, there I was, even deeper in a situation that I had no idea how I was going to get out of, while at the same time almost relishing the challenge ahead of me. I was hoping that somehow Charlie was going to be happy that she had me and then move on; as most people do to each other on ships; all before Lauren found out. After all, Charlie and Lauren would only be on the ship together for one week. How hard could it be to avoid Charlie while still keeping her happy and also being with Lauren and not letting her know about Charlie?

I think we all know the answer to that.

The Ultimate Betrayal

"My god. What sort of boss was I, not only allowing my team to act like this, but actually encouraging them."

"Hell Week" becomes the week from hell.

By now, you know why we refer to this week as being "Hell Week." It was always a very challenging time for everyone involved in "bumping in" a new cast or new shows. Even though I was not involved in the shows in a major way, I once again had to ensure that the new cast got settled in, had reasonable time to get rest, and had plenty to eat. The usual platters of food and drink and endless supplies of coffee had to be made available. I had to make certain that they had time to do safety training and inductions as well. Add to this, the fact that I had to make the most of my limited time remaining with Lauren, while also keeping Charlie in her place. I was beginning to wonder when I was going to get any sleep.

It became a game of juggling between spending time with Lauren, then, when she was sleeping; in my cabin most of the time, going down to the Galax lounge during the new cast's rehearsals. This was so that Charlie thought that I was showing a little interest in her, in order for her to chill out and not cause a fuss with Lauren. Luckily for me, I had the "we have to play it professionally" card at that stage, and this seemed to be keeping Charlie at bay for the moment. The "Not until Lauren has gone, so she doesn't get hurt" card, was the other one I used.

Lauren was spending more time with her cast, in their final week together, while also packing, so this helped my cause. They say love is blind, but what they really mean is that love blinds your judgment. No stable person would believe this situation was going to have a happy ending. Ok, so "happy Ending", may not be the correct term to use; because I was hoping for lots of happy endings. A peaceful outcome and not one that resembled world-war II, was more what I meant.

Only someone who was in love / lust, or "in-sane" would even contemplate getting themselves into such a predicament. Well, whether it was love, lust, or just plain lunacy, that is exactly what I had done. I must have been fucking crazy to think this could work. I mean, it's hard enough trying to juggle two women in the same city when they live miles apart and don't know each other, let alone living on the same goddamn floating tin can that is not much longer than a football field and both of them knowing each other. Having said that, for the most part, I was somehow surviving; well, at least I thought I was.

Two nights before Lauren was due to get off, I was in the Galax lounge with the new cast at about 3:00 a.m., rehearsing. I had a few minutes to spare until Deb needed me on stage, so I thought I'd run up to my cabin and see if Lauren was awake. As I opened my cabin door, I was stunned to see that she was not in my bed and even more stunned to find a pile of seductive photos that Stephanie had sent me lying on my bed. These photos had been sent by Stephanie in previous weeks. I was not sure how to dispose of them, so they had been in a draw, along with a note from Stephanie, which said that she couldn't wait to come and visit me.

It was obvious that Lauren had been going through my things, in another one of her jealous moments and found what she thought was the smoking gun, that would prove that I was guilty of being with someone else. The photos had arrived a few weeks prior, and I had not yet had the chance to dispose of them. I certainly didn't want them, but I couldn't exactly just put them in the bin, for anyone to find. When Lauren found them, she automatically presumed that all the things Ricky was saying about me being with Stephanie, were true. I guess part of it was true, but it certainly wasn't as bad as it looked. Either way, this was not the way I wanted Lauren and I to say goodbye to each other after seven turbulent months together.

I ran downstairs to see if she was in her cabin and used my master key to open her door; after several times knocking with no response. She was not in there, so I went to see if she was in Ricky's cabin, which she wasn't either. *Where else could she be*, I thought to myself. I knew Debbie needed me back soon for rehearsals, but this was something that was a priority for me, right at that moment. I frantically ran to almost all parts of the ship—both inside and out—and looked in all the usual places Lauren could be, before finally finding her in the very spot at the front of the ship where I was, the night Stephanie made a move on me. Lauren was sobbing, and as I approached, she saw me and stood up, screaming, "Stay the fuck away from me," as she began throwing punches at me.

I tried to calm her down, but it was to no avail.

She yelled, "I knew you were like this, and I never should have left Barry."

To which I replied, "You never left Barry, so what are you talking about?"

This argument went back and forth for a few moments, with both of us bringing up the ways that the other person had contributed to the demise of our relationship. I'm not sure how Lauren was viewing the situation, but to me, it was obvious we had both created such a destructive relationship, that there didn't seem to be any way of reversing the damage done. Somehow, we both managed to calm down to the point where we agreed, that the best thing to do was for Lauren to go back home and for us both to have some time out with the view of possibly starting fresh at a later date.

C.R.U.I.S.E

Do we have any monkey masks?

It was now early August, and Lauren had been off the ship for a few weeks. We'd been talking quite a bit on the phone, and things were looking up. I had my suspicions about her and Barry being together, but I was trying to give her the benefit of the doubt. She told me that she saw Barry the night she got home. She denied that anything happened between them, but sometimes you just get a feeling about things. My gut was telling me she was lying, but I put it behind me and hoped she was doing the right thing.

Charlie had been making several attempts to sleep with me since Lauren had left, and I was quite proud of myself, for not giving in to her recent advances. On a few occasions, she came up to my cabin in need of a cuddle and someone to talk to, all of which I helped her out with, as I was trying to be a caring, supportive boss to all my cast. This was despite the fact, that I felt that Charlie was taking advantage of this and trying to use it as a way to seduce me again. I had told her, that if she had issues that she needed help sorting, that she should go through her dance captain; Leanne, who would either take care of them, or come to me to take care of them. I made it clear, that I didn't think it was appropriate, for Charlie to come directly to me.

Discipline on a ship is so important, and the way things are dealt with, is also important. There are certain politics and a way that things need to be handled. Like any job, if you have an issue, you go to your direct supervisor, then if they are unable to fix it, you then go to your manager; in this case, me. On a ship, there is the chief purser and then the staff captain, and then finally, the captain, but only as the last resort. The captain is not to be bothered with day-to-day running issues from each department. After all, the captain is the master of the vessel and is not only responsible for the safe navigation of the ship, but he is also the law, the police, and the judge and jury, should the need arise.

Either way, it is the captain's responsibility to ensure the safe transportation of the ship, its passengers, and crew, so they do not have the time to deal with issues that can be dealt with, by a supervisor or department manager. Likewise, each department manager has a lot to deal with and

The Ultimate Betrayal

does not have the time to be sorting out personal issues that, in my case, the dance captain can take care of. Despite me explaining this to Charlie, she persisted in coming directly to me. She kept looking for ways to get my attention, to spend time with me, in the hope that I would give in to her advances, which, at that point, I wasn't.

As cruise director, I worked a little different to other managers. In most cases, if a crew member was not performing their job properly, or if they did something wrong, they would receive either a verbal or written warning. Each warning would then be sent back to the cruise line's head office and kept on file, for future reference. It was my opinion, that this may then be looked upon detrimentally, when that crew member was looking for re-employment, or promotion.

The way I used to deal with matters of discipline was totally different. I would give the crew member some sort of duty, or punishment, that made them think twice about doing it again, while not hampering their future employment prospects. For example, we had a mascot for the kids' club on board, which was a dolphin, called "Dodger." We had a character suit of the dolphin, and each time we had a children's disco, someone would have to wear the dolphin suit and dance with the kids.

Inevitably, the kids would always punch and kick Dodger, so badly, that no one ever wanted to do this job, so this became the best form of punishment for the crew. If they missed their duties, or failed to do their job, they would have to wear the suit, for one of the kids' discos. I must say, that very rarely did anyone wear the suit more than once, so it seemed to work, and was fucking hilarious to watch too.

One of the new cast members was Lee, a very talented singer and dancer, with a bright future. However, Lee spent most of his time in the nightclub, trying to pick up female passengers. Even though there is an unwritten rule on ships, not to "tamper with ship's cargo," I didn't have a problem with this, until Lee started missing safety drills and duties, due to late nights in the club pulling women. In this case, I thought that instead of giving him "Dodger duty," I wanted a punishment, that would get right to the heart of what he wanted, which was his ability to pull women.

C. R. U. I. S. E

I banned him from going into the nightclub at night, for a period of two weeks. Of course, he was absolutely gutted about this, but he understood and took the punishment like a man. Each night, Slim and I would egg him on, about how many hot women were in the bar, just to wind him up even more.

On this one particular night, we were having a crew party down in the spa/sauna area. Most of the entertainment team sat around a huge, round table, drinking. We were all having a great time, but I could see that Lee was itching to get upstairs amongst the women. It had only been five days since his two-week ban had begun, and he turned to me and said, "Boss, do I really have to stay away from the bar for another nine days?"

"Yes, you do." I said; with a smile on my face.

"Isn't there some other way I can pay my punishment off?" Lee asked.

I thought to myself, "if you knew how much fucking money I was making through bingo scams, you would know, that I don't need money." Slim could see me contemplating Lee's comment, and at that moment, Slim leaned over and whispered a funny alternative for Lee's punishment to me. I thought for another moment, laughed, and said, "Okay, Lee, if you want to get out of this, you have to do one thing." Lee sat up attentively, in anticipation, of the solution to his problem. I continued, "You have to run around the entire promenade deck once." Lee smiled, thinking that this was a sure thing.

"No problem," he said.

"Naked!" I rebutted.

"You're fucking kidding." he said.

"Did I stutter?" I laughed; along with everyone else, as Lee slumped back in his chair. I explained to him, that this was the only way I was going to allow him to go back to the nightclub, before his two-week suspension was served. He was reluctant, and it looked like he was going to have to serve his time as previously agreed, until Charlie stood up and said, "If Lee does it, I'll do it."

I looked at Slim, who was grinning like a Cheshire cat, at the thought of Charlie being naked. Slim laughed, as he looked at me rubbing his hands

The Ultimate Betrayal

together. What the hell was Charlie thinking? This had nothing to do with her. I guess she was looking for a way to impress me, seeing as her various other attempts to get me into bed again, had failed. I turned to Nick, who was my new compère, and said, "Do we still have those monkey masks in the deck six locker?"

Also smiling, Nick nodded, then jumped up and took off to get the masks. I explained that if this was going to happen, I didn't want anyone getting recognized, which would lead to them being disembarked and subsequently more rehearsals for the cast and I. Lee finally agreed, and we set a time of 2:00 a.m. that night, which was a few hours later, to do the nudie run. We agreed to meet at the dressing room, which was directly below promenade deck and had easy access to the fire escape.

At 2:00 a.m., Slim and I sat in the fire escape, next to the dressing room, waiting. A few minutes later, Lee arrived, followed by Charlie, and then Nick arrived with the monkey masks. Lee was still not happy at the thought of exposing himself in the cold night air, in the Bay of Biscay. He knew however, that he had no other hope of getting amongst the smoking-hot women on that cruise, if he didn't do the run. We stood talking for a minute or so, before Charlie said, "Well, are we going to do this or not?" She undid her top.

Lee hesitantly followed, by removing his shirt, then in one swoop, Charlie dropped her dress and underwear and stood there totally naked; much to Slim's pleasure.

"Weeheey!" Slim shouted. "Nice little puppies."

Having seen Charlie naked before, I was not too bothered with staring at her, like Nick and Slim were, so I handed her and Lee the monkey masks and motioned for us to get moving. They both put them on, at which time Nick said to Charlie, "Hey, now that's a huge improvement."

Charlie began stumbling around, trying to see Nick with the mask covering her eyes. "I'll kick your short arse if I can find it." (Nick was only five-foot-four-inches tall, and Charlie was maybe five foot eight).

"Right, let's do this then," I said, as I made my way up to the fire escape. I opened the door and waited for the others to arrive. We all gathered at the top of the stairs. I said, "One lap up the port side, through the middle of the ship near the games room at the front, and then back down the starboard side."

"This is fucking hilarious." Slim laughed. "I'm glad I brought my video camera." He turned the camera on and prepared to film.

Off they went. Lee sprinted down the deck, with his hands covering his crotch. Meanwhile, Charlie didn't seem in too much of a hurry, nor did she seem bothered to cover herself up either. I think she was hoping I'd get so turned on from watching her, that I'd not be able to resist having sex with her again. To be honest, I was far too busy pissing myself laughing, at what I was encouraging my team to do, to even think about Charlie as a sexual object. She did look hot though. She had an awesome, slim dancer's figure, perky little tits and a really hot little ass.

My god! What sort of boss was I, not only allowing my team to act like this, but actually encouraging them. It was one of the funniest things I had ever seen and one that I just had to include in this book. Slim, Nick, and I sat waiting, as Lee and Charlie did their lap around the ship; which should have taken two minutes, max. Within a few minutes, Lee came around the corner and ran straight past us and into the fire escape, to get dressed.

We expected Charlie to be not too far behind him, but after a few more minutes, there was still no sign of her. It had been more than five minutes from the time they set off and more than enough time to make it around the ship; even at walking pace. Finally, Charlie came running around the corner yelling, "Quick, get inside; there are two kids chasing me."

Without question, we raced inside and shut the fire escape so they couldn't follow. We got down to the dressing room and shut the door behind us.

"What happened?" I asked.

An out-of-breath Charlie explained, "As I walked past the games room, I heard a young boy's voice say that he saw a naked girl walk past, so I decided to hide behind one of the lifejacket cabinets out on deck, hoping that they would not see me. They just happened to sit on the chair right beside me and were talking. They didn't seem to be leaving, so I thought I should make a dash for it, before anyone else came out on deck. I ran for it, and they gave chase."

By the time she was halfway through this explanation, Slim, Nick, and I were in hysterics laughing. We honestly laughed for what seemed like an eternity. I am kind of curious, what sort of parents let their children (aged approximately twelve years old), run around a ship at 2am. But who was I to question someone's values, when I was encouraging my team to run around a cruise ship; butt naked? Nick binned the monkey masks the following day, as we could no longer use them on stage, for fear of someone recognizing them.

The funny tag to this story, though, was that five years later, when I returned to the UK for another contract, I turned my hotel TV on, one Saturday night and saw Lee being crowned the winner of a singing contest, run by Sir Andrew Lloyd Webber called "Any Dream will do." Lee, subsequently, starred as the lead, in one of Sir Andrew Lloyd Webber's musicals in London's West End. He also went on to marry one of the West End's biggest female stars; so, he "pulled" the ultimate girl, in the end.

Even though it was five years later, I once again pissed my pants, recalling the night of the nudie run. I rang Slim, and he too was watching the program. He mentioned that he still had the video footage of that night, but in case you're wondering, Lee, we promise it will never, ever be shown to anyone. I think, anyone who worked with Lee on that cruise ship contract, could see that the guy had incredible talent and was always going to go a long way in his career. Perhaps, in some small way, that discipline, that I forced onto him, at that young age, when he was twenty-one, may have helped in him reaching the pinnacle of the entertainment industry. If anyone from the UK knows exactly who I am talking about, then please go see Lee in the show, and ask him about his nudie run in the Bay of Biscay.

A new start…or more of the same problems?

The whole situation with Lauren and I being on again, off again was starting to do my head in. It seemed like we spent more time discussing whether we should get back together, or break up than we actually spent being together or making the relationship work. This wasn't helped by the fact that we had not seen each other in over a month. I don't think it helped that her parents had recently broken up and that her mum had started sleeping with her dad's best friend. Lauren's dad, was not aware of this, and I think the pressure of Lauren knowing, but feeling like she was betraying one of her parents, by saying or not saying anything, added to her frustration.

Add to this Charlie's constant advances, and I was beginning to wonder if I should have ended my contract after six months, instead of extending for a further three months, like I had. I think I needed a change of scenery or something, and just as I was thinking that one night as I stood at the back of the Galax lounge, Nick walked up to me with a cute young blonde.

"Hey boss, this is Becky," he said. "She is the new beauty therapist who joined us today."

Yes, that's right. By this time, Colleen had left and Becky was her replacement. As you may have realized, Colleen and I didn't really have much to do with each other for the rest of the time she was on board, hence the reason why she hasn't been mentioned too much in recent pages. Coleen did, however, get disembarked (fired) from the ship, for being pissed one night in an officer's crew cabin.

Crew parties were the norm and sneaking alcohol in, was a common occurrence. This particular night, Coleen was absolutely hammered and unfortunately for her, Lauren got wind of this and anonymously called the bridge, to report a drunk crew member; which was a case for instant dismissal. I guess that Lauren wanted to "eliminate" any possible competition, so that I wouldn't be tempted.

Fast-forward more than a month and Becky had arrived onboard. Becky was very cute, and on first impressions, she seemed very nice. We chatted for a while and seemed to hit it off. You know when you meet someone and there is just that "spark." Well, Becky and I certainly had it. As we chatted, I found out that she was twenty-one and lived in the same town as Colleen, but thankfully, they didn't know each other. As we were chatting, I thought to myself that she could be the answer to all my problems with Lauren and Charlie.

It could be a new start, so to speak. I could move on from Lauren, and Charlie would surely leave me alone, if I was with someone else. Or maybe she would continue to stalk me as only Charlie can. Either way, I fancied the pants off this girl Becky, and as it turned out, the following day, we literally "fancied the pants off" each other. It turned out, that Becky was not as innocent, as I first thought. She was a wild little thing, with an insatiable appetite for men. To be honest, it was kind of nice to have some fun with someone and not feel the pressure that I had felt for the last few months.

About a week into us hanging out, Becky told me she didn't want it to be serious between us and that she just wanted it to be casual. I was happy with that for now, even though I'm not one to have meaningless relationships, despite my behavior so far in this book, so I went along with it. Meanwhile, Charlie had given me a little more space. She had not been coming around at all hours of the night for a week, and she was generally laying off, when it came to demanding sex. I thought to myself, *finally, things have settled down*. Well, so I thought, anyway. As it turned out, Charlie was scheming and trying to work out a way to get me to sleep with her again.

Naughty school girls.

It was our usual Friday night party night, and I was down in the club with Slim, having a drink at about midnight. When everything seemed to be under control, I decided to head back up to my cabin for a quiet night. I arrived at my door, and as I opened it, I saw Charlie and Kara (another dancer) sat on my lounge, dressed up as school girls. Even though I was surprised they were dressed like that in my cabin, I was not surprised they were there, as I never locked my cabin door. They both had very short skirts on, no underwear, and see-through white tops, that tied up in the front (with no bras). Add to this the cute pig tales they both had, and it was like seeing two cute Britney Spears; aka her first music video clip, "Hit

C.R.U.I.S.E

me baby one more time." The only thing the girls had, that Britney never had, were the huge, bright red pairs of C.F.M boots that each of the girls were wearing ("Come Fuck Me" boots for those who didn't work it out). These boots were costumes from one of the shows on board.

As I stood there in the doorway, they both walked over to me and said, "We've been such naughty girls, Mr. Cruise Director; we need to be punished." Although I thought Charlie was not quite the brightest girl in the world, it seemed that I underestimated her ability to get what she wanted and her ability to come up with a fresh way to get my attention. After all, she knew I was no longer interested in sleeping with her on her own, however, she figured there was very little chance I could resist her and another girl at the same time. I think most men would find it hard to resist that, if it ever happened.

So, with that, Charlie and Kara sat me in my chair in the middle of the room, and before I knew it, they had tied my hands to the chair. Charlie distracted me by kissing me, as Kara tied my legs to the legs of the chair, also. Charlie straddled me and rubbed her tits in my face, as Kara undid my fly and began performing oral sex on me. I'm presuming that anyone reading this book would be thinking one of two things: If you're woman, you're probably thinking, *You're sick, that's disgusting*. But if you're a man, I'm certain that you're thinking, *now that is every man's ultimate fantasy*, and yes, at that point, it was mine too.

This was something that I had never had happen to me, but having had it happen, without even planning it, I have to say, that while it was fun, it wasn't all it was cracked up to be. Pleasing one woman, can be difficult at times, so imagine trying to satisfy two women at once. It's not as easy as you may think. Having said that, I think that the girls pleasure that night, was coming from the fact that they were also living out a fantasy, so I don't think anyone left unsatisfied.

The girls entertained me, into the early hours of the morning, and this was not the last time we spent the night partaking in such activities. Charlie was spot on in thinking that this plan would work with me, and in fact, it also helped to convince me she was worth spending time with

The Ultimate Betrayal

alone, as well. So once again I found myself in a situation whereby I was stretching myself between two girls, and occasionally three, when Kara joined us. Neither Becky, nor Charlie really seemed too worried that I was spending time with the other. I'm not sure if either of them knew, but neither of them ever asked and I wasn't trying to hide the fact, so to me, the situation was better left as it was, for the time being. I often thought about seeing if the two of them would be interested in a threesome, but I figured that I was on a good thing as it was, so I didn't want to run the risk of losing it.

Busted big time.

One night, Charlie rang and said, that she and Kara wanted to come up and "play." I was not really up for it that particular night, but then Charlie told me that Leanne, the dance captain had heard about our little threesomes and was keen to be a part of it. I was starting to wonder, just how far this could go, and I wasn't even trying hard to get it. It was just falling in my lap; literally. I agreed, and about an hour later, Charlie came up and said that Kara and Leanne were on their way. Charlie and I sat and watched TV, waiting for the others to arrive, but after half an hour, they were still not there. Charlie rang down to Kara's room, and Kara told her that they were coming now, so Charlie and I decided to make a start, right there on my lounge.

To give you an idea of my cabin, if you open the door and look straight ahead, you will see a desk, followed by my bed on the right and the lounge directly in front of you along the back wall. I sat in the middle of the lounge and Charlie had undressed herself and straddled me. We were going for it "full out with feeling", as entertainers would say, when the cabin door flew open. Charlie and I stopped and both looked to see the rest of the cast standing in the doorway staring at us. There was no point in Charlie and I trying to hide, or act shy, as they had all seen just about as much as could be seen already.

I popped my head to one side of Charlie, so the cast could see me properly and said, "Well, you have two choices. You can come and join us, or shut the door," at which time Phil grabbed the door handle and shut it. We could hear them laughing, as they disappeared down the corridor as we continued what we were doing. This appeared to be another one of Charlie's ideas, to sleep with me and clearly, neither Kara, or Leanne, had actually agreed to what Charlie had promised me, was going to happen.

Almost happy families.

At that point in time, life seemed pretty good. Becky and I were having such an amazing time together, and Charlie was keeping me occupied on nights when Becky wanted to be alone. Charlie was still quite needy and would come to my cabin wanting to talk or cuddle or have sex and she was actually starting to creep back to the slightly psychotic behavior of a few weeks earlier, but I was dealing with it. I never questioned if Becky was seeing someone else on board and didn't really need to know either, until one night when she arrived at my cabin with the news that I really didn't want to hear. She asked if we could talk, and when we sat down on my lounge she uttered the words that every unmarried man dreads hearing.

"I think I'm pregnant."

It was a good thing that I was sitting down, otherwise I would have been on the floor. I was totally speechless.

We both sat there in silence, for what seemed like eternity. She could see that I was obviously shaken by the news, and she was still trying to fathom the situation herself, so she said she was going to go down to her cabin to rest. Becky needed a little time to herself and so did I, so she kissed me goodnight and went back to her cabin.

Not ten minutes after Becky left, my phone rang. It was Charlie, and she needed to see me urgently. I tried to convince her, that now was not a good time, however, she said that it was an emergency, so I agreed she could come up. Charlie arrived a few minutes later, and as the door opened I aggressively said her, "This had better be good," to which she replied, "Well I'm pregnant. Is that good enough"? Now that one did floor me.

The Ultimate Betrayal

What are the chances of that happening? The strange thing, was that not for one minute, did I think that either of them were lying; not even Charlie. We discussed things for a moment, but very quickly things heated up and we ended up in a screaming match. I'm not sure if it was from my shock of this happening twice in half an hour, or if it was her being over emotional, as some women can be when their hormones shift like that. (I can hear women around the world cursing me right now for that comment—LOL)

Either way, Charlie and I were getting nowhere. The conversation ended with Charlie accusing me of manipulating her and forcing her to have sex with me. With those words being her last, she then stormed out of my cabin. Of course, I was stunned at her accusations, given that she had blatantly gone out of her way to be with me.

I immediately went down to deck two, where the entertainment team lived and knocked on my kid's club leader, Hayley's, door and asked her if she would accompany me to Charlie's room, as a neutral witness to this conversation. If Charlie was going to play mind games, I was going to make sure my backside was covered, because a woman like that, can be extremely dangerous on a cruise ship. Accusations like that can cost someone their job, even if they are not true, because the captain will always err on the side of caution in these kinds of situations.

Some women on cruise ships think that they can have sex with a guy and then manipulate him in any way they like. I have seen this occur on several occasions, and if they come unstuck they simply cry sexual harassment, or rape, which inevitably gets everyone's attention, including the captain. A classic case of this, was when two married women went with two male entertainers back to their cabin one night, while their husbands were gambling in the casino. The women seduced the men (I don't think it took much work though) and ended up having a foursome with them.

Meanwhile, their husbands began to panic, when they could not find their wives after some time. When the women finally appeared, and were questioned by their husbands, they told them that the male entertainers had lured them back to their cabins, under false pretenses and tried to have sex with them. Not wanting to have such a fuss made it to the media, the captain instantly dismissed both entertainers, leaving a huge hole in the entertainment program for that cruise, which lead to massive passenger complaints and dissatisfaction. This was all because the two women were covering their own butts.

Back to deck two, though. I knocked on Charlie's door, and we discussed the situation and argued back and forth for some time, but unfortunately, the only agreement made, was when I told her that she was not to come anywhere near me, for the remainder of her contract. I made it clear, that if she needed anything, she was to go through her dance captain, Leanne. Hayley bore witness to this, and I returned to my cabin to put these events, in my cruise report, in case anything came of it, so I had the evidence to provide the office with; if need be.

A wake up call.

The following day, we arrived in Spain, and as normal, I went to the internet café, to check emails. As I arrived at the internet café, I noticed Charlie sitting at the computer opposite me. I thought nothing of it and commenced checking emails. A few moments later, I received an email from Charlie. Given the circumstances of the night before, I simply deleted it. I was not interested in anything she had to say. I finished checking emails and left. The following day, as we approached England again, I received a text message from Lauren, asking if I could call her, as soon as I got signal. When we got closer to England, I rang Lauren, and as she answered the phone, I could hear her crying. She asked me if there was anything I wanted to tell her, to which I said, "No." She asked me again and I gave the same answer.

Lauren then told me that she was sorry that she had done this, but that she was also glad she did. She explained that the night before, which was the day Charlie sent me the email, Lauren broke into my email account and went through my inbox, looking to find any information to suggest that I was with Charlie. There was nothing to suggest this, however, as she was about to log out, she saw one unread message in my deleted mail. She opened it and saw that it was from Charlie. Now, if I had read the email, I would have deleted it totally and not just from my inbox as the contents were quite damning.

The email read:

> Dear J. D., I want to tell you how sorry I am for last night and that I hope we can sort things out. You are the most amazing lover, and I hope that we can do it again soon. The sex we have is so amazing. I don't want to lose you as a lover or friend, Love Charlie.

Now what could I say to that? I had to come clean with Lauren. Surprisingly, she was quite calm about it. She was obviously upset; however, she was remarkably okay. At the end of the day, her and I were not really together, and let's face it, there was a very good chance, that her and Barry were fooling around too. While I'm not saying that what I did was right, from the first day Lauren and I met, we had been as bad as each other, so neither one of us could get too upset at the other for these sorts of indiscretions.

Either way, it certainly gave me a wakeup call, and I decided there and then that I was no longer getting involved with either Becky or Charlie at all. I needed to sort my head out, and it was not going to get any easier while I was playing the field.

The Bilbao mafia.

After all the high dramas of the past few weeks, I needed some time out. I was approaching the end of my contract, and I don't think a week went by in the nine months I was on board, that I didn't have some sort of drama, involving a girl. They say that we attract into our lives what we think about most, so my predominant thoughts must have been on women and troubles, because that is all I seemed to get at that time in my life.

After the show one night, Slim called me and asked if I could give him a hand. One of the woofers in the huge speaker bins in the showroom had blown and he needed me to help him replace it. Knowing Slim, I'd say there

C.R.U.I.S.E

was a good chance that it was blown because Slim and Dom were blasting the music during the disco, way too loud. The only time we could do the repair was 2:00 a.m.; once the disco had finished. Just to give you an idea of what we were doing here—imagine your car stereo with the little woofers that sit in the door. These woofers that we were dealing with were 18-inch woofers and weigh somewhere around thirty kilograms each.

We had to remove the damaged one and then wire up and install the new one. It didn't take that long, so once the job was finished, we sat and came up with some funny things to do with the broken speaker.

Slim jumped up and said, "Come with me, boss. This will be piss funny."

We picked up the speaker and went up to the back of the promenade deck. Slim left me there with this huge bloody speaker, as he ran down to the sound booth, to get a piece of rope and an octopus strap. He came back and tied the rope to the octopus strap and then hooked the hook of the strap to the speaker. He then lowered the speaker down, over the back of the ship. This particular ship had a flat back that went down for about eight decks below. Of course, it is highly illegal these days to dump any rubbish over the side of a ship, so I had to stop Slim there. In the old days, most ships would dump all their rubbish overboard once out to sea, but these days, you can't even dump the "grey water" from showers and galleys, unless it is 1-1 million. That's one bad particle to one million good particles.

The grey water and sewage on ships, goes through such a full-on series of treatments, that the final product is often better than your drinking water at home. There are some instances where dumping of certain rubbish is permitted, but it has to be more than a certain distance out to sea. For any ships not complying with these international laws, heavy fines apply. So, there I was, trying to stop Slim from dropping this speaker into the water.

"Slim. You can't drop it. We'll get in so much trouble," I said.

"I'm not dropping it, boss. I'm sticking it to the back of the ship," he said.

Just in case you're not aware, speakers have a magnet on them and the bigger the speaker, the bigger the magnet, so you can imagine how big this one was. Slim slowly lowered the speaker down to three decks below, before swinging it away from the ship and then back, until the magnet attached itself to the steel hull. He then lowered the rope a little more so the hook unattached itself from the speaker, then he pulled the rope and strap back up. We both ran off laughing like a pair of school boys, who had just egged somebody's house.

The following morning, I received a call from the captain, asking if I knew why there was a giant speaker, stuck to the back of the ship. I explained to the captain, that Slim and I replaced it the night before, but that the storage cupboard had a broken lock and that it was more than likely that some young passengers on a buck's night, had gotten in there and done this with the speaker. The captain bought my story and nothing more was said. Shortly afterward, Slim and I went into town, and as we walked past the back of the ship, we couldn't help but laugh at the engineering team hanging from harnesses and using mini cranes to try to remove this giant magnet and speaker from the ship. Unfortunately, neither Slim nor I had our camera with us, so we have no photo to share this hilarious event with you.

As if this was not enough fun and near trouble for one week, Slim went out shopping that day and bought two of the biggest Super Soaker water pistols ever made. These things each had a four litre water tank in back packs, attached to the guns and a pump action, that if hit at close range, it actually bloody hurt. I'm actually very surprised he even got them on board the ship as it wasn't that long after 9/11 and security measures on cruise ships around the world, were beginning to tighten. He managed to convince me to use my master key, that opened every cabin on the ship, to gain access to the other entertainer's cabins while they were sleeping. He wanted to wake them up with an almighty fright.

It was 2:00 a.m. in the morning, a few weeks later, which seemed to be our favourite time, to cause trouble. As usual, Slim and I were almost the only two people still awake on the ship. We dressed ourselves in "urban water assault" gear and made our way down to the entertainers' corridor. We cased the place out, to see who we should get wet first and both decided that Nick was the obvious first target. Firstly, because he had a great sense of humour and secondly, because Slim is twice Nick's size, so Slim could sit on him as I soaked him.

I quietly inserted my master key, into Nick's door and unlocked it ever so quietly. Slim stood with his water cannon loaded, and as I flung Nick's door open, Slim unleashed what seemed to be a bathtub full of water, all over Nick, as he lay sleeping. Within in instant, Nick was completely soaked, the door was shut, and we were off. As we ran off, we could hear Nick swearing at the top of his voice, "you fucking arseholes!"

Slim and I scurried around the corner to hide for a few moments and make sure he didn't come out, before moving on to our next victim. We decided Lee was the next one to feel the power of our water blasters, so we crept around toward his cabin. Again, I quietly opened Lee's door then *BANG!* Both Slim and I unleashed our water tanks on Lee, as he lay in bed. Two from two and we needed to re-fill. We went around to the laundry and re-filled the tanks, then headed around to Charlie's cabin. Just as we were approaching Charlie's cabin, her door opened and there she stood in the doorway with nothing but a cute little pair of panties and a white t-shirt on.

This distracted me for a moment, however, it didn't deter Slim in the slightest, as he unloaded his entire backpack full of water on her. You'd think at this stage, that Charlie would try to run for cover, but no, she stood there, with her hands outstretched allowing Slim to plaster her dripping wet t-shirt to her toned body.

As both Slim and I stood there admiring Charlie's fully erect nipples, that protruded through her top, we felt a huge gush of water hit us in the back. It seemed that Becky and another Steiner girl had heard the noise and decided, that they wanted to get in on it. Slim and I turned around to see Becky and the other Steiner girl standing with Lee; all with empty buckets in their hands. Slim and I immediately gave chase for Lee. The two girls ran into their room and locked the door. Even though we had a master key, this would have been no fun. The fun was in the chase with Lee.

The boy showed some balls, so now the hunter becomes the hunted.

I unlocked Lee's door, but he had himself wedged up against it, so we couldn't get in. He stupidly dropped his bucket as he ran off, so Slim filled it up, before using his weight to barge through Lee's door. To Lee's credit, he held Slim out, but eventually Slim managed to get the door open enough to get his big leg, between the door and the wall. This allowed me to throw the bucket of water, up over the door and onto Lee standing on the other side.

Neither Slim nor I thought about the light switch, situated just inside the door, so when it began sparking, zapping, and smoke began coming out of it, we thought it best to bail out. Just as we did, the circuit shorted out and Lee was left standing there in the dark, soaking wet, with nowhere to sleep and no lights until the electrician could come around in the morning. That will teach him to mess with the "Bilbao Mafia"… ha-ha.

Back to a normal (ish) life.

After a long and exhausting contract and what seemed like an even longer flight home, I arrived back home in Brisbane. It was so great to be home. I arrived with lots of fun stories to tell and a shit load of cash to have fun with. Getting the amount of cash that I had earnt back into the country was a feat in itself, but well worth it, when I knew what I had planned for it. I was spending most of the money on recording my debut CD and some more on a funky ski-boat, so I could enjoy the beautiful Broadwater on the Gold Coast. The boat was the coolest boat with a huge engine. I was racking my brains trying to work out what to name it, when Slim's voice came into my head, reminding me of how Lauren and I ended up together. So, with that, the boat was named "D'ya like that."

Lauren and I had been chatting on the phone and things had settled down between us. She was due to arrive in Australia, in a few days, for a holiday that I had paid for, several months earlier. We enjoyed each other's company, but during her visit, while we were in Sydney, she let the cat out of the bag about her and Barry. The reason I knew she was still with Barry, was because she accidently sent me a text that was meant for Barry, stating her love for him and how she was looking forward to having sex with him in a few weeks. I knew the text was meant for him, because she signed the text with "luv ur weesaks," which was the same sign off that Barry used in the Valentine's Day flowers that he sent her earlier in the year. Lauren went home a few days later and as expected, we broke up.

It was a few days later, that I received a phone call from Charlie from the UK. She started by saying that I was such an arsehole and that she couldn't believe I would stoop so low, as to be cheating on her. Um, last time I checked, I was running away from her, not in a relationship with her. She abused me some more, then said that someone else wanted to speak to me, at which time Becky got on the phone and also began to abuse me. I was shocked. Not at what Becky was saying, but at the fact that her and Charlie were actually speaking, as they had never spoken a word to each other when I was on the ship. It seemed that the two of them had started chatting and discovered that I was sleeping with both of them at the same time.

Once Becky had finished having her say, she handed the phone back to Charlie, at which time Charlie informed me she had Lauren's number and that they were going to call her and tell her all about what I had been up to. After all, at that stage, Lauren thought that I had only slept with Charlie once, and she certainly didn't know about Becky or Kara. I told them both to "knock themselves out," as I presumed they were both full of shit anyway and wouldn't have the balls to call Lauren.

I honestly didn't think Becky and Charlie would call Lauren, but they did. Lauren called me the next night and unleashed a barrage of abuse over what the girls had told her. She knew everything, so there was no point in me denying it. Things were over between Lauren and I, so while I wasn't happy about that, there wasn't much point in continuing to argue with her on the other side of the world. I'm not too sure if she was actually angry at me for being unfaithful, or if it was a case that I was doing exactly the same thing as her, as she was doing to me and she didn't like it. Either way, I absorbed Lauren's abuse for about ten minutes before she abruptly hung up on me.

The Ultimate Betrayal

I thought it was best to let Lauren calm down before trying to talk to her. I had no doubt that if she wanted to talk, then she would call. Sure enough, a few hours later (at 3:00 a.m.) she rang and began another barrage of abuse, calling me every name under the sun. This type of abuse carried on for a few days with Lauren calling me at all hours of the day and night screaming abuse at me, then hanging up. After four days of it, I decided enough was enough.

"Hold it right there," I said. "Don't you think it's time we move on from this, Lauren? I understand that you're upset, but this is not getting us anywhere."

"You can fuck off," she replied. "I'm going to make you pay for this so bad. You're going to wish you never screwed around on me."

"Hang on," I said. "You were sleeping around on me too."

"You're such a cunt," she said, before hanging up the phone yet again.

A few days passed and I had not heard anything from Lauren, so I figured that she had finally gotten over things. Then, four days after I had last heard from Lauren, I received a call from Mark in the office in London. As Mark began talking, I could tell in his voice, that something was wrong. He explained to me that an unidentified Scottish man had made several calls to the head office of the cruise line, to the home of the director of entertainment (he had obtained her personal details illegally), and to the captain on the ship itself.

In each call, he claimed that I had threatened to return to the ship and rape and kill two of the female crew members. The unidentified man continued to say that if I was to rejoin the ship, that he would personally make sure that no ship in the fleet would sail due to bomb threats and other terrorist threats that he would instigate.

From what Mark told me, it appeared that this Scottish guy was very heavily intoxicated and seemed to be under the influence of drugs during each of these reported calls. Needless to say, Scotland Yard was involved, and they were investigating who this clown was. Straight away, I had no doubt in my mind, that he had something to do with Lauren. Either way, the problem was that I was due to return to the ship as Cruise Director in

C.R.U.I.S.E

February (two months later), and the other ship that our company provided cruise directors for, already had Steve on there, so now there was no chance for me to return at all. Mark finished up by saying that he and the cruise line knew that these allegations were not true, but given the nature of the threats, they just couldn't risk putting me on board for my safety and for that of the other crew and passengers either.

I was devastated by these events, but as is always the case, life guides us in the direction we are meant to be, by way of subtle, or in this case, not so subtle hints.

Redemption

Another chance to get it right.

It was now May, and I had not worked for nearly six months. After everything that had happened on my previous two contracts, I felt that I needed to take some time to do absolutely nothing. Thankfully, I had enough cash from the last contract to get by. I had auditioned for an Australian company, a month earlier, that provided many cruise ships with entertainers. This was my first proper audition, so I was blown away, when the director, pulled me aside, right after my audition and offered me the choice of two ships. He said, "we never usually offer singers a contract, on the spot, but we are so impressed, that we want to make sure we don't miss the opportunity, of having you work for us."

I was shocked. I was happy with my audition, and knew that I had talent, but this was beyond, what I had thought of. The director continued, "You can either have the Pacific Princess, sailing around the pacific islands, or, the Tahitian Princess, sailing through Tahiti." I knew which one, I wanted right then and there, but none the less, I had a think about it for a day, before confirming that I wanted to go to Tahiti.

C. R. U. I. S. E

Both ships were identical and both itineraries, were nice, but Tahiti, just had that special appeal to me. This time, it was as the lead male vocalist, in the production shows and not just a singer, among others, or a cruise director. This contract, was not on some "two-bit ferry", or a budget cruise line. This was Princess Cruises, which has some of the best production shows at sea. They say that "everything happens for a reason" and this was proof. If things had not have gone pear-shaped in the UK, then I would not have had this opportunity. The ship was almost brand new, and at the time, was considered one of the most technologically advanced ships in the world.

I received a package, containing scripts and musical arrangements and CD's, a few weeks later, so the following few weeks, were spent learning songs and lyrics, before rehearsals started. I left for rehearsals in Sydney, at which time I had the absolute pleasure of working with a man, who I consider to be one of the greatest and most inspirational choreographers, not only in Australia, but in the world. His name is William Forsythe and this man has such a knack of bringing the absolute best out of the people he works with. William has worked with some of the biggest names in the music world and has worked on world-class events. Working with William, is still to this day, one of the highlights of my career. I know that I became such a better performer, for having worked with him. Rehearsals were a pleasure to turn up to each day, and the five-week period flew past, with barely a hitch.

The company put us all up in our own 1-bedroom apartments, right in the heart of Sydney. Our rehearsal studios, were a fifteen-minute train ride away, but on weekends and at night, we were right in the city, if we wanted to explore. I have been fortunate over the years, to be able to temporarily live in some great places during rehearsals. London, Orlando and Sydney were all great places to hang out for six weeks.

I had an amazing cast in Sydney, who were all so talented, and while the four girls in the cast were all attractive, I was certain not to make the same mistakes as I did with Lauren and Charlie. Personally, my time exploring in Sydney, was always brief, because, myself and my female singer, always used our day off, between shows, to start learning the songs, for the next show. This was, so we didn't slow the dancers down, by fumbling over lyrics, while being blocked into dance numbers.

The Legend of William A Forsythe.

During rehearsals, we had a great choreographer, Julie and an awesome music director, Scott. The two of them took as through the five shows that we had to learn. Most days would start with Nat, my female singer and I working with Scott in one room, while Julie taught the dancers the routines. After morning-tea, we would usually come together as a cast, so Julie could block Nat and I into the show, with the dancers.

This was pretty much how the six weeks went, apart from the second last Friday, before we left for Tahiti. On this day, legendary Australian choreographer, William Forsythe, who was half owner of the production company, was coming in to teach us the "Welcome Aboard" show. This show was only ten minutes long, but was dynamite. The show was (as the name suggests), the show that was to be performed on the first night of every cruise. This music for the show was the same on all Princess ships, however, William's choreography was more spectacular than the shows that were rehearsed in California for the bigger ships.

Anyone in the entertainment industry in Australia, knows who William is. Everyone knows how amazing his choreography is and they also know his reputation, in rehearsals. Early on in his career, William had a reputation for throwing shoes at performers and using quite colourful language towards them; regardless of their age. That morning, we were all on edge, before we met William, because his reputation preceded him. It didn't help that Julie, had warned us to be prepared and not slack off.

We all came back into the studio after lunch, and William was warming up and going through some dance moves in his head, facing the mirrors at the front of the studio. He was wearing tight jeans and a white t-shirt. Not exactly dance attire, but he could do what he wanted; he was William Forsythe. He had the stereo remote in one hand and his phone in his back pocket. The cast all stood in silence, at the side of the room, trying not to look like we were obviously watching this legend of a man. The nervous tension from the cast, was obvious.

As William went through some choreography, we watched in anticipation, waiting for him to start teaching us the routine. I'm sure the dancers were studying his every movement as he went about things. After a minute or so, William threw his right leg high above his head in a kick, but unfortunately for William, either the floor was overly slippery, his jeans were too tight, or he was simply not warmed up enough. As his right leg went high above his head, his left leg slipped from underneath him and in an instant, William became horizonal in the air, then landed flat on his back.

We all stood in silence, not sure if we should help, or not. I mean, this was William Forsythe; dancing royalty. After a moment laying on his back, William lifted his head and looked towards us and said, "Well don't I feel like a right cunt now." We all burst into laughter, before myself and Ashley went over and helped William up off the polished timber floor. Even though William's ego was severely bruised, along with his ass, this was precisely what we needed to break the ice.

The afternoon, was great. William was at his brilliant best, teaching us the routine. I found myself laughing hysterically on more than one occasion at his antics. At one point, he was trying to teach the three girls, Olivia, Melina an Imogen a particular move, where they were doing circular hip motions, as they lower themselves down towards the floor.

Imogen, who was only eighteen during rehearsals, was not really doing it the way William wanted, so in his infinite brilliance, William simply said, "Like you're trying to rub your cunt on the floor." *Oh my fucking god William!. She is eighteen.* I thought to myself, as I pissed myself laughing. *You can't say that to an eighteen-year-old.* That was William though, and love it or loathe it, that is part of what makes the man so special.

A few moments later, William was trying to teach Nat and I our entrance onto the stage. I say trying, because neither of us were getting it and William was showing signs of frustration. William is a dancer and he loves dancers and while he loves singers too, I think he thinks singers

Redemption

need to spend more time learning to dance, to make his job easier. After we finally got it, the show was ready to run from the top. We all went to our starting positions awaiting the music to start.

As the music of Ricky Martin's "Cup of life" began, one by one, the dancers went on stage; as choreographed. Once the dancers were all on stage, it was time for Nat and I to enter from opposite sides of the stage, before commencing singing. As Nat and I "slinked" on (This is the best description I could find to explain, sort of how we were coming on stage), William looked at us, tilted his head to one side, screwed up his face, then banged his hand on the mirror behind him; which was the queue for Julie to stop the music.

We all stopped in the positions we were in. William glared at Nat and I, who were side by side at this point. He looked unimpressed and said, "Let's go from the top once more, FOR THE STUPID FUCKING SINGERS." (obviously yelling the last part) While there was obvious venom in his voice, Nat and I knew, that this was also William's sense of humor. William is a funny fucking man; even when he's cranky.

We managed to nail the start the next time and after a few more run-throughs, the show was spectacular. Even though William's past reputation precedes him, on both occasions that I worked with him, I have always found him to be funny, sincere, very caring and a brilliantly creative man. Yeah, we saw glimpses of his temper and tantrums, but they were more funny, than they were scary. I say all of this with such love and respect for the man, because, if I had not had the privilege of working with him, I might not have reached the heights in my career that I did.

Everyone who has worked with William, loves him and I am no different. During our last week of rehearsals, we had to do a full run of every show, from start to finish; without stopping. On the final day, William was coming in to watch two of the shows. Also coming in, was the other owner, the office staff and some family members. Julie asked us all to wear all black for the runs. Nat and I thought it would be funny to create our own shirts, paying homage to William's outburst the week before. It was 2004 and the UK brand, FCUK had just launched in Australia. I had been wearing their shirts from the UK for a few years, but it was only starting to take off at home. Anyone who knows them, knows that they are famous for the play on words slogans.

I came up with the idea to paint on our black shirts, "Stupid FCUK'ing Singer" in white writing on the front. I went to the markets, bought some fabric paint, three black shirts and started creating. They were pretty basic, but still looked awesome. Nat and I wore them on the final day and when William walked in and saw us, he pissed himself laughing. We handed the third shirt to him and from what he tells me, he has often worn it, so that singers know his true feelings for them.

After six fun-filled, but very strenuous weeks of rehearsals completed, the cast and I headed to Sydney airport at 5:00 a.m.; bound for Tahiti. We were all so excited, at the prospect of coconuts on the beach and the general lifestyle and hospitality of the Tahitian people. But before that, we had to endure a thirty-hour flight to get there. Yes, that's right, thirty hours. The thing about cruise lines is, that they fly so many crew members around the world each and every day, that they get massive discounts off their airfares, with all the major airlines. The downside of it is, that sometimes the flights that the crew members have to endure, are not always the best.

For example, to fly from Sydney to Tahiti, you would normally fly to Auckland and then Tahiti, which should take no more than eight hours total. On this occasion, Princess Cruises booked us from Sydney to Auckland, then to Los Angeles, then back to Tahiti. A total of thirty hours, but somehow that worked out cheaper. Go figure.

As any group of young entertainers would do in this situation, we made the most of it. The flight to L.A. was empty, so we each had four seats in the middle of the plane, and the three male dancers and I, managed to knock back copious amounts of free beer, in the first few hours, before passing out for the remainder of the flight. We may not have beaten Australian test cricketer David Boon's record of fifty-three tinnies from Brisbane to London, but we certainly gave it a good nudge.

We arrived in L.A. a little worse for wear, but somehow straightened up enough, to get off the plane, before making our way to the baggage

Redemption

claim area. In the customs line, Josh (dancer) and Olivia (dance captain) had a fight over something stupid, which led to both of them storming off in a huff. Meanwhile, my female singer, Natalie, who was married to a Texan, had forgotten that her green card had expired and was detained by authorities.

I went through without any hassles and was at the baggage carousel, collecting mine and Natalie's luggage, when Josh returned, from his tantrum. He grabbed a trolley and went around to the other side of the carousel, to get his bags. At the time, Josh was twenty-one, and for some reason brought with him a "Scooby-Doo" pillow. This thing was huge and in my opinion, was ridiculous to carry through airports, by a five year old, let alone a twenty-one year old. At this point, it seemed to be keeping Josh calm, so I left him alone.

Shortly after collecting all the bags, I heard Josh swearing—fuck this, fuck that—over the other side of the carousel. I couldn't actually see him, but all of a sudden, I saw the Scooby-Doo pillow launched over the baggage carousel, like it had come to life; yelling, "Raggy!" I nearly pissed my pants thinking, *what the fuck is wrong with this cast?* Thankfully, that was the end of the drama at L.A.X, apart from the fact that Natalie was not going to be joining us in Tahiti straight away.

Natalie had to fly back to Texas, to have her green card renewed, before she could join us. What we had forgotten, though, was that we did some shuffling of luggage, before we checked our bags in at Sydney airport, and when doing so, I placed all of my toiletries in Natalie's bag to make my bag lighter. I only remembered this when we were halfway across the Pacific Ocean, on the way to Tahiti.

I spent the next few days borrowing everyone else's toiletries, as they are ridiculously expensive to buy in Tahiti. The upside of Natalie not flying to Tahiti with us, was that with the plane totally full, but I was the only person who had two seats to spread out. The other benefit of travelling the long way around to get to Tahiti, was that the company got us our own rooms, at the Sheraton in Tahiti the night before joining the ship. This was worth the pain, to have a nice night relaxing in luxury. We made the most of it, taking advantage of the amazing facilities, including the awesome spa that was right on the water.

The following morning, we were picked up early and taken to the ship, which was only a few miles away. As we arrived at the quay side, where the ship was docked, we all knew, that the next six months, would be something special. The ship was absolutely breathtaking and looked like a floating Versace Hotel. We dropped our gear off and got straight into rehearsals that morning. On the way to the show lounge, I stopped at the officers' mess to grab a coffee, to give me a kick start, for what lay ahead. As I was making my coffee, a gorgeous Egyptian looking girl stood waiting for me to finish.

I said, "Hi, I'm J.D., the new singer." She laughed and said in a British accent, "Oh, so you're J.D. Your ex-girlfriend Colleen, told me to watch out for you."

Oh great, I thought. Not only is each ship very political, but apparently, this kind of politics also jumps from ship to ship. The worst part of this situation, was that she was simply breathtaking. Her name was Sarah, and she was also a "Steiner" like Colleen. I guess it was a good thing that she said this, as it saved me as lot of time and embarrassment, trying to impress her. What I found amazing, was that she was literally the first person I had come into contact with on board. She just happened to be the only person, that Colleen shared a room with, on her very next contract, after leaving our old ship. What a small world we live in. The scary thing about this kind of thing, is that even though there are hundreds of cruise ships around the world and thousands of crew members at any one time, the chances of stepping onto a totally new ship, in a new company and knowing someone from past contracts; is quite high.

A classic example of this, was in 2013, when I travelled on an Australian P&O ship as a passenger. I had previously had an awesome cabin steward, on a contract (That I will get into later). The steward's name was Suresh. He was my steward for a few months, in 2006, but seven years later, I walked into my cabin on the Pacific Dawn, as a passenger, and who walks through the door to introduce himself, but Suresh. Of all the

Redemption

ships, he was on my ship, but what was even more bizarre, ws that on each ship, there are hundreds of cabin stewards, but I ended up with him. The industry really is a small world of its own.

Back in Tahiti, myself and the new cast, met the current cast, who all seemed lovely, and the female lead singer, Stella, was kind enough to stand in for Natalie, until she arrived from the USA. It was crucial to the shows being ready, that I had a female lead to work with, while blocking the shows in. Even though Natalie would be under prepared for opening night, at least the rest of us would be ready, so the show should still be of a high standard. It was evident to Stella and I, along with everyone else, that Stella and I, had a great chemistry together on stage, straight away.

According to Michelle, who was the current dance captain, helping to bump in the shows, we looked as though we'd been working together for years. Stella had been in the industry for years, so it was great working with her, and I learnt a lot during those few days. The first few days of rehearsals went very smoothly, apart from Sheldon dropping a female dancer on her head, during a lift. She recovered in a few days, as did Sheldon's ego.

This ship was certainly not as bad as "hell week" on my first ship, so after a few days of hard rehearsals, it was now time to relax at the "Island Night" deck party. The crew usually decorates the pool areas, with local palm leaves, there are copious amounts of summer cocktails, and everyone (passengers and crew) party until the early hours of the morning. Quite often, you can buy grass skirts and floral shirts, in the port, that day, but if not, the shop on board, always has some in stock. Island night is so much fun and everyone gets fully into the spirit of it. Passengers dress up in grass skirts, coconut bras and leis (and that's just the men), but seriously, it's one of the highlights of any cruise itinerary, so if you're planning on going on a cruise and you haven't already got yourself a decent Hawaiian shirt or dress, then you'd better get one.

The cast and I had a few drinks in my cabin then went upstairs to join the party atmosphere with the passengers. Everyone was dressed up in Island Night attire, which gave it a great atmosphere, and all the passengers were having such a great time. The fact that we were in Tahiti, made Island Night even more fun. It had a genuine tropical feel to it, especially when the local dance troupe came on board to perform for the passengers.

The local show anywhere in the world, is special to see, when they come on board. Whether it be in Russia, Scotland, or Tahiti, the local shows, are always enjoyed by the passengers. What made this really great, was that the locals would bring on a whole pile of handcrafted items, which they sold earlier in the afternoon, including grass skirts, leis, crowns, and other amazing pieces. The local dance troupe consisted of around thirty performers, ranging in age from forty years old, right down to little Leilani who was just over a year old. This little girl was totally adorable.

Leilani, had not even been walking for that long, but let me tell you, she could shake her butt like crazy. She would take center stage, with her tiny little grass skirt and coconut bra on and shake her little tosh so hard. At the end of the routine, the crowd went absolutely crazy, clapping, cheering and whistling, and on this particular occasion, little Leilani got so shocked, that she left a big puddle in the middle of the dance floor.

Later in the night, the party out on deck was going off and pretty large amounts of cocktails were consumed by all of us. Somehow, Stella and I ended up back at her cabin. I say "somehow," but I think we both knew how it happened. We both ended up messing around on her bed and were in the process of getting naked, when something bizarre happened. We were almost totally naked, when suddenly I had a manic sneezing fit and Stella started to get really itchy eyes. We tried to continue, but it just became unbearable. Stella's eyes had puffed up like balloons, and for more than ten minutes, I could not stop sneezing.

We eventually gave up on the idea of doing anything and lay there laughing in disbelief at what happened. It was like we both had some crazy allergic reaction to each other. God knows why, but nevertheless, we realized it was a sign. I returned to my cabin later that night and neither of us dared make a move on each other, for the rest of the cruise, for fear of it happening again. Since then, Stella and I have remained very close

Redemption

friends. We often end up crossing paths, on ships, or in the same city, but to this day, we have never been in a cast together; nor have we had sex together. We still laugh about that night, each time we see each other.

As soon as Stella's cast left the ship and my cast took over, we all began enjoying the wonders of Tahiti. The ship did ten-day itineraries, so we had four shows, to perform each cruise. This meant that, for the most part, I had as much free time, as the passengers. While in Tahiti, we sailed from Papeete, to Rangiroa, Rarotonga, Huahine, Nuka Hiva, Fukarava, Hiva Oa, Moorea, Apia, Pago Pago, Raiatea and the stunning island of Bora Bora.

If you're wondering why I've not mentioned any ports of call previous to this, well, my first two contracts at sea, only went to Bilbao, in Spain and Cherbourg, in France. In both cases, the ports were ferry ports and quite boring, with nothing nearby to see. In hindsight, it was probably a good thing, because it forced me to focus on becoming a better performer, rather than spending all of my time sightseeing. This contract in Tahiti, however, was a whole new world.

Tahiti is one of the bucket list destinations for many people. Not only did I get to experience it, but I was lucky enough to stay there for six months and get paid to do so. The place is even more beautiful, than the pictures or videos portray. It really is breathtaking. The turquois coloured water, the coconuts, white sandy beaches; it really is paradise. Papeete itself, is nothing special, but once you sail out into the islands, you feel like you're in heaven.

Even though, I wanted to experience all there was in Tahiti, I still had a lot to learn and a long way to developing my craft to the level, where it was world-class. I was determined to make a name for myself in the cruise industry and even though, I had the choice of which ship I chose for this contract, I wanted to be able to choose, any ship, in any part of the world, next time.

My cruise director was an English guy, named of Chris. Chris was well spoken and confident. He was a singer himself, who had only recently stepped away from the production shows, with Princess Cruises. Chris knew all the shows that I was doing and in fact, had premiered most of them too. There was no doubt that Chris was a great entertainer, however, at the time, he appeared to be having a little trouble accepting the "transition period" from singer, to cruise director.

I don't blame him. Even though cruise director pays better, the job of singer on most ships, is really something special. You are almost revered as royalty and treated accordingly, by passengers and even crew, to some extent. Singers are usually picked up from the airport in a limousine and taken to a hotel, the night before boarding, then collected once again in the morning and taken to the ship. On some ships, you get your bar bill paid each month, and in almost all cases, you get all of the privileges that the passengers get, as well as the discounts that crew receive, in the bars and shops. As the lead singer, in the production shows, you generally have, a nice outside cabin, in a passenger area, that either has a large window, or a balcony.

With all the perks of the job, as a singer, Chris seemed reluctant to let go of the singer status. He began criticizing my ability and in particular my vocal range in the shows, to the point where it was noted, that if I couldn't rectify these issues that he felt I had, then I might be sent home early. On some contracts, while the cruise director oversees all of the entertainment, unless there is something majorly wrong, the cruise director leaves all issues and corrections, in the hands of the dance captain.

In this case however, Chris saw it as his right to hand out notes to the cast, whenever he felt it was needed. He particularly said that the lower end of my vocal range, was not very strong. Well, I am a tenor, not a baritone, so that is to be expected and given how low the key of some songs in the shows are on Princess Cruises are, he felt this was more than just a minor issue. Some people might take these sorts of comments personally and tell him to stick it where the sun doesn't shine, but I decided to see if there was any way that I could develop this area of my range, to prove him wrong.

I began working on this, and before I knew it, I had a range that spanned from Baritone to high tenor. It seemed that Chris saw something special in me, but he also thought, that perhaps I was a little lazy in the way that I sang. He was right in regards to my range needing some work, but cer-

Redemption

tainly not in regards to my passion and effort to succeed. Now, thanks to Chris, I am fortunate to have a range, that is wider than most male singers. As a singer, I am what's known as a true tenor, and the Princess shows tend to be written in strange keys, that were more suited to a baritone, than a tenor. So, I am now fortunate enough to be able to sing low enough for these types of shows, while also having a very high range. This enables me to be able to adlib and add my own spin on some of the songs in a way, that most other male singers can't.

Thankfully, it wasn't just criticism, that Chris shared with me. I was fortunate enough, to benefit from his experience, as he assisted me in many costume change tips and other helpful areas of the shows, that he had spent years perfecting; and which I was able to learn, without the trial and error. An even happier outcome for this story, was when I saw Chris, a few years later, on a different ship, when I was on board as a headline act, with my own show. Chris was the cruise director and after watching my own show, Chris let me know, how proud of me he was and how much that he thought I had grown, both as a singer and a performer. This was a huge compliment, coming from a man, who once didn't think I was worthy of being in this industry.

Speaking of costumes and shows, the shows that are on board cruise ships (for the most part) are truly spectacular. Quite often, passengers would ask me who does the choreography, who designs the costumes, how much do they cost, etc. Well, when you think about how long a show stays on any ship, which is usually five years, then each costume would be worn probably six hundred times. If the show is transferred to another ship, then the costumes, are possibly worn another six hundred times.

This means that the costumes really have to be made well in the first place. They have to be designed for maximum "wow" factor for the audience too. To design costumes for these shows, the companies contract famous designers such a Bob Mackie or Nolan Miller, to ensure the that shows look spectacular. Each show can cost anywhere from around USD$200,000 to design, and the sets can cost from tens of thousands right up to millions to create. Add to this, the direction and choreography of some of the biggest names and you realize why cruise lines try to get a long life out of each show.

If you add up the cost of putting these shows on these ships and then recasting every six months, plus the cost of flights, accommodation, and rehearsals for the performers, this takes up a huge chunk of any cruise line's budget each year. The thing that sets the entertainment apart from other departments, is that even though the entertainment costs so much to produce, it is one of the few departments, that does not generate revenue for the cruise line. Sure, the reputation of the shows and overall experience is what draws passengers on board, but it doesn't bring in on board revenue like the salon, shops, shore excursions, or bars.

I have to say that I absolutely loved most of the costumes I was lucky enough to wear. They were all so brilliantly designed and crafted and felt and looked amazing on. The choreographers from London, Florida, and Australia that I worked with, were all world class, and I am very fortunate to have learned my craft from them. When I finished up performing on ships, production shows, were just beginning to take off, so far as the scale of the productions. These days, there really is no limit to the things that we are seeing so far as shows on cruise ships. Full blown Broadway musicals such as Cats, Hairspray and Grease are onboard Royal Caribbean Oasis-class ships, while, ice-skating shows and even high-diving aqua shows are all becoming part of the norm.

During my first eight years at sea, I was fortunate enough to star in over twenty-five shows and even premiere three. Premiering a new show, was a magical process to be a part of. To be part of the first cast to create a show, meant that you were not only the first performers to perform the show, but the process became more interactive. The staging and choreography, was, for the most part, adapted to suit the first cast. Each and every one of the shows that I performed in, had at least one moment, that I absolutely loved performing.

The Tahitian Princess' home port of Papeete, was where we would start and finish the cruises, every ten days. Turnaround in Tahiti was awesome. "Turnaround" is where each cruise ends and begins and where the ship refuels, restocks, and passengers disembark and embark. In most cases, this occurs all in one day, but in Tahiti, it happened differently.

The ship would arrive in the early evening and the passengers were able to enjoy Papeete in the evening, before returning to the ship. The following day, the next group of passengers would arrive on a charter flight from Los Angeles. Later than night, the previous group of passengers, would leave on the same plane, that the new passengers arrived on. The ship would stay docked for another night and leave the following day. That's forty-eight hours in that awesome place.

The nightlife was not great, though, and the only bar nearby charged nearly ten dollars for a beer and was a little seedy looking. The bar was called "Les 3 Brasserie," which from what we understood, translated into English as "Three Tits". This may not be totally correct, but it was the best translation we found locally. Papeete wasn't a great night out, but each night, more than forty food vendors, would set up on the quay side and sell anything from Chinese, to seafood and the most amazing crepes, anywhere in the world.

All the crew, passengers, and of course the locals, would go there and sit under the stars, to enjoy the atmosphere and great food, served from the vans. There was usually a local band or a group of musicians playing all night, and almost all the passengers and crew, would join the festivities on the quay side. I promise you that you will never find a better Oreo and ice cream crepe anywhere in the world. When it came time for us to go "out", we would first go back to the crew bar and fill up on a handful of cheap drinks. Any drink at the crew bar was USD$1, so it was often a case of everyone shouting each other drinks, at that price.

A Tahitian princess.

A few months into our contract in Tahiti, we were in the Marquesas Islands and I was enjoying the sunshine of the Polynesian weather up on the top deck of the ship. I walked around the corner of the sun deck and saw the most beautiful woman, I had seen in some time. This girl had beautiful olive skin, dark brown eyes and a smile, that would melt any heart. At that moment, it certainly did melt mine, that was for sure. I watched, as she walked past me, with an older man and a lady. I presumed that they were her parents. I admired her, as she walked past and went to the deck below.

After my show that night, I quickly got changed out my costume and went to the front of the show lounge to de-greet the show. I always made a habit of de-greeting the passengers after the show and the passengers always seemed to enjoy seeing me there. As the last of the passengers, left the lounge, I saw this girl, from earlier. I could not resist the urge to go and speak to her, but before I got the nerve to do so, her mother was pushing her to, come and say hello to me. The girl reluctantly came over and said hi. I say reluctantly, not because she didn't want to talk to me, but because her mother was being embarrassingly pushy; as only a mother can.

She came and introduced herself to me. Her name was Claudia, and she was a lawyer from Florida. I don't remember much more of what she said, because, up close, she was every bit as beautiful, as from a distance. From the moment, we met we both knew, that there was a serious attraction between us. Not just physical, but on a much deeper level. It's quite amazing how you can meet someone on a cruise ship, or on holidays anywhere, for that matter, and suddenly it turns into the most amazing love affair. I have yet to pinpoint why this is, but I think most people have experienced this kind of thing, at least once in their life.

Claudia and I had the most amazing ten days together, and to this day have an amazing friendship, based on the total honesty and naivety of the time we spent together. Out of complete respect for Claudia and our time together, I prefer to keep the details of this between her and I, as it really was beyond anything I had experienced with someone before and don't wish to cheapen the situation by going into details. When Claudia left Tahiti, we began making plans to see each other again, at the end of my contract; with a view to seeing where things could possibly lead. Sadly though, that never happened, for reasons that I will explain shortly, and it has been one huge regret of mine, that we've never had the opportunity to see each other since.

Redemption

To this day, Claudia continues to be such an amazing source of inspiration to me and the way I live my life. Claudia herself always laughs when I tell her that she is my inspiration, because in her eyes, she is just a normal woman, who lives her life as best she can. That is what makes her so inspirational, because even her "normal life", is one that is truly inspirational.

Claudia is now a very successful vice president for a massive financial advising company in America and has achieved success, worthy of her hard work. She dedicates so many hours each week, to giving free legal advice to women, who have been involved in domestic violence as well as any other charities and organizations, that ask for her help. It is for these reasons that I have no doubt that Claudia and I will remain friends, for a very long time. Even though we hardly speak these days, I think she knows, that she is in my heart always and most certainly always on my mind.

Dolores (like clitoris).

At any time, while working on a cruise ship, you could have someone walk into your life whether it is for a week, or a lifetime and your life will never be the same again. For better or for worse, it never ceased to amaze me, how many totally amazing people, I've managed to meet on ships. Some people, like Claudia, will be in my life always, while others, I will never see again. Regardless, all of them have influenced me and inspired me, in some way. By this stage of the contract we were heading toward Christmas and I was not sure what to expect from my first Christmas at sea.

It was a hot, sunny first day of the Christmas cruise, which left Papeete a week before Christmas Day. I was sunbathing on the sun deck, with Shani, who was one of the cruise staff. The new cruise sales girl, Dolores, who joined the ship, the cruise before, walked over and joined Shani and I. As Dolores introduced herself to me, I didn't quite catch her name properly. I politely asked her to repeat it, at which point she said, "It's Dolores, like clitoris." I couldn't help but laugh. She then explained that this was a joke she shared with everyone she knew, after an episode of the TV show "Seinfeld", where they used the same explanation for a girl with the same name.

C.R.U.I.S.E

Dolores was Canadian, but of Portuguese parents. She was five feet, four inches tall, had awesome brown curly hair, beautiful olive skin and curves in all the right places. On first impressions, Dolores was full of energy, somewhat loud and quite a handful of a personality. I don't mean any of these things in a bad way. She was just not the quiet, reserved type; that's all.

As I laid back down and continued to get nice and brown, from the gorgeous Tahitian sun, Shani and Dolores, started discussing the lack of eligible single males, for the women on board the ship. Dolores was stating how things were about to heat up, with several women, all having their eye on two different men. Dolores and Emma (a nurse), apparently both had their eye on the same guy and not for the first time either.

According to Dolores, she had slept with a guy, that Emma fancied, on the Dawn Princess a few months prior. So, this was looking like it was going to be an interesting rematch, with them both setting their sights on one man. To be honest, even though, I wasn't paying a great deal of attention to their conversation, I was still getting quite hot under the collar. Dolores as I said, was Canadian and very attractive. Shani was a cute blonde from Essex in the UK and the both of them, seemed to be up for some fun. They were only wearing skimpy bikinis and were very nicely oiled up in the sun, as well, so it was no wonder I was getting hot under the collar. Emma, the nurse, was also a very cute blonde, so whoever the guy was that Emma and Dolores were going to fight over, was a very lucky guy.

It was several days later, during one of the shows that my dresser, Lorette, mentioned to me, that two female crew members were keen on me. She told me this, in the middle of her reaching for my zip and pulling my pants off, during a fast change. Because I was in the middle of a show, I was a little distracted, but none the less, I got the message, loud and clear.

For those of you who are unaware, most shows have "dressers." It is the dressers job to assist the performers during fast costume changes during the shows. I have had some great dressers, both male and female, over the years. Without them, I would not have made many of my super-fast costume changes. A good dresser is one who can have your pants unzipped

Redemption

and around your ankles by the time you have ripped open the Velcro on your shirt and undone your bowtie. At first, it was a little strange having a male do this job, but I have to say, Danny, who was assistant cruise director on this ship, was probably the best dresser I have had. He had me undressed faster than any woman ever has; and he wasn't even gay.

Lorette was also very good and during this change, while pulling my pants down, she refused to tell me who the two girls were that fancied me, but did mention that one of them had stolen the other one's boyfriend, on a previous ship. I instantly recalled the conversation from a few days prior and realized that it must be Dolores and Emma. Looking back, I am certain that Dolores brought that conversation up with Shani, in front of me as a way to drop the hint that it might be me. As is the case though with most males, I suck at taking hints and it went right over my head.

Wow! I thought to myself, as Lorette adjusted my fly, trying not to bump my tackle. They were both cute. *How do I choose?* I certainly didn't want to make the same mistake as I did, the year before with Colleen and Lauren. After much deliberation (actually after a flip of a coin really), I thought that Dolores was more my type of girl. Looking back now though, Emma is definitely more my type. Besides, what man doesn't have the "naughty nurse" fantasy and want sponge baths from a hot nurse. I could have had all of this, in real life, but such is life and Emma is now very happily married with children now.

Now if "apparent time" on cruise ships moves three times as fast as on land, then it was no wonder that within a few days, Dolores and I had completed the five "Fs" with each other (Found, Fancied, Flirted, Fucked and Fought). That meant, that things were right on track, as per cruise ship style relationships. Dolores was a crazy Canadian girl who was not shy to admit, that she had slept with more than fifty men by age thirty. According to her, most Canadian girls were like this. Now I am not willing to have an opinion on if Canadian girls are really like this, however she said that all of her friends were the same, so there you have it.

You're probably wondering why I got involved with a woman like this, after all the trouble I had with Lauren being unfaithful. Well it's simple. It's a thing called "ship goggles." It's kind of like beer goggles, but it lasts much longer. You see, when you get beer goggles, you think the girl (or guy) is hot and then in the morning, or a few hours later, you realize that they aren't, so you leave. The effect of the beer that, creates the "beer goggles", usually only lasts a few hours. On the other hand, when you have "ship goggles" it's like a gradual deterioration of your eyes ability, to judge a good catch, from a bad one. This type of condition, can last for an entire contract, or in this case; much longer.

Let me clear something up, before Dolores travels across the world to kill me, for what I just wrote. Dolores is by no means ugly, or even close to ugly. She was very attractive and one of the sexiest women I had ever been with. What I mean by ship goggles is that with my ship goggles, I was blinded to the fact that, she was bio polar. She alerted me to this, when we first met, but as expected, I chose to ignore it, thinking that this would have no bearing on our relationship.

I'll come back to this part of the story shortly.

To be continued…

Ship board relations

Apart from the "Ship Goggles," working on a cruise ship seems to make things become so crystal clear, when it comes to relationships. I have seen many relationships crumble, when there is one partner on land and the other at sea. At the same time, I have also seen many relationships grow and get stronger, during this time apart. One thing is for certain, when you're in a relationship that has one of you on a ship and one not, you *will* get clarity; one way or the other.

During this contract, on the Tahitian Princess, two of our dancers, Olivia and Melina, both had boyfriends back home (Chris and Kelt). Both were young couples in love and while they all struggled with the distance between them, their love grew and became so much stronger for the experience. As part of my contract as a singer, I was able to bring a partner or friend on board for a cruise; virtually for free. I could literally have a

Redemption

girlfriend come on board and stay for every cruise, for $10 per day. One of the singers on our sister ship, had his girlfriend stay on board for more than four months.

Because I was single, both Olivia and Melina, asked me if I could put in an application for their boyfriends to come on board for a cruise. Technically, any of my guests that I brought on board, had to be accommodated in my cabin. However, there was always a spare cabin on the ship, so the hotel director, would always put my guest in there, while they were on board. This meant that Chris and Kelt were able to spend valuable time with Olivia and Melina, during the contract in Tahiti.

On both occasions, when the guys came on board, I wasn't even charged the $10 per day and the girls were kind enough to buy me a bottle of alcohol to say thank you. I also helped out one of the engineers, getting his girlfriend on board for a cruise, at which time he bought me several bottles of alcohol, so I was happy to help. Having the guys on board was also handy if I wanted the shows filmed for my show-reel. I knew Chris from playing indoor cricket with him many years earlier, so it was also good catching up with him.

I'm happy to say that I went to Melina and Kelt's wedding and there is no doubt in my mind, that they will be together forever. Chris and Olivia also got married recently and started a family. They too, seem to have a very happy future ahead of them. So distant relationships can work, however, from my experience, these were the exception.

On the very same contract, my female singer Natalie, as I mentioned early, was married to a Texan. Throughout the course of the contract, their marriage deteriorated. So much so, that they broke up during that contract and are now divorced. While a normal marriage break-up on land, is always going to be hard for anyone, a breakup at sea; is so much worse. The demise of their marriage also happened in front of almost every crew member, while Natalie's husband, Doug was on board, for a few weeks visiting Natalie.

We all knew there were problems, and I especially knew something was not right, when I heard noises and banging from Natalie's cabin, which was next to mine; late one night. The following afternoon, Natalie appeared for rehearsals, with a really bad black eye. When questioned about it, she said that it happened as an accident, when Doug threw a bottle of water at her, during a play fight. I personally didn't buy it and quietly questioned her side stage, when no one else was around.

She denied any wrong doing by Doug, but that suddenly changed, when Doug came storming into the theater, looking for Nat. She quickly ran off stage, locked the dressing room door and cowered inside. Seeing the look in both Nat's eyes and on Doug's face, as he marched towards where I was standing, I stopped him and suggested that he talk to me for a bit, instead of making the situation worse for himself. Even though my loyalties lay with Nat, as my singer, I didn't care who was right or wrong. I just knew that nothing good was going to come of it, while Doug had that pissed off look on his face. Olivia instantly alerted Chris, the Cruise Director and within an two minutes, Chris and the head of security, Liam, ran into the showroom and defused the situation.

Over the next twenty-four hours, Nat gave a damming statement of what actually occurred that night, to Chris and Liam. Doug was put under cabin arrest and disembarked at the next port, while Nat was left to pick up the pieces. While Nat put on a brave face and appeared to be coping okay, on the outside, the inside was apparently a much different story. This was evident by the fact that her performance on stage declined terribly. The one thing you need to maintain as a singer on a cruise ship is consistency. No one says you have to be absolutely brilliant every single show, but you need to set a good standard and maintain it.

Unfortunately for Nat, she was more up and down than a yo-yo. This didn't just fluctuate from night to night, but it even fluctuated from first show, to second show; in the same night. Nat's pitch and vocal control was up and down, to the point that she was averaging five negative written comments from passengers, each cruise. I felt for Nat, because it is really difficult, dealing with something like that privately, while still having to be so vibrant and perform publicly, while you're dying inside.

As a performer, I am very supportive of my team, as I know how important it is to stick together especially on a ship. The cast are the only group on board a cruise ship, that arrive together and leave together. This can often lead to jealousy and spitefulness shown towards casts on cruise ships, by other crew members. It is for this reason that you all need to stick together.

A few weeks later, our new cruise director, Sammy, had brought Natalie's problem to my attention, so I sat down with Sammy and discussed how we could help Natalie turn this around. Her performance was affecting the overall quality of the shows, not to mention the cast's moral, as a result of the negative comments that we were getting each cruise, from the passengers. The main problem we faced, was that Natalie was best friends with the dance captain Olivia, who ended up shielding Natalie, rather than trying to make her aware of the issues.

Isn't it better to face the facts and improve, if you are falling short of your own potential? I know that us entertainers, can sometimes have fragile egos, but accepting responsibility for our shortcomings, will make us better performers, in the long run. No one was trying to hurt Natalie, or make her feel unworthy. We were simply trying to show her, that there was a problem and then assist her to fix it. In this case though, Natalie herself, somehow could not see, or more to the point "hear" how bad she had become. If she could hear it, she obviously was ignoring it.

When Nat heard that Sammy and I had been discussing this matter, she made such a fuss and became quite the "diva", making everyone else's lives, apart from Olivia's painful, for having to work with her. When it became apparent that Natalie was neither going to improve, or realize how bad she actually was, it became my job to somehow try to lift the standard of the shows, with the help of the dancers.

In a small, eight-person cast, like ours, it is vitally important that the two lead vocalists do exactly that; lead. So now it was my job to do that for both of us for the remaining two months. Looking back now, I'm so glad that things went this way, as it helped me to grow as a performer for the second time in the same contract. I look back at that contract as such an amazing contract for my development as a singer and am grateful for these challenges.

C.R.U.I.S.E

This was the first situation of this type, that I had witnessed on a ship, but since this, I have noticed that every cast has similar situations. If you look closely in every cast at sea, the weakest cast member, always attaches themselves to the dance captain; sort of like a sucker fish. This is a way of survival. They rely on their friendship, to assure their safety in situations, like what was happening with Natalie. They become the first person the dance captain protects, should any trouble arise. I know that this also happens in work environments on land, but on ships, it seems more obvious.

Do I hear bells of some description?

By now, Christmas day was fast approaching, as was New Year's Eve and then Australia Day, soon after. This was party / festive season, so we were gearing up for all of the parties on board. The festive season is such a crazy time at sea, with each department holding their own party, of which every other department is invited along. With this being the case, December and January seem to be one constant hangover. I remember Christmas day that year, when I was walking along a section of the ship, that the crew referred to as the "M1." On American ships, they refer to it as "I-95", after their major highway. Most ships have one and it's usually a wide corridor, that runs almost the length of the ship. The M1 or I-95 is in crew areas, and is where most of the stock gets transported, to various parts of the ship. It is also where crew are often seen transiting, from one area to another, without having to go into passenger areas.

This Christmas Day, I was walking down the M1, not paying any attention to what was ahead, when suddenly before me, appeared our chief engineer Enda, holding a full glass of mulled wine. He stuck it right under my nose, where I could smell the overwhelming flavor, and in his thick Irish accent said, "Drink up lad." I tried to politely say no, at which time he pushed my head back and tried to pour it down my throat, while muttering like a drunken pirate, "Just drink it, ya pussy."

The chief engineer is in charge of the entire mechanical running of the vessel and in fact is third in charge of the entire ship, in most cases. He is

Redemption

in charge of anything from blocked toilets, lights, computers and air-conditioning, to how much power the captain is given from the engines at any particular moment. Truth be known, the chief engineer drives the ship and the captain just steers it.

Enda had obviously had a few of these drinks himself that day, so I was a little curious as to who was keeping the engines running at that point, given who else I was about to discover, was with him. Enda was a top guy and a barrel of laughs, so I could hardly refuse his generous festive offer. I threw my head back and slammed down the contents of the glass and as I looked back down again, I saw another senior officer, stood directly in front of me. Actually, he was the *most* senior officer; the captain.

I almost choked on the contents of the drink, at the sight of the master, no more than a foot away from me. Captain Bomarco simply handed me one of the two glasses of mulled wine he was holding, and ordered me to follow him, as he skulled the drink. I reluctantly obeyed the captain's orders as Enda laughed. He could see that I nearly shit myself, before I realized that the captain himself, was enjoying the festive spirit and was not there to discipline me, but rather celebrate with me.

For the rest of the day, anyone who passed by this drinks table on the M1, would have to stop and share in a festive drink with Enda and the captain. Needless to say, after a few times down the M1, I began going the long way around to get places, for fear of not being able to perform on stage that night. That night the entertainment department put on a Christmas show for the passengers, at which time I really needed to sober up. It was a bit of a thrown together variety show of which one of the numbers was the brain child of our cruise director, Sammy.

The number involved me and the other male cast members, all wearing women's underwear. While the gay dancers, may have enjoyed this, myself and Josh, who was also straight, were not too impressed. We had to sing a parody of "Walking in a winter wonderland," which was actually "Walking round in women's underwear." With much reluctance we did it, and as the curtain went up, I was oh-so-elegantly positioned on the grand piano (A la Shirley Bassey) as I sang the opening lines of the song. After a few lines, I gracefully slid off the piano and briskly walked down toward the front of the stage.

The combination of a beautifully polished solid timber floor, along with my new socks (I have no idea why I was wearing socks with a nighty) meant that when I tried to pull up, at the front of the stage, one of two things was going to happen. I was either going to go ass over tit, or slide right off the end of the stage and into someone's lap. Either way, neither outcome was going to be a happy one for me. As it turned out, I ended up flat on my ass with Sammy's purple, full-length nighty up over my head and my bright red jocks on show for the entire audience. I really need to think about matching underwear next time I do this kind of thing, don't I? As a complete professional (cough cough), I continued singing, as I elegantly removed the dress from over my head, crossed my legs like a lady, and continued singing as Josh, Joel and Sheldon stood there laughing at me.

Not long after that, we were back stage preparing for our next number, which was slightly more normal than the last one, when I heard someone snoring outside the dressing room door. Melina and I went outside and found Josh asleep on a chair in the corner, still dressed in fishnet stockings and a silky black negligee. He too had obviously found himself at Enda's mulled wine table a few times throughout the day and was feeling the effects of it now.

Melina grabbed her camera and took a picture, which woke Josh up. He stood up dazed and looked around at us for a moment. In that moment Sheldon grabbed the chair that Josh was sitting on for his next number on stage and took off toward the wings. Josh went to sit back down on it, but ended up on his ass on the floor, with the black number up over his head and his fishnet stockings and matching black panties on display for all to see. He sat there for a moment in a daze, before nodding back off to sleep, while we went on and did the next number without him.

We survived the festive season and by this stage, Dolores and I were very much loving being together. So much so that I had found, chosen, and arranged for my biological mother to purchase on my behalf, a ring

Redemption

so that I could propose to Dolores on board. Sue (my mother) was coming on board a few weeks later for a cruise, so it was a perfect opportunity. The only problem with this, was that I could not tell anyone on board. As soon as one person knew, the entire ship (including Dolores) would know. I had to plan the whole thing by myself. I knew exactly how I was going to do it and as the time drew closer, I began to enlist key people to assist me. Each person had to be sworn to secrecy.

The first person I told, was Sammy my cruise director. She had to know, because I needed her permission to do it during my cabaret show. My plan was to bring Dolores up on stage and sing a song that I wrote to her and then propose to her, in front of the theatre full of passengers. Sammy was totally cool with this and was ecstatic at the thought of this happening. Sammy was a big romantic and loved this kind of stuff. She had seen how crazy Dolores and I were about each other, so Sammy was all for it.

It was the day of my show and I was as anxious as anything, because if things didn't go to plan, the whole ship was going to be watching. That morning, I enlisted my next person, Tim. He was the assistant cruise director and one of Dolores' best friends on board. It was Tim's job to make sure that Doloires was watching the show and that when I called her up on stage, that she actually came up. Tim arranged for himself, Dolores, and Sue to all sit together, at the back of the room for the show. That afternoon, I rehearsed with the band and I told the musical director, Sarah, what was happening so she knew her part in the plan.

After dinner, Dolores and I were in my cabin, and I was gently trying to persuade her to make sure that she was dressed nicely that evening and in particular, that she was wearing underwear to the show. Dolores hardly ever wore underwear, which wasn't normally a bad thing, but I was planning on having her sit on a stool, while I sang to her, so it was probably best for all concerned, that she wore some that night. She was wondering why I was so keen on what she was wearing on this occasion, so I didn't push it. I think I gave her some lame excuse about Sue wanting to get some photos of the two of us together.

Even though I had only told Sammy, Tim, and Sarah there seemed to be

C.R.U.I.S.E

a "buzz" around the ship that evening. I think Sammy had mentioned in the Heads of Department meeting that afternoon, that something special was going to happen during the show that night. As it turned out, when the show got under way, the back of the theater was unusually filled with almost every senior officer on the ship.

Just before the show began, I was sat in the dressing room with Scotty McLean, a magician, or as he calls himself a "deceptionist". Scotty was the headline act and I was the opening support act for him that night. Scotty could see that I was extremely nervous. He asked me why I was so nervous, so I told him about what I was about to do. Scotty had been married for several years and had been through all of this already, so he took it upon himself to give me some words of wisdom. His words calmed me down and out I went and performed a cracking show.

I performed four numbers, then it was time for my last song; the one I wrote for Dolores. I gave the audience a brief idea of how the song came about and told them that I would like to bring someone special up on stage, so that I could sing it to her. As I called Dolores on stage, I could hear her at the back of the room saying, "Oh my god." As planned, Tim made sure that she came up on stage and as she sat down on the stool beside me, she mumbled, "I'm going to kill you." I turned to her, smiled and whispered, "This is why I wanted you to wear underwear," as I laughed. The music began, and I sang the song. Throughout the song, I could feel my heart racing at an unbelievable rate. Not only was I singing my original song for the very first time to an audience, but I was also about to do something else that I had never done before.

Dan, who I wrote the song with, was also in the room, as the orchestra played the music that we had written, beautifully. As the song came to the end, I held Dolores' hand as I continued singing. At the completion of the song, we both stood and Dolores went to walk away, thinking that this was the end of her being required on stage. I gently pulled her back toward me before letting go of her hand, to reach into my suit pocket. I dropped onto one knee, which made it very obvious to Dolores and the audience what was coming next.

Redemption

The crowd let out an instantaneous gasp, realizing what was about to happen. I opened the box and popped the question; "Dolores, will you marry me." The room sat in absolute silence, awaiting her response. It seemed like an eternity before she said anything. She was obviously in shock, as was the rest of the room. She smiled and said, "I don't know what to say," at which time Sammy yelled from the back of the room, "Say yes." Dolores nodded and said the word that I and everyone else in the room were hoping to hear; "Yes." The crowd simultaneously erupted into applause and cheers as Sarah cued the band, to play a reprise of the song. Dolores and I kissed before I grabbed her hand and led her backstage.

Dolores, Sue, Sammy, Tim, Tim's mother (Who was also on board) and myself, went up to the nightclub to celebrate the occasion. Dolores and Sue got on so well, and in fact seemed like best friends, not mother in law and daughter. The two of them were hilarious as they began getting drunker. After a while, I thought it best for Dolores and I to go to bed. We excused ourselves, while Sue, Tim and his mother continued partying. All of the crew knew that Sue was my mother, so I knew she was in good hands.

A few hours later, at about three in the morning, I received a phone call in my cabin, from the bar manager in the club. He said that my mother was dancing on top of the bar and he asked if I could come and get her. I laughed and simply said, "Just tell the bitch to go to bed," before hanging up. He knew I was joking, but at the same time, instructed her (in more polite terms that I suggested), that she should call it a night.

The following morning, I was due to meet Sue in the show lounge at nine, so we could go ashore in Bora Bora together. She was watching the art auction that was taking place and was obviously still feeling the effects of the night before when I arrived. As I approached, a beautiful piece of art, by Scarlet Chow, was being paraded across the floor as the next item to be bid on. The auctioneer started the bidding at four hundred dollars (USD), at which point, I said to Sue, "That's a really nice piece." Like a reflex reaction, Sue's hand shot up to bid on the item, and as it turned out, no one else even bid for it.

Sue decided that it would be a nice engagement present for Dolores and

C.R.U.I.S.E

I, and I agreed. It reminded me of Sue, from the night before, when she was dancing on the bar, drunk. The piece is called "Golden Fan". I must say, that fifteen years later, this piece is now worth a lot more than the four hundred paid for it. More than that though, this piece sits proudly over my shoulder, as I type these words. It is a beautiful part of my collection now and is a constant reminder of my time on the Tahitian Princess. If anyone is ever onboard a cruise ship that has art auctions, I highly recommend, that you purchase a piece of art, as there are some incredible bargains for both collectors and investors. Sue herself purchased several pieces by the artist "Martiros" that she has throughout her home.

Sue enjoyed the rest of her cruise getting to know Dolores, then Dolores and I spent the last two months of the contract side by side. We were inseparable and were blissfully happy. We had discussed our future and made plans for Dolores to move to Australia, where we would both find jobs on land. To be fair on both families and not expecting either of them to travel across the globe, we thought it was best to have a ceremony and party in each country. The plans for these were in full swing as we thought about settling into life together after ships.

At the end of my contract, I went home for a few weeks to find a place for Dolores and I to live, before I had to fly to Canada, to help Dolores make the big move, to the other side of the world. A few weeks later, I arrived in Vancouver, and Dolores and I began sorting out her life, for the move. I met all of her friends and a few nights later, we had a going away party at her place. When I met her friend's partners, they all shook my hand and said, "Dude, thanks for making us all look bad." What they meant by that, was that when Dolores showed them all the video of me proposing to her, all of their girlfriends, said, "See? That's how its supposed to be done." The guys were all cool and were of course joking though, and they actually thought it was quite legendary.

During the party, I secretly took each of Dolores' friends into the spare bedroom, so they could record a personal video message for Dolores. The plan was, that I would play that videos for her, once we were in Australia, to

Redemption

remind her how much her friends cared about her. It was supposed to be a secret, until several weeks later, when she was missing home.

I had managed to get most of her friends to record a message and was in the spare room with her best friend, Kristine, when Dolores walked in. We had finished recording, so we were sat on the floor talking. Dolores had drunk quite a bit by this stage of the night, so the moment she saw us in the room together, she went absolutely crazy. She thought that I was trying to sleep with her friend, so she went nuts. She began swearing and screaming at both of us, and before I knew it, things turned into a massive fight. Kristine and I were literally sitting in the middle of a completely empty room, so it wasn't like we were in bed, or even close to each other, when she walked in.

I decided to go bed, to try to defuse the situation, while Dolores stayed in the lounge room with a few friends. I could hear from the bedroom, as she continued to scream abuse at me and opened up with a barrage of abuse about me to her friends. She must have slagged me off to them, for at least an hour, saying the most horrible things, I think I had ever heard anyone say. Prior to this, Dolores had told me that she was bi-polar, but until this moment, I had not seen any indication of it. I had witnessed her acting irrationally on a few occasions, but as an overly trusting person, I turned a blind eye. At this point though, what I was witnessing, was some scary shit and not what anyone should be subjected to in a relationship. With that in mind, I made the decision to cut my losses and return home; without Dolores.

The following morning, I woke up early and began packing my things to leave. Once I was ready, I thought I should wake Dolores to at least say goodbye. I really did care about her, but given the situation, I saw no way out of it peacefully. As I was about to leave, I noticed her half-naked, passed out on the bed in what would only be described as a "Frog-position." I chuckled quietly at the view, then grabbed her camera, to take a pic, so she could see what she looked like, after I was gone.

As I took the photo, the shutter on the camera, woke her up. From the moment she opened her eyes, she re-launched into the barrage of abuse from the night before. After a few minutes of this abuse, I grabbed my bag, told her I was leaving, and headed for the door. She jumped out of bed and stood in front of the doorway of her apartment, so I could not get past. I tried peacefully to try to get past, at which point she became even angrier. She then began to get seriously violent and started throwing punches at me.

I've never been one to enjoy violence of any kind, but at this point, there were only two options as I saw it. Either I stay there and get punched and kicked for god knows how long, or I use force myself, to force my way out of the apartment. I don't believe in hitting a woman and never have, but she had made it clear that she was wanting me to fight back. She may have been only five-foot, four- inches tall, but with Portuguese parents and a Canadian upbringing, she appeared to me like she was Mike Tyson at that point.

With that, I let go of my suitcase and used every bit of strength I had to throw Dolores out of the way. There really was no other option. She was not a big girl, but when someone wedges themselves in a doorway like that, there is no way you can get through. She had literally wedged her legs and arms across the doorway, like a cat clinging onto something for dear life. It was killing me to see this situation unfolding with the woman that I loved, but I knew that I had to do this. As I picked her up and threw her away from the doorway, she screamed as she landed heavily on the floor in the hallway, hitting her head on the wall.

I quickly grabbed my bag and opened the door. By this time, Dolores had gotten back to her feet and ran back over to me, even angrier than before. She proceeded to punch me a few more times before biting me on the lip, causing blood to gush from the wound. If it was a guy acting that way, I would have punched the absolute crap out of them, and even though Dolores deserved to have the shit beaten out of her on this occasion, I managed to refrain from retaliating. Again, I pushed her away and fled out the door of the apartment.

I got downstairs and assessed the extent of my injuries. I was more shaken than injured, but nonetheless, I did have a badly cut lip and a huge scratch on my right hand, that was bleeding.

I was about to find a taxi to take me to a hotel or somewhere away from there, when I noticed that during the struggle, I had managed to drop my bum bag, which contained my wallet, keys and passport. There was no way I

Redemption

could get back in, because it was a secure building and I was already out the front. I used the phone at a local shop to call Dolores so I could hopefully get my things back. Of course, when I rang, I got the same attitude and a "go fuck yourself," in response to my request for my belongings. She was seriously psychotic, and it totally shocked me to see her like that. She was laughing down the phone in an evil tone and continuing with abusive comments.

After several attempts to get her to cooperate, I had no other option, but to call the local police. They promptly arrived, and as they took a look at my ripped shirt and cut lip, they questioned me about what had occurred. I explained the situation, at which time the officers said that they were going to arrest her and charge her with assault and domestic violence. Now, I was really faced with quite a dilemma. Even though I never wanted to be with Dolores again, I certainly didn't want her to be charged with these offences.

After much negotiating with the police, I managed to convince them not to take any action against Dolores. I simply wanted my stuff and wanted to leave. They collected my bag and took me to a nearby motel, where I was able to stay for a few nights as I planned my trip home. A few days later, Dolores called and we spoke about the whole situation, at which time she was extremely sorry for what happened. I too was sorry that I was unable to make her feel secure enough, or loved enough so she wouldn't "tip over the edge" in such a way.

Somehow, over the course of the next few days, we remarkably managed to sort through a whole lot of issues and actually decided to give things one last shot, which would be the life we had planned in Australia. A week later, Dolores moved to Australia, and we lived together for six months, until things turned sour yet again. I have my opinion and Dolores has hers about what went wrong, so I'll simply conclude this chapter by saying that once the ship goggles wore off for Dolores and I, it became glaringly obvious, that we were not as compatible as we had first thought.

A New Beginning

"The most important piece of advice I could give any budding entertainer, is to learn to accept criticism and to use it to better themselves as a performer."

Back where I belonged.

After Dolores went back to Canada, I continued working on land for a further six months, before I began getting itchy feet. I was working full-time as concierge, but also filling in for several six-week stints at a 1,000-seat theatre restaurant, when the male performers took holidays. This situation worked for me and the venue was able to replace their talent with someone more capable than just an understudy. I knew the guys in the show and Melina from my Tahitian Princess cast, was also in this show, so it felt like home.

After just over a year on land though, I was well and truly missing being at sea. Once again, the ocean was calling, and I had to answer it. I made a phone call to my old choreographer, William Forsythe and told him that I wanted to go back to sea. William was happy that I called and informed

A New Beginning

me that he had a place for me, in a few months. I had just bought my first apartment, and had a friend who could rent it, so the timing was perfect. For the last three months before I went away, I took over as manager of a motel. I lived on site and while I was always on call, I mostly had my afternoons and evenings free; even though I was not able to leave the property.

I wasn't happy running the motel, but it was a secure wage and I had nights off to rehearse for my next contract. I received my pack of CD's and music scores with lyrics, and I was completely focused on being ready on day one of rehearsals. A few weeks later, I was heading back into rehearsals in Sydney for my next ship. It was a new cast, with three new shows and a brand-new start. I felt energized, and I was ready for whatever life and ships was willing to throw at me. My new cast members were all great, as well as being extremely talented. We had a brand-new show, which we were premiering. This meant that we had two weeks to put the show together, instead of the usual one and I got to work closely with William Forsythe again.

Rehearsals went off without any major dramas, and we joined the ship in Melbourne on a warm summer's day, five weeks later. James, the male singer who I was replacing, was giving me a guided tour around the ship and introducing me to some of the crew. When we arrived at the gym and salon reception, on the bridge deck, I was almost flawed with what I saw. There before me, stood a young woman with the most amazing grace about her. She stood no more than five feet two inches tall, but she was meters above others, when it came to her presence. She had long, blonde hair and the most piercing blue eyes, which complimented her stunning smile.

As we left the area, I asked James who she was. He could tell by my tone of voice, that I was more than slightly taken by her. He informed me that her name was Klara. She was twenty-one and was from Sweden. He then told me not to even bother trying to get in her pants, because every guy on board the ship had tried; and failed miserably. I was instantly deflated, but none the less blessed for the fact of having met her.

James and I continued downstairs to have some lunch, where we met up with the rest of the cast. As we were eating, two girls approached the group and introduced themselves to us. They were Carly and Cassie. They had also joined that day and were cruise staff. The cruise staff are like activity hosts. They are employed primarily for their personalities, to run all the activities, game shows, and theme nights on board. Carly made a point of coming over to me and introducing herself personally.

"Hi, I'm Carly, but everyone calls me Charlie," she said.

Oh fuck, I thought to myself. *Not another "Charlie."*

"Hi. I'm J.D. Nice to meet you," I said.

The two girls left, and I continued eating my lunch. A few nights later, Carly and I bumped into each other on deck and decided to go for a walk together on the quayside in Auckland. The ship was docked overnight, so it was a great opportunity to have a nice, relaxing walk along the water and get to know each other, seeing as we were both new. We walked for a while and chatted about what we had done before and what we liked etc. We stopped on a log seat on the end of the quayside and sat for a bit.

I remember thinking to myself, that I was wasting my time making a move on Klara and that Carly seemed like a nice girl; despite sharing the same nickname as the "bunny boiler". She was quite cute too, so maybe I should show some interest in her. See what I mean? Within forty-eight hours, the ship goggles were taking affect once again. Just as I turned towards Carly, she did exactly the same thing, which put our faces, and in particular our lips, within centimetres of each other. The electricity was apparent, and we kissed, right there under the moonlight, with the ship in the distance; lit up like a Christmas tree.

We kissed for a while and laughed and talked, before heading back to the ship. We went back to my cabin and almost as soon as I closed the door, Carly threw me on the bed and undid my jeans. I'm not sure if Carly always moved that fast, but that's ships for you. As I've said before, things move very fast on ships. Carly surprised me, by giving me head, not more than thirty minutes after kissing me for the first time and no more than a few days after we both boarded the ship. We messed around for a bit, before Carly went back to her cabin and I went to sleep.

The following morning, I woke to a phone call from Michael, the cruise

A New Beginning

director. He was asking why I was not at the safety induction at 9:00 a.m. I looked at my watch and according to it, the time was 8:15. I told Michael that it was not for another forty-five minutes, at which time he reminded me that the ships clocks went forward an hour the night before, which made the time 9:15. It is a common occurrence that the ships clocks are moved forward and backward throughout a cruise, depending on the ships direction. Even though I had experienced this on other ships, it was a rookie mistake this time around.

> *If the ship heads east, the clocks usually go forward an hour and subsequently, when the ship heads back west, the clocks go back an hour. On Atlantic crossings (From Southampton to New York), it is not unusual for the ship's clocks to go forward an hour every night for the 6 nights of the crossing to match up with the time at your destination.*

Later that day, I had to see Michael regarding my lateness and subsequent absence, at which point I got a written warning for not getting to the second induction. I would have gotten away with it, but the first officer knew me from the Tahitian Princess and knew that I was absent. That night, I sat in the crew bar after rehearsals talking with Morgan, who was in his sixties and was cruise staff on board.

Let me detour for a moment.

To best explain Morgan, simply take Slim and add thirty-five years (he even had the English accent, even though he was an Aussie).

Morgan was known as the "Ratman" and was the ultimate player on cruise ships. In all my time on ships, I don't think I have ever seen anyone come close to Morgan, when it comes to pulling women. The man has more front than a butcher shop, and this works for him. Morgs is like the Babe Ruth of pulling women, and just like Babe Ruth, he has the same theory about success. They know that the best way to hit the most home runs, is to swing the bat at everything.

Both Morgs and Babe Ruth struck out more than anyone ever remembers, but what people do remember, was how many times they scored. This was despite Morgan being married for several years. His real name was Peter, but his middle name was Morgan. I guess this helped in disguising his extra-marital affairs at sea. Because he went by the name of Morgan, women were not able to find him on land if they wanted to, and his wife was none-the-wiser to his behaviour on board. I'll explain more about him soon.

So, there I was, telling Morgan about my written warning and the head job from Carly, in pretty much my first conversation with him. He called Matty over, who was another cruise staff, and said, "Hey, Beast, (Matty's nickname) I think we've got a new member for the "rat pack." J.D here, has got a written warning and a head job, before he's even sung a note on stage." Both Morgan and Matty pissed themselves laughing and both shook my hand. I guess I had been accepted so far as the lads were concerned, even if others didn't agree with my start to the contract.

The rat pack.

Survival on cruise ships is all about alliances. You need to develop and nurture the right relationships on board, in order to get by and have peaceful and enjoyable life at sea. You must always try to never piss people off and although that is almost impossible at sea, if you are to do so, make sure that you have a good network to cover your ass, if this does happen. Probably the best network I have ever seen in action at sea, was aptly named the "rat pack" and was the group of guys who befriended me very quickly, when word got out about my before-mentioned written warning and a blowjob, before singing a note on the cruise ship, The Pacific Sky.

Let me explain something before I go any further. If you are to find yourself in trouble, when you're on your own on a cruise ship, then you have to deal with it yourself, but if you're part of a group like the rat pack, then they deal with it for you. This group was under the guidance of Morgan "Ratman," or as we called him, "Morgs." He really was the leader, so far as setting the benchmark for the type of behavior that they got involved in. I don't want you thinking that the rat pack was serious by any means.

A New Beginning

It was a total piss take. It was simply a group of guys having a laugh and watching each other's backs. As I mentioned a moment ago, Morgan was in his sixties and was one of the cruise staff on board the Pacific Sky.

He was once a headline entertainer and had also been a cruise director, but was starting with a new company and had to work his way up again. As a headline entertainer, he was brilliant. His show was a mix of Rod Stewart (which he looked a lot like, as well as Jerry Springer) and raw comedy. Morgan was a very smart man when it came to the rat pack. Kind of like a good businessman would do, when putting together a board of directors for a company, Morgan had people around him who had strengths, where he had weaknesses. Before I explain, let me introduce you, to the other members of the rat pack.

The ratpack consisted of, Paul. He was the security guard and was better known as "Patch"; because he "patched" things up. Joel, was the photographic manager. He went by the name of "Flash"; for obvious reasons. Ian, was the casino manager and was known as "Chips". Matty, was cruise staff and went by the title of "The Beast". Morgan was "Ratman" and then there was me; affectionately known as "Vermin".

Everyone's names were all relevant to them or their position on board, except for mine. My nickname stuck, after Sheldon, a dancer on board the Tahitian Princess, gave me this name one day. Sheldon said that he called me vermin, because I had the voice of an angel, but the mind of a two-dollar whore. Now, while I wasn't too flattered about the second part of that comment, even though it was true, I certainly liked that he thought so highly of my voice, so I embraced the name and it has stuck ever since. The name even became my character name when back on land, in the cabaret theatre restaurant in Australia.

Each one of the rat pack had a particular role in the team. For example, Patch would always be aware of security patrols in crew areas late at night and would warn the rest of the group, so that they could get rid of the female passenger they might have in their cabin, before security patrol busted them. If caught, this was grounds for instant dismissal. Flash had the job of getting incriminating photos of any senior officers on board, that could be used, in the case of one of them wanting to rat on us for something. Flash's photos were amazing blackmail material and got us out of many sticky situations.

Chips would provide the cash flow for the group, by way of the arcade machines, that he had to empty on a daily basis. This would allow our bar bills to be paid each month, despite them being so high, from constantly being in the bars chatting to women. The Beast, Ratman, and I were all responsible for entertaining the ladies and being the face of the group. The passengers would all know who the three of us were, so we would often initiate a conversation between girls for the other rat pack boys and then leave them to it.

The rat pack would always meet as a group, on the first and last night of every cruise. This usually occurred at midnight, on the mooring deck located at the aft of the ship. The code for a meeting was "The Chinese junk is in the harbour." Any one of us could call a meeting, by spreading the "code," but usually it was only on these two nights of each cruise. The reason why we used the code, was because female crew members, were always trying to find out what we were up to and what this whole "rat pack" thing was about. They knew it existed, but no one knew what it was about, or where the meetings took place. We kept things on the down low, simply because, if people knew what it was about, then it just wouldn't work. The power was in the element of surprise.

The meetings would run as follows: Once we were all present, Ratman would begin with his "Ratman" chant. Once again, none of us took this whole thing seriously; or ourselves, for that matter. It was a total piss take and a case of seeing what we could get away with while having a laugh at ourselves. So Morgs would start by repeating "rat rat rat rat," then someone else would join in with "Scurry scurry scurry scurry," at the same time, then when we were all singing something different, Morgs would start his chant-like song, singing, "Rat, there is nothing like a rat, there is nothing like a slut, there is nothing like a mole," etc., until we all ended up pissing ourselves laughing and stopped.

Why? Who fucking knows, but like most things in life, we didn't ques-

A New Beginning

tion why we did it; we just did it. If the meeting was on the first night of the cruise, then we'd discuss what sort of talent there was on board and each member would declare which girls they were chasing. We tried not to chase the same girls, unless they were total whores and wanted a bit of everyone. If it was the last night of the cruise, then we'd all say how many and who we had been with that cruise and whoever had the most, or in some cases the best stories, would be given the perpetual "rat towel."

This was a hand towel that had the word "Ratman" embroidered on it that Morgan had got from somewhere. The towel was given to the most successful member, for the duration of the next cruise. The significance of the towel was so that they could wipe their dick on it, when done with a girl (not that anyone actually did). Disgusting, I know, but hey, like I said, it was the fact that it was so pathetic, that made it so funny.

I know this is all beginning to sound a little sick and more like something out of "American Pie", or some fraternity movie, but it was quite funny to actually witness. I'm not trying to make myself look any better than the others here, but I can honestly say that I didn't reach the levels of "success" the others had. This was for two reasons. Firstly, because even though I've racked up more than my fair share of women on ships, I'm not about numbers. I've actually been looking for love, but obviously had been going about it in the wrong way. On this occasion, I had been voted in, because of (as I mentioned before) the fact that I got a head job from Carly and got a written warning, before I started singing in the shows.

The other reason I never did too well in the same way that the other boys did, was mainly because I'd already been with Carly and was thinking that maybe she would be worth holding onto. I had also declared at my first rat pack meeting that my target for that cruise (but more realistically, that contract) was to be with Klara. The one that everyone said was untouchable. Most guys on board actually called her "Elliot Ness" (The Untouchable). The other boys in the rat pack, were happy for that to be my mission for the contract and weren't too bothered that I wasn't notching up dozens of women each month like they were. This left more women for them.

C.R.U.I.S.E

Cabin renovation rescue.

If you've ever been on a cruise ship, you will know that the cabins on board, in most cases, are quite small. These days, mega-ships, like the Oasis class ships, with Royal Caribbean, have two-story "loft suites", and other ships have very large suites, but for the most part, cabins are pretty basic. For the crew, this is even more so the case. Crew cabins are the smallest cabins on board. While the above-mentioned suites can cater for up to eight guests, the crew cabins, which sometimes sleep four people, are as small as the smallest passenger cabin.

It would be remiss of me not to give you a brief description of what the crew and officers accommodation was like on board, as most people have a very hard time grasping what it is actually like to live on a ship. To give you an idea, most crew cabins are actually smaller than most people's main bathroom in their house. It is big enough for four bunk beds, about two feet between them to walk down and they have a cupboard and a set of drawers. In my opinion, they are not enough for one person; let alone four. Quite often, all four crew members also have to go down the hall to a communal bathroom and toilet. Apart from officers and entertainers, crew cabins, are almost always inside cabins, with no windows, so they are usually dark and very stuffy. Given that most of the crew work thirteen-hour days on board, I guess it's sufficient, even though it's nowhere near ideal.

I remember hearing a story, about the man who designed the interior of the Grand Princess. After the ship had been completed, he went on board to visit the crew quarters, and he was so shocked at how small the areas were, that he promised that he would never use the same dimensions, when designing ships. He stated that he didn't quite realize, how the actual dimensions transferred from paper, to real life.

Officers' cabins, on the other hand, are quite good. On many occasions, I have visited the captain's quarters for parties and social gatherings, and they are of course very lavish and spacious. You would expect this, for someone who is in charge and has such a high-pressure position. The higher-ranking officers, such as Staff Captain, Chief Engineer, First Officer,

A New Beginning

and Staff Engineer, also have well-appointed cabins, with all the facilities, required to make their time on board comfortable.

The cruise director and other senior officers also do well, when it comes to cabins, but as you move down the chain of command, the standard of cabins deteriorate, until you get to the ones I mentioned in the beginning of this chapter. For the most part, crew members share with one other person. Any concessionaires, such as entertainers, casino staff, beauty therapists and shop workers, all share with one other person. This is apart from managers of each department and the singers, who all have their own cabin. All of these cabins do have their own bathroom, unlike the quad share cabins of the wait staff, bar staff and galley cooks, etc.

One thing that I am very particular about on board, is my cabin. I have been very spoiled on a few occasions with cabins. On the Tahitian Princess, my cabin was glorious. It had a huge, king-size bed, full-length mirrors, a huge window, with a great view over promenade deck. It had a TV, DVD player, mini bar etc. Now while this was great, it wasn't always the case, that I would inherit a fantastic cabin. Sometimes, I had to make it that way myself. For example, on the Pacific Sky, I almost fell over, when I saw the state of my cabin, so I thought, *well, it's an old ship, so I'm sure no one will mind if I do some renovations on it.* By the time I boarded the Pacific Sky, the ship had been in service, for twenty years, so she was very dated, to say the least. The day I moved in, I found the carpentry workshop and borrowed some nails, a hammer, a saw, and some wood. I then went about rectifying this sad excuse for a singer's cabin.

As a carpenter, I made a very good singer, however I was handy enough with tools, to make this wreck look half decent. I started by ripping the single bed off the wall (yes, beds are attached on ships so they don't move) and began building an extension on it. I then ripped the bulkhead off, along with all of the PA it's the wires off with it, then moved them across to accommodate my now double bed. I found some great curtains from the laundry and I permanently borrowed a huge TV, from the piano lounge. This in itself was funny, because I literally went up to the piano bar at the front of the ship on deck fourteen in the middle of the day to acquire it.

C.R.U.I.S.E

The passengers were reading books and relaxing when I strolled in to the lounge. I unhooked the TV and removed it from a shoulder height cabinet, that it was sitting in. As I was about to walk off, an older male passenger, sitting nearby said to me jokingly, "You're not stealing that are you?" I turned and said, "As if I would do that in broad daylight." We both laughed as I headed off down the fire escape with my new large TV.

Back in my cabin, the TV looked great and I then installed a fully stocked bar, DJ set up with mirror ball and lighting, all to create a party cabin, for my fellow crew members to enjoy. The great thing about all this, was that it all tucked away very easily behind fixtures, that I built, so that at any time, there was a cabin inspection, the cabin would look perfectly normal. When it became party time, cabinets would drop from the roof, doors opened, revealing a fully stocked cabinet and curtains revealed a cocktail bar to rival any nightclub. Thus, turning my cabin, into party central, in two minutes flat.

My other great cabin renovation, was on the Saga Ruby (a ship I will get into later in the book). On this occasion, though, I didn't do much of the renovation, because the hotel director, Dawn, was kind enough to have the carpenters do it all for me. The cabin was originally run down and the deal was, that if I moved in there (because it tended to be quite noisy at times), Dawn would fully renovate it for me. Once they had finished, it had the softest plush carpet, with double underlay (to dull the noise from boiler rooms below), a huge bed, huge desk, new paint, bathroom, mood lighting etc. The cabin itself was huge and the biggest crew cabin in the area, but now that it was brand new, it was totally awesome, and I was the envy of all the crew.

Ports of call.

One of the things I've not really mentioned so far, are some of the amazing places that cruise ships travel to. There really aren't too many places in the world that cruise ships don't visit. There are the obvious ones that they go to, like the Caribbean, Alaska and Mediterranean, but then there

A New Beginning

are the not so common places like Greenland, Norway, Fiji, Thailand, and even Antarctica. The amazing thing about travelling to these places on a cruise ship, is that one day you could be sailing from one country and the following morning, you're having breakfast somewhere totally different.

Over my time at sea, and since, working in the travel industry, I have been fortunate enough to have seen more than four-hundred destinations. As much as I would love to share my experiences of each and every one, it would honestly, fill an entire book, in itself, so below are some of my favourites.

Bora Bora, is one of the most sort after destinations in the world; for good reason. It has the most stunning water, it is so peaceful and the locals, are super friendly. Oh, and don't forget those awesome over-water bungalows. When we sailed in Tahiti, we had two full days in Bora Bora, every ten days. This allowed us plenty of time to explore the island, by local car, or by jet ski. The beaches are simply breathtaking in Bora Bora and the turquoise coloured water, is always a nice bath temperature.

One place, that is a must-see in Bora Bora, is the restaurant and bar called "Bloody Mary's". Legend has it, that this is where the famous drink was invented and also where the inspiration for the character's name in the movie "South Pacific", came from. Bloody Mary's has the coolest atmosphere, with sandy floors and a large round bar in the middle of the venue. While the drinks and food are great, the highlight, is the interesting toilet decorations, that they have.

When going to the toilet, in order to flush the toilet, you must yank down on a rather large wooden cock, which is attached to a chain, that flushes the toilet. This is a hit with guests. Even my mother, got a picture of her yanking on the cock, when she visited.

Gibraltar, may be famous as a war time landmark, but to visit this incredible city, is something you will never forget. I was lucky enough to visit there on a ship and even though it is a huge hike, up the mountain, the views at the top of the rock of Gibraltar, are spectacular. My advice, is to get transported up the mountain, then walk back down. The monkeys on the rock are super friendly, very cheeky and extremely talented at steeling things; so hold onto your belongings.

One very interesting thing, that you notice from the top of the rock, is that whenever a plane comes in to land at the airport below, both directions of traffic are stopped. This is because the runway, goes directly across six lanes of their main highway.

New York is a city that is spoken about in every travel guide or book, but to sail into this iconic harbor on a cruise ship, is an amazing experience. As you sail past the Statue of Liberty and see the Manhattan skyline in the distance, you can't help but be impressed. On both occasions that I visited New York on a ship, we had overnight stays. This meant that it became a race to see as much as possible in just over twenty-four hours, while there.

St Petersburg, may not be on everyone's bucket list and it certainly wasn't on mine, prior to visiting, but now that I've been, I am so glad I did. Just like New York, the two times I visited St Petersburg, the ship was docked overnight. This allowed me to do as many shore excursions as possible. The highlight for me, was of course seeing the Bolshoi Ballet, perform Swan Lake. Even though I was only thirty, and fairly uncultured, I was truly blown away with the spectacle of the show and its performers.

Rome is a city that is on everyone's bucket list; and for good reason. There is so much to see and do in Rome and even though it is a three-hour bus ride from the cruise ship terminal, into the city; it is well worth it. I was lucky on one occasion to visit the Vatican, St Peters Basilica, along with the Trevi Fountain and various other tourist attractions. On my other visit to Rome, I packed a good book, found a quaint little authentic Italian restaurant, grabbed a pizza and coffee and soaked up the Italian hospitality.

Some other honorable mentions include:

- **Rangiroa; French Polynesia** – Picture postcard beaches and stunning turquoise water.

A New Beginning

- **Isle de Pines; New Caledonia** – Stunning beaches and awesome snorkeling.
- **Barcelona; Spain** – Great food and Spanish hospitality.
- **Quebec; Canada** – So cultural and quaint.
- **Amsterdam; Netherlands** – I'm still speechless, from my visit there.
- **Sacred Island; Yasawa Islands, Fiji** – A breathtaking, uninhabited paradise.
- **Edinburgh; Scotland** – Don't miss the underground tours or military tattoo.
- **Tallinn; Estonia** – A beautiful old-world city.

One place, that deserves a special mention, is **Port Vila**. It's not the place its self, but one particular venue there, that is very memorable.

Port Villa is not the most exciting place on Earth, however, it did have this one bar in the main street called "Mamu Bar." It was a tiny little bar that was really nothing special, apart from the fact, that each day at 2:00 p.m. it became a "wet bar." By wet, I mean that the bartender covered everything behind the bar in clear plastic and then handed out buckets. At this point, all the patrons begin launching buckets of water, as well as beer, all over the place. It doesn't matter if you want to get involved or not, or whether you're eating or not. If you're in the bar at 2pm, you're going to get wet.

When the cruise ships were in port, the place was always packed with pissed crew members, letting their hair down. Even innocent pedestrians got dragged in and drenched. Nobody got away dry. If you were ever walking down the main street of Villa after 2:00 p.m., you always made sure that you were on the opposite side of the street to Mamu Bar, otherwise you'd get drenched. Even the Captain had been dragged in and soaked on occasions.

Once everyone was totally soaked to the core, what usually happened, was the bartender would bring out the dishwashing liquid and gives the long timber bar top, a good drenching in detergent. Then, volunteer female patrons, were placed on top of the bar, laying down (usually in a bikini or very little clothing), before being launched down the length of the bar. The bar was about twenty feet long. The girls slid down the bar and into the waiting arms of somewhere in the vicinity of six men, who had their arms interlinked to catch the girls.

During one New Year's cruise, we had more than four hundred passengers ranging from age eighteen to thirty on board, and the day we were in Villa, Mamu Bar was full to the rafters. People were dancing on the bar and furniture, and everyone was generally running amuck. We had this one young passenger who was wheelchair bound, but had been at every party and every event throughout the cruise. He was a really top guy and had such a good laugh. He came on the cruise on his own, which in itself was very brave, but even more so for the fact that he had no legs at all.

As I said, he'd been a part of everything, so when people started getting hurled down the bar, he too wanted a shot. Two guys lifted him up on the bar and then flung him down the timber top, to be caught at the other end. I'm not quite sure how or of the technicalities behind this kind of trick when you have no legs, but he somehow broke a few ribs on the way down the bar top. At the time, he winced a little before carrying on drinking for the rest of the afternoon. He went to the doctor's later that night but didn't seem too fussed when he was told of the damage he had done to himself. Well, if he was concerned, it certainly didn't stop him from drinking himself unconscious later, anyway.

Unfortunately, the last time I was in Port Villa, Mamu Bar had been pulled done. It was probably due to all of the timber in the building being rotten, but it did look like they were rebuilding it on the same block. So, if you're ever in Port Villa, do yourself a favor and get down to Mamu Bar. But remember to wear your bikini or board shorts.

Until recently, my favourite destination in the world was a tiny little island called **Ouvea**. It is situated in the Loyalty Islands, in the South Pacific. Prior to seeing Ouvea, Bora Bora was my favorite, but as I arrived at the beach, I was blown away with Ouvea's natural beauty. The beach, was everything that you would expect from a deserted island in a movie. The

A New Beginning

water was so stunning and the beach was incredible. The local kids played, while their dogs roamed the beaches, looking for scraps from the tourists. Fortunately for me, I got to experience this paradise, but unfortunately, for most people, cruise ships rarely visit Ouvea anymore.

Nanuya Lai Lai, may not be a famous name to you, but if I call it by its nickname of "The Blue Lagoon", you instantly have a picture of the most breathtaking place on earth. Nanuya Lai Lai, is the island paradise, that was famously called the blue lagoon, when filming of the 1980's movie of the same name, that was partly filmed there. It is a private island, that is somewhere I could easily live forever. Just like Tahiti and other parts of Fiji, Nanuya Lai Lai, has the golden white beaches and turquoise water, but somehow, it seems to be on a whole new level.

The only way to visit Nanuya Lai Lai is to fly in by seaplane from the main island of Fiji, or by small ships, such as "Blue Lagoon Cruises". They do seven-night cruises, leaving from Denarau in Fiji and make their way up into the Yasawa Islands, to the north. The ship has less than eighty passengers, so it is very intimate; just like the island itself. When we arrived at the island, the ship, backed up to the beach, cast a rope out and tied up to a large coconut tree. Passengers, then had the option to be taken ashore, by small boat, or to jump off the back of the ship and swim to shore, which was less than fifty metres away. Of course, I took the swimming option, because the water below, was far too inviting, to knock back.

Nanuya Lai Lai, in my opinion, is the most beautiful place on earth, and while I am yet to see every single place on earth, I am sure that when I do, there won't be too many above Nanuya Lai Lai, when it comes to natural beauty and tranquility.

Along with my favourite destinations, I thought that I would share a list of the many ports of call, that I was fortunate to visit during my time at sea. I've included these, to give you an idea of some of the incredible places that you too could visit, if you were to work or travel on board various cruise ships, small ships or river cruises around the world. Obviously, there are many more that ships visit, but this is my list thus far.

C.R.U.I.S.E

CARIBBEAN: Montego Bay | Labadee | Cozumel | El Cielo | Falmouth

FIJI: Denarau | Nanuya Lai Lai | Sacred Island | Naviti | Viwa | Sawa-i-Lau | Monuriki | Tamasua | Suva | Yasawa I Rara | Dravuni

PACIFIC ISLANDS: Lifou | Vavau | Nuka Alofa | Luganville | Port Vila | Noumea | Mystery Island | Isle de Pines | Ouvea | Champagne Bay

EUROPE: Frankfurt | Vienna | Nuremburg | Budapest | Regensburg | Passau | Linz | Melk | Durnstein | Bratislava | Salzburg

ASIA: Bali | Jakarta | Tokyo | Hong Kong | Singapore | Langkawi | Phuket | Pattaya | Kho Samui | Port Penang | Port Kelang | Melacca | Quantan

USA: Fort Lauderdale | Cape Canaveral | Miami | New York | New Port | Boston | Portland | Bar Harbour | St Johns | Maine | New Brunswick | Los Angeles | Honolulu

CANADA: Montreal | Quebec | Halifax | Vancouver | Sydney | St Pierre | Bay d'Espoir | St Johns

POLYNESIA: Papeete | Rangiroa | Rarotonga | Bora Bora | Moorea | Huahine | Raiatea | Nuka Hiva | Hiva Oa | Apia | Pago Pago - **ITALY:** Naples | Pisa | Florence | Civitavecchia | Livorno

MEDITERANEAN: Rhodes | Piraeus | Port Said | Alexandria | St Lucia | Sardinia | Nord | Palermo | Cairo | Lisbon | Cypress | Gibraltar | Valetta

ATLANTIC: Akureyri | Reykjavik | Ponta Delgada | Iraklion | Cape Farewell | Qaqortoq –

ENGLAND: Dover | Portsmouth | Southampton | Falmouth | Guernsey | Newcastle

IRELAND: Dublin | Cobh | Foynes | Killybegs | Belfast | Galway | Ringaskiddy | Kilkenny | Arklow | Cork | Foynes | Limerick | Sligo

SCOTLAND & WALES: Kirkwall | Invergordon | Leith | Glasgow | Shet-

A New Beginning

land Islands | Edinburgh | Inverness | Lerwick | Loch Lomand | Pembroke | Cardiff

FRANCE: Lexois | Le Harve | Bordeaux | Nice | Brest | Marseille | St Malo | Cherbourg | Lorient | Le Palice Toulon | Saint Nazaire

SPAIN: Santurtzi | Barcelona | Malaga | Bilbao | Vigo | Maloy | Granada | Cagliari | Massina | Alicante | Moville | Safaga | Gijon | Categena | La Coruna | Ajaccio | Motril | Mahon | Cadiz

NORWAY: Oslo | Svolvaer | Hammerfest | Northcape | Olden | Geiranger | Fredrikstad | Bergen | Flam | Skjolden | Stavanger | Torshavn | Isafjordur | Odense | Trondheim | Tromse

DENMARK: Keil Canal | Copenhagen | Kalundborg | Alborg

BALTIC: Stockholm | Helsinki | St Petersburg | Tallinn | Riga | Berlin | Szczecin | Estonia | Warnemunde | Saarema | Turku

AFRICA: Tunis | Al Khums | Algiers | Casablanca | Morocco | Limasol | Tangier | Melilla

AUSTRALIA: Brisbane | Sydney | Melbourne | Perth | Cairns | Exmouth | Albany | Heron Island | Hamilton Island | Moreton Island | Port Douglas | Burnie | Fremantle

OTHER: Sadane | Ceuta | Amsterdam | Portree | Gdynia | Dubai | Sogne | Aqaba | Muscat

Filipino takeaway.

On most cruise ships around the world, the majority of the crew are either from India or the Philippines. This is for several reasons, but mostly because the positions such as waiters, cooks, deck hands or cabin stewards, require sometimes up to thirteen hour days, for not a huge amount of money. It is for this reason that Westerners generally steer clear of these jobs, as they have better pay and better conditions in their own countries. This does not mean that there are no Westerners on board cruise ships. There are plenty of us, but usually only in the shops, salon, the entertainment team, photographers, security, purser's department, and the bridge. The rest (bar, kitchen, floor staff, and cabin stewards) are all either from India or the Philippines.

In the cases of the Indians and Filipinos, the pay and work conditions tend to be superior to their own country, even with the long hours that they work. My hat goes off to all the galley staff, waiters, bartenders, cabin stewards, garbage men and women, and all the other positions that require these long hours and generally very long contracts of up to ten months at a time. These guys and girls work their butts off each and every day of their contract, so they can provide for their families back home. They usually have no deck privileges whatsoever, which means that they cannot be in passenger areas off duty and are confined to either their cabin, or the crew bar when off duty.

Having said that, if they are to work a few contracts on board a cruise ship, they can pay their house off, put their children through school, and set their family up really well. There are many cases of women from the Philippines, who have had babies and gone straight back out to sea within a month, leaving their mother to take care of the baby while they earn the money. From what I understand, it is a common practice anyway, as many grandparents from these countries, often raise the children, regardless.

To them, each US dollar or British pound that they earn, is like gold. They save their money and spend as little as possible during a contract, so they can take as much home as possible. At the end of most contracts, I give away a lot of my older clothes to my cabin steward, and I know they are very much appreciated. There was nothing wrong with these clothes, but during the contract, I had more than likely bought new ones, and I didn't want to carry all that excess luggage home with me, and I figured it would be appreciated more by them.

Each cent counts to these guys, so it's no wonder, that on many ships, there are many little side deals going on, or moneymaking schemes be-

A New Beginning

tween the crew. It's almost like the black market or underground market. Anything from haircuts to cigarettes they deal in. All crew get extremely cheap drinks and cigarettes from the crew bar or officers' bar on board. For example, a shot of whiskey is around one dollar, and a pack of cigarettes is no more than two dollars. The reason ships get such cheap goods, is simply because they don't pay any sort of duty on these items, as they are leaving the country that they are bought from straight away.

On board a ship, crew can buy a carton (10 packs) of cigarettes for as little as USD$8 and a carton of Heineken beer for USD$20, or a liter of spirits from USD$8. What usually happens is that the crew member buys bulk and sells them to friends on land for a profit. This occurs on board every ship, and for the most part goes totally undetected. Either that, or senior officers simply turn a blind eye to it. There was one setup that was quite extraordinary though, that had been running for some time, that I must share with you. When it was unearthed, it had the entire senior management team on board speechless.

It involved a group of Filipino staff who had set up their own "takeaway delivery service" on board. Each night, two of the galley cooks would make a box of chicken wings disappear from the galley, and reappear in their cabin on deck two. Two of the deck guys, had smuggled a gas cook top on board and a huge pot, was stolen from the galley; which they would fill with cooking oil. The ship's printer designed and printed out flyers and put them under all the other Filipino crew's cabin doors. These menus had a list of their chicken wing meals, with various sauces, along with their cabin telephone number. When a call came in for an order, they'd deep fry the wings in their cabin and have their girlfriend deliver it and collect the cash.

Now, none of this sounds too bad, until you realize how much of a big deal fire is on a cruise ship. Fires are the number one danger to the safety of passengers and crew at sea. It was only a few years ago that the Star Princess had more than one hundred cabins destroyed in a fire caused by a single cigarette. It is for this reason that no crew members are permitted to have candles, incense, or naked flames of any kind in their cabins, other than a lighter if they are having a cigarette.

As you can see, there would have been quite a concern with this little business going on, which involved fire and hot cooking oil. If, at any time, the ship hit a wave and pitched or lurched suddenly, the cooking oil or the flame, could easily ignite a fire. Even though the crew in this particular story got caught and were disciplined accordingly, they have to be congratulated for creating such a brilliant business on board with their "Hooters' style" wings and sauce. I'm sure that being caught didn't deter them, or anyone else, for that matter, as this type of thing still goes on regardless of how many times people get caught.

The curse of the "Pacific Sky."

I remember my father once telling me, that it was bad luck to change the name of a ship. He told me this, just after we bought a twenty-eight-foot boat, that had its name changed, just before we hit a large turtle and almost sunk it. As I got older, I was not totally certain that this sea fable was always the case. I had seen many cruise ships undergo name changes, that didn't seem to have too many hassles. For one particular ship though, what my father had said, was absolutely correct.

This particular ship was originally built in 1984 for the Sitmar Line and was called the "Fairsky." It was later bought by Princess Cruises and renamed the "Sky Princess" before being sent down to P&O Australia and once again renamed. This time as the "Pacific Sky." From the time that P&O took over this ship, it was apparent, that if ever there was a ship which was haunted or cursed, then it was this one. Rumour has it, that the ship had a long history of mechanical problems and that it was better off being on the bottom of the ocean, than sailing on top of it.

My chief engineer, from the Tahitian Princess; Enda, had told me that when the Sitmar Line had the ship, the engineers tampered with it mechanically, before it was given to Princess Cruises. Whether or not, this was true, the ship was lucky to be still sailing. For all its problems, this ship was a great ship. It had a whole lot of character and was a great ship to work on. The ship did, however, seem to have a horrible curse when it came to public relations.

A New Beginning

A few years prior to me joining the ship, there was an incident in the news that involved a lady being found dead in another passenger's cabin. Over several years, it was found that several illegal substances, including Rohypnol, were found in her system. It was also discovered, that prior to dying, she had engaged in sex with several different men. The interesting part is, that more than fifteen years later, neither the coroner's inquest, or the legal system, has been able to determine whether or not, she took the drugs willingly, or if she was a victim of foul play.

There were eight "persons of interest", who were being investigated in this matter, but it must be said that even now, none of these men, have been found guilty of any wrong doing. This case has been in the media in Australia for several years now, and throughout the case, P&O's name has been well and truly dragged through the mud. There have also been several attempts by various TV networks to infiltrate the crew, with journalists, getting a job on board. This was in an attempt to get inside information, regarding ship life and to find out if rumors of excessive drug trafficking and so called rampant mass orgies, were true.

In all my years at sea, I have never seen, or been offered any type of drugs, or been invited to, or heard of any such orgies, other than what you have already read about in this book. I am not so naive to believe, that there are no drugs on board cruise ships, but there certainly would not be the amount, that the media claim. It is extremely difficult to smuggle anything on board a ship, so it is simply not possible, for anyone to be dealing in large amounts of drugs, as the media have claimed. We all know how misleading the media is and this particular current affair program, are truly, the bottom-feeders, of the media industry. I have approached this show and challenged them on their stories, but they are not interested in the truth, nor do they want to be made to look like fools, which would happen, if I went on their show.

With all the media hype surrounding the Pacific Sky in the years prior to me joining, the ship was finally beginning to enjoy a slightly less dramatic few months so far as bad publicity. We had sailed throughout the Pacific for a few months and were about to relocate up to Singapore, for the remaining three months of my contract. We were on our way back to Melbourne and were right in the middle of the Pacific Ocean, when the ship suddenly stopped; dead in the water. We had limited power and no engines at all.

The engineers managed to rectify part of the problem, and the ship limped back to Melbourne for proper repairs. We headed off a few days later bound for Singapore, but a few days after arriving in Singapore, the same problem occurred. It seemed that the mechanics that repaired the ship, who were not P&O engineers, had only done a "band aid" type job. This was because, the company knew that the ship was being sold within a few months and didn't want to spend a great amount of money on it. Once again, the ship was dead in the water, but this time it was in the Malacca Straights, which are known for having pirates.

I have to say, that at that point, it was a little unnerving, as the ship had only four days prior to this, brought on board, a dozen armed guards and anti-pirate sonar equipment, in case of any threat from pirates. Just seeing them on deck, twenty-four hours a day, made us all realize, just how real the possibility of an attack was. It was only a few months earlier, that the small Seabourn Spirit cruise ship, had a huge hole shot in the side of it, by pirates off the coast of Madagascar. With that, both the passengers and crew, were all feeling a little apprehensive, about floating with no power.

Thankfully, we had no such trouble with pirates on this occasion, but nonetheless, the ship was not going anywhere fast. At the time, the ship had quite a few passengers from Perth, and I'm not sure if they're more prone to over dramatizing things, but it appeared that a few of them had phoned their local TV news stations. They told the news, that the ship had broken down and that there was no food or drink and no electricity, or water either. All of which, I must add, was total rubbish. This time, everything on the ship was working, except the problem with one of the engines.

The captain made extra efforts to make the passengers comfortable, by providing free drinks with dinner for a week and even having two hours of free drinks for everyone, each afternoon. By this stage, the passengers did drink the ship dry. On top of this, each passenger received a refund of

A New Beginning

$500 for the inconvenience. There really was nothing else that the company could do, but the media still had a field day with the story.

Several days later, passengers were still getting angry and complaining at every opportunity, so one afternoon, the captain made an announcement, asking passengers not to vent their frustrations on any of the crew. Apparently, several passengers had taken it upon themselves, to abuse the crew, with some passengers even turning violent. The captain told the passengers that he would not tolerate such behavior, and if anyone had a problem that they wished to discuss, he would be in the purser's square in one hour, at which time, he would talk to each person individually.

When the captain arrived an hour later, he was bombarded with a barrage of abuse from almost one hundred passengers. They shouted obscenities at him and called him every name under the sun, including a *cunt*. Let's be serious here for a moment. While this was probably most upsetting for these people, because they had saved their money to come on this trip, it really wasn't the end of the world, and it certainly wasn't the captain's fault at all. He was not in any way responsible for an engine fault that was basically caused by old age.

Unfortunately, the worst of the media frenzy was yet to come for the public relations department at P&O Australia. It was only a few weeks later, when the ship had yet another fatality. The ship was in Port Penang in Malaysia, and I was in a taxi on my way back to the ship, when I heard a news report on the radio. I couldn't quite hear it properly, but I did manage to hear something about a Jet Ski accident off the coast of Port Penang, involving a tourist. I'm not sure why, given that it is a very busy tourist area, but I instantly knew that it was someone from the ship. I arrived back at the ship a short while later, to see some of the crew looking quite downcast. There was no official word, but rumours had started to filter through to us, that passengers and crew members had been involved in an accident.

A short while after, the captain made an announcement over the ship's public-address system, informing everyone that there had been a Jet Ski accident. He said that two Jet Skis, carrying three female passengers and one male crew member, had collided. A group of four girls had all been

C.R.U.I.S.E

together on this cruise, so the crew all knew who they were straight away. According to the captain, the female driver of one of the jet skis, was killed instantly, while her pillion, was in serious condition, with broken legs, pelvis, and collar bone. On the other Jet Ski was Carlos, one of the ship's shore excursions staff members.

Carlos too, had very serious injuries and was in fact in a coma. His passenger, was the luckiest of the four, sustaining only a broken leg. As you can imagine, the entire ship was in total shock. The ship was due to sail late that night, but didn't do so, until the early hours of the following morning. The captain went to the hospital to visit the victims, and a few company representatives from the ship, were left in Penang, to assist with legalities, once the ship had sailed.

For the three girls, it must have been horrendous to deal with, knowing they had to return home, with one less friend than they left with. For us, we all had to come to terms with one of our own being in a life-threatening condition. For several weeks after the incident, the captain would give us regular updates on Carlos. The captain also visited Carlos, whenever we returned to Port Penang in the following weeks.

Within a month, Carlos had regained consciousness, and within two months, he returned to his home country of Mexico. What was even better news, was that when I was on the Pacific Star, twelve months later, his shore excursions colleague, from the Pacific Sky was on board and informed me that Carlos had made a complete recovery and had returned to work on ships, which I thought was fantastic news. The company once again suffered some hideous publicity, from the media, but it has to be said that once again, it was not even close to being warranted.

The Jet Ski accident happened with an independent operator, that the ship had nothing to do with, and even though this was the case, P&O Australia went so far out of their way, to ensure that the victims and their families, were all taken care of in every way possible. The lesson in this particular case, so far as the three girls though, or for anyone ever thinking of travelling, is that you just never know when something can go wrong on holidays. No matter where in the world you are, it is totally crazy to ever

A New Beginning

leave home, without very comprehensive travel insurance. Not just the one that the bank offers you on your credit card, as it really is not suitable.

As far as I am aware, the four girls did have suitable coverage, which ever so slightly lessoned the burden of the incident. The good news for P&O was that they sold the ship soon after. It sailed under the name of the "Sky Wonder" as part of Pullmantur Cruises in Spain, for a few years, before being cut up into scrap.

Another unfortunate incident with the Pacific Sky, that most people would never have heard of, was when it ran aground at Isle of Pines in New Caledonia, a few years prior. The ship was anchored in the bay at Isle of Pines, on a beautiful day. Everything was quiet and there was no sign of the trouble that was coming. To be totally honest, I don't have too many details about how it happened, as that too was kept quiet, even from the crew (other than those who were involved).

From what I can gather, though, the ship's engines somehow dropped into forward gear and propelled the ship toward the island. It started off slowly, but very quickly began picking up speed, as it dragged its anchor off the floor of the ocean and headed straight for the coral. It is believed that it got up quite a head of steam before coming to rest, wedged up on a massive piece of rocky beach. The crew and few passengers that were on board at the time, recall quite a jolt, as the ship was abruptly halted by the rocks.

The ship was gently removed from the rocks, but not before quite a bit of damage was done to the bow. Some pictures were circulating between crew members, but none managed to make it to the media. So, for the most part, any subsequent stories by the media seemed to be nothing more than speculation. Nevertheless, the ship limped back to Brisbane on that cruise, on a serious list, to avoid too much water getting into the hole in the portside bow. The ship went straight into dry dock and stayed there for several weeks, meaning a shortened contract for many crew. Luckily for P&O, it happened when ninety-nine percent of the passengers were on shore, so most of them simply thought it was a mechanical issue that forced the early end to the cruise.

At the end of our contract in Singapore, when the ship sold, the crew had begun a mission a few weeks prior, to find souvenirs to take home as keepsakes. The day before the ship docked in Singapore, for the last time, every crew member's suitcase was searched for stolen items from the ship. Some crew got caught, but I think most crew were as smart as I was and off loaded the souvenirs beforehand, knowing that these baggage inspections would happen. I took my items off in Penang, a month before and posted them home, so they would be there, when I got home.

I have a plague from the corridor on deck ten, that has an outline of the ship and cabin numbers, directing passengers to their cabin. I also managed to get one of the plagues that the ship was given, on its inaugural journey into each port around the world. The one I got was for Manila, which I was offered huge money for, from many of the Filipino crew, but money was not my motivation, but rather nostalgia was.

Always cover your arse.

The heading for this section says it all. Cover your arse at all times, when working on a cruise ship. As I have mentioned, the politics on board a cruise ship, can be quite a big deal and can take a lot of getting used to. Remember - "Think fast, speak slowly, choose your allies carefully," these are the essential rules of engagement, when working on a cruise ship. You have to be so careful who you associate with, or align yourself to. It seems that for every friend you have on board, you also have an enemy or someone who is jealous of you, your position, who you're sleeping with, or spending time with.

As you know already, I managed to get myself caught up with quite a nutcase in Charlotte when I was Cruise Director. After that, I always kept one eye on what people were up to, as well as their hidden motives. Even the sweetest person, can turn into a vicious dog on a cruise ship, as I found out for the second time in my career at sea.

I'd been dating Carly for a few weeks by and already I had begun seeing signs that suggested, that she was not the most stable girl. She was becoming extremely clingy and possessive, even to the point, where she

A New Beginning

was going around the ship, telling all the passengers that she was dating the male singer and how in love we apparently were.

This, among other things, was a little too weird for my liking, so I decided to end things between us. I cut my losses and moved on, much to the delight of the guys in the rat pack. They all thought she was a freak. A few nights later, I was having a drink with Klara in the crew bar, chatting about various things, and I learned that she was quite an amazing young lady. We made plans to have lunch on deck the following day, and this became our regular thing. I'd bring her coffees in the salon and we'd also have lunch and occasionally watch a DVD together at night. We became quite close, and the more I got to know Klara, the more I wanted to know about her.

Unfortunately though, Carly was not letting go of things between her and me. I was still getting passengers coming up to me a month later saying, "Oh, I met your girlfriend Carly earlier." This baffled me, given that we had not been together, or even spoken for that long. I spoke to her a few times and asked her not to say that to passengers, but of course she denied doing it, even though I knew she had. Why else would random passengers say something like that, if no one had said anything?

It seemed like more than just a coincidence, that Carly would appear, at the same place, that Klara and I were; all the time. If we were out on deck; Carly would walk by. If we were having dinner in the officers' mess; Carly would be there too and stay, until we left. If we hung out in the crew bar; so would Carly. As I said, there was nothing I could do, but it was beginning to border on psychotic.

It was only a few weeks before Klara finished her contract and we were both wishing she wasn't leaving. She had been on board for eight months though and was ready to get back to her family and friends in Sweden. With only a few weeks to go, we were worried about getting together, because it would only make things harder for both of us, when the time came for her to leave. At the same time, there seemed to be an undeniable connection between us.

Klara and I began dating, but kept it fairly secretive, so that Carly didn't turn even more psycho, than she already was. The night before

C.R.U.I.S.E

Klara left the ship, we went up to the piano bar at the front of the ship, late at night, for a drink. I had offered for Klara to come back on board as my guest, for a few cruises, if she wanted, so we could spend some more time together and explore our feelings some more. Klara left the following day, and it was like I instantly knew, that I wanted to see her again.

One of the hardest things about working on a cruise ship, is saying goodbye to people whom you get close to. You meet so many people and make some amazing friends, but then you have to say goodbye. The opposite happens, as well. You meet people you can't stand, but thankfully they too have to leave, eventually. It was almost instantly after Klara left, that Carly began hanging around again. I'd managed to avoid her for the few weeks before Klara left, because Carly's mother had been onboard, but now that her mother was gone, I was being targeted even more. Carly and I had several disagreements over the next few weeks, but none of them were even close to this next series of events.

I was in my cabin one night when Carly came around and needed to talk about something. To be honest, I still don't know what that something was. I think it was just an excuse. It was a formal night, and she was dressed up, in a nice dress and mentioned something about a female passenger, that I had been talking to. We ended up in a fight, then, she stormed out of the room. I went after her and caught up with her, at the bottom of the stairs near my cabin. It was a steep stairwell, in crew areas and we both stood at the bottom, as we continued to argue.

Carly made some rude remark about Klara and took off up the stairs. I reached out to grab her arm, as she ran off, but I accidentally caught the back of her dress instead. She was still in motion, at the time, so her dress tore ever so slightly. At that instant, we both got a shock, and I let go. Carly screamed and ran up the stairs. I tried to catch her, and then made several attempts to call her and talk to her, to make sure she was okay. All these attempts were unsuccessful. I think she was looking for attention more than anything and wanted me to chase her now. Obviously, I was concerned about her, given that I had probably frightened her when I accidentally grabbed her dress. I also frightened myself at the same time, but I was not going to continue to play mind games like that, so I left it alone.

A few days later, I was walking away from the officers' mess on deck nine when Carly approached me from behind and began abusing me, for talking to another female passenger, that morning on deck. By now, I was totally over this whole obsession and insecurity. I would never tolerate this kind of behavior from a girlfriend, let alone from a coworker, that I slept with twice, almost three months earlier. If this was a guy doing this to a female on land, or a ship, he would be dismissed, or charged with sexual harassment. I continued down several flights of stairs, to the crew door on deck three, which led to our separate stairwells and our cabins on deck two.

I knew Carly was not too far behind, because I heard her mumbling something along the way. I opened the door to the crew area and walked past the stairs that led to Carly's cabin and began heading down the next set of stairs, that led to mine. As I took my third or fourth step down my stairwell, I heard Carly scream, and then it sounded like she fell. I ran back up the stairs to see if she was okay. When I got to the top of her stairs, I saw her halfway down the stairs and Morgan at the bottom, asking if she was alright.

"No, I'm not alright," she said. "He kicked me down the stairs," looking up in my direction.

I was stunned. She hobbled off, around the corner and into her cabin. Morgan looked up at me quite puzzled, not knowing what happened, and of course not knowing if I was there all along, or if I turned up at the top of the stairs (which was the case) when I heard Carly scream. Morgan hated Carly with a passion, but he also knew that despite neither of us giving a shit about her, I would simply not do something like that to her, or anyone else. He kind of had a little chuckle to himself and disappeared, towards his cabin, which was located next to Carly's.

I left it at that, as I presumed it was another one of Carly's attention-seeking stunts; which it was. I just didn't realize how far she was prepared to take it on that occasion. I went ashore that day in Koh Samui in Thailand and had a great day riding around the island on a moped and just relaxing on the beach. As I returned back on board, the machine on the gangway, that you swipe you cruise card in and out of, said for me to contact the head of security. I contacted security, and Liam (yes the same Liam as the Tahitian Princess. I told you it was a small world on ships). Liam advised me that Carly had made a formal complaint of assault, and that I would have to go before the captain the following day.

I was in shock. This girl was unbelievable. The lengths that she was prepared to go to for attention. Thankfully, I had been keeping a detailed log of every single incident that had occurred with Carly, as I had a feeling something like this might happen. I learned from my best mate a long time ago that a diary is admissible in court, so I thought surely it would also apply on a cruise ship.

The longest hearing in maritime history.

The following morning, I arrived at the captain's office, to put the matter to bed. Present at the hearing was the captain, the first officer (who also doubled as the ship's lawyer in any matters), my cruise director, Michael, and my dance captain, Deb. The captain read me the complaint and went through the "Captain's standing orders" to give the official subsection, etc. The captain's standing orders are in essence the laws that the ship and all of its crew and passengers must abide by. The captain explained that Carly had claimed I had "forcefully kicked" her down the stairs. If this was proven to be the case, it would be grounds for instant dismissal.

The captain explained Carly's allegations and all of the issues at hand, at which point, he allowed me to put my case forward. I think the captain thought I would simply admit to those false allegations and take my punishment. He was certainly shocked when I not only refuted Carly's claims, but countered her allegations with a comprehensive history of unreasonable behavior, on her part. The captain clearly understood my version of events and was beginning to see there was not really a case to answer here, however, he was intrigued, as to why I had broken up with

A New Beginning

Carly and then taken her back on more than one occasion; which ultimately led to this situation.

He also couldn't understand why, if I wanted nothing to do with her, that she was in my cabin the day before. I explained that it was my stupidity, that led to me taking her back, but her being in my cabin, the night before, was because, she was abusing me about talking to a passenger. The captain and I went back and forth, for nearly half an hour, with neither one of us giving an inch. I knew he was the captain and it's not wise to argue with the master of a ship, but this was my career we were dealing with, and I was not about to let some crazy woman, with mental issues, try to ruin my career.

I was prepared to fight to the end, to prove my innocence on this occasion, and that is exactly what I did. Now was not the time to play nice, or even fair, for that matter. I needed to prove to the captain that Carly was more than capable of concocting such a malicious scam. I went on to explain Carly's background and the things she had done to me in the lead up to this event, all of which went toward proving, that it was totally possible she was also capable of such a vindictive act.

I then went on to mention the fact that Carly was partially blind in her right eye. If I ever stood on the right side of her, she would ask me to move to the left, because she couldn't see me on the right side. Carly had somehow managed to slip through the required ENG1 Medical, that all seafarers must pass, without this defect of hers being detected. I explained this to the captain and pointed out that the staircase Carly fell down, was on the right side as you walked along the corridor. Therefore, it was highly possible, that Carly may have misjudged the first step—which I had seen her do on many occasions, when approaching raised door sills or stairs on the ship. It was my opinion, that in this case, this led her to fall down the stairs.

After more than two hours of discussing the matter, the captain ended the session and advised that he would require a further few days, to go over all the evidence. He wanted to speak to Carly and Morgan, to find out some more information. I spoke to Morgan a few days later, and he told me, that the captain had asked him about the incident. Morgan had given the captain a full run down of Carly's behavior up to that point, and that even though he didn't see the incident properly, he was of the belief that Carly fell down the stairs and was not pushed or kicked as alleged.

Two days later, the captain called me to his office and explained to me the seriousness of the matter and that he would prefer it, if I stayed away from Carly, so as to not risk exposing myself to any similar situations. He then explained there was simply not enough evidence to suggest I had committed the assault, that Carly had alleged. I was obviously relieved and thanked the captain for the fairness of the hearing and advised him that I would most certainly be avoiding Carly. I went straight down to my cruise director's office, to let Michael know that I was staying. Michael was pleased, even though he knew he would now have to deal with Carly throwing tantrums about the outcome.

A short while later, the captain advised Carly of the situation, and as expected, Carly decided to leave the ship immediately. We were all extremely relieved, as she had been quite a pain on many occasions, and all the men on board, were now worried that she would try this type of thing with them. She was so embarrassed by the situation that she could not bear to stay for the remainder of her contract. Several other entertainment staff were also elated that Carly had decided to leave.

Matty even offered to pay her airfare home before, he'd heard the outcome just so (in his words) she would fuck off, as we didn't want her on board. I know I can speak for the male members of the entertainment team, when I say that we were extremely happy she was leaving, so we celebrated heavily that night. Carly's replacement from Canada, Lisa, arrived a few days later and was so much more suited to the team so all is well that ends well.

New opportunities.

With this unfortunate incident behind me, there were now two things I wanted to concentrate on; finding a way to be with Klara and creating my own cabaret show. By that stage, I had been on ships for nearly five years as a production show singer and I felt that I was ready to become

A New Beginning

semi-permanently based on land. Over the years I had seen many different guest entertainers perform their shows, and I was super keen to become one myself. Guest entertainers worked less than I did (which was very little anyway) and got paid even more that I did; so why not? Having said that, as a singer, I was the least worked person on board any ship. Myself and the female singer, would be lucky to work six hours a week on most ships, and we got paid anywhere from $140 - $220 per day. That's seven days a week, regardless of whether we work or not, so it's hard to believe that anyone could have it better than that.

Well, guest entertainers do. Having seen so many acts come on board, I had a fair idea of what worked and what didn't work. I was also very fortunate to have two mentors during this period, that had both been guest entertainers and were more than happy to hand their knowledge and expertise on to someone starting out.

Morgan had spent years performing his cabaret show "Tonite's the Nite," which was a Rod Stewart show. Morgan had a great act, which he often performed on board while I was there. Morgan was not only a good singer, but also a fantastic comedian. We've had so many comedians come on board, and I have to say that Morgan was better than almost all of them. Michael, my cruise director was also a guest entertainer before he became Cruise Director, so the two of them were instrumental in the creation of my own show.

The concept I had come up with, was a "swing" style show, with all the favourites from Frank Sinatra, Dean Martin, Bobby Darin, and Sammy Davis Jr. All of these types of songs, had been recently redone by Michael Bublé and Robbie Williams, so I knew the genre was popular. I'd seen all of these types of songs go down so well with passengers and I thought they would combine well, to be a great show. I had been performing a small "rat pack" section in one of the productions shows on board, so I knew that I very much enjoyed this type of music.

I ordered enough band music, for a forty-minute show and convinced Michael to give me a shot at it. Normally, a cruise director might give a production singer a twenty-minute spot opening up for a headline act,

C.R.U.I.S.E

but Michael was good enough to give me a shot, as top of the bill one night, with my own show. I spent the next week learning all the songs and rehearsing with the six-piece band on board to get things right. I spoke several times with Morgan and Michael, to see what they thought would work so far as format, etc.

On the day of the show, I woke up and under my cabin door, was the daily program. This program gets printed each day for the passengers and explains what is going on for the day. It's like the daily newspaper on board and had everything the passengers needed to know for the day. This included, where the ship was, the local currency, any activities that were on that day, what themed menu it was, and of course, what the show was that night. I opened it up and in the middle page was a huge banner which read: Showtime this evening featuring vocalist J.D Moorea, in "A Little Bit of Swing."

From that moment on, I was as nervous as hell for the rest of the day. I found it hard to concentrate on anything. I had my last rehearsal with the band in the afternoon, then at 8:00 p.m., it was show time. Apart from my obvious nerves in the first few numbers, the show went down without too many problems. I hit the occasional bum note, but all in all, my first outing with my own full show, was a success. The feedback from the passengers in the cruise ratings, was quite positive.

Throughout the next two months on board, Michael gave me a few more opportunities to perform my show and fine tune it. On these occasions, I asked any other guest entertainers that were onboard, to come and watch my show and give me their feedback. I felt so lucky to have such amazing entertainers, from all areas of the industry, take the time to assist me, by giving me their time and experience. They were all so helpful and were brutally honest on many occasions, which I very much appreciated. I was not looking for people to tell me that the show was great or good. I wanted them to see where I could improve, which they did.

The most important piece of advice I could give any budding entertainer, is to learn to accept criticism and to use it to better themselves as a performer. People will always have their opinions, and you can't take everything personally, but if you can take feedback on board and use it to your advantage, you will become such a better performer and enjoy a lot of success.

With my show, I now had something to move toward, rather than dwelling on the past troubles I had found myself dealing with. Klara and I had been keeping in touch, and it was becoming more apparent that the more time we spent apart, the more we wanted to be together. Klara was planning on visiting Australia, and I thought it would be a great opportunity for her to come and stay with me on the ship for a few weeks, on the way to Australia.

We were currently cruising out of Singapore, so it was in her flight path anyway. Klara joined the ship a few weeks later and from the moment we saw each other again in Singapore, we knew that we had made the right choice. It also became very obvious to me, that the past drama with Carly, had served a purpose in the big picture. If Carly had not caused the trouble she did, then she would have been around, when Klara came back on board, and I have no doubt that she would have caused all sorts of trouble for Klara and I. Thankfully, Carly and her psychotic behavior was long gone, and Klara and I had an amazing three weeks in Thailand and Malaysia.

Thailand—another world.

During our cruises in Thailand and Malaysia, we had an overnight in Pattaya every fortnight, which gave all of the crew the opportunity to get off the ship for a night and totally unwind. It was a great chance for the crew to let their hair down, without having to worry about getting breath tested, or being seen by passengers. We'd spend the entire day in Pattaya or Bangkok. We would then come back to the ship in the afternoon, to freshen up before going back out at night. Sometimes, we would even get a hotel in town, so we didn't have to come back, until the following day. Either way, it would be an all day and night party. I'm sure most people have heard about the fun that goes on at night in Bangkok and Pattaya, so I won't go into it in too many details about the ping pong shows, etc. but I would like to share a couple of stories though of our time in Pattaya.

The very first day we arrived in Pattaya, myself and the cast, got off the ship and caught a local "tuk-tuk" into the city. We were walking along the streets, checking everything out, when I thought to myself, *this is not what I was expecting from Thailand.* I'd heard so many stories of how wild and crazy Thailand was, but at that point, the place looked like any other city, and to be quite honest, it seemed very boring. I turned to Anthony and said, "Mate, I don't get what everyone raves about this place for. I just don't get it."

No sooner had I opened my mouth, as we turned the corner, then bang! There was everything people had talked about. As we walked down the street, lady boys and Thai girls were hanging around outside bars and clubs dressed in skimpy dresses. One girl pulled her tits out and started, squeezing her nipples, while another motioned, like she was giving head and said, "Me suck you for fifty baht." "Fifty baht, for suck your big cock," she said. As we walked past her, another girl walked up beside me and grabbed me on the crotch and said, "Me give you very nice time."

At that stage, it was hard to tell which ones were male and which were female. Anyone, who laughs at a guy, for not knowing straight away, has obviously never been to Thailand, because I can tell you, it took me quite a while to work it out myself. Unless you grab them between the legs, it's quite difficult to work out. The rule of thumb though, is that the hotter ones, are usually always the males.

Later that night, the dancers led us all into "Boystown," which was a section of gay clubs, in the main area of town. It wasn't the sort of place I'd normally visit, but hey, it's Thailand, and most of the girls you saw on the streets, were guys anyway, so it couldn't have hurt. We walked into this one club and as you entered, there was this massive fish tank built into the wall. The tank was at least eight-feet high and around twenty-feet long. Inside the tank, were several "girly boys" swimming around, wearing nothing more than a pink G-string, with a number attached to it.

At first it seemed a little confusing what they were doing, but after a

A New Beginning

minute, we figured out that this was very similar to your typical Chinese restaurant. You know the type, where you pick your live lobster out of the tank, before it is cooked and severed to you? In the same way, these girly boys were on display, until someone picked them out and took them away, for some fun. Having travelled to most parts of the world, I thought I was pretty well travelled and was not easily shocked, but this had me stunned for quite a while.

I sat with the others, having a few drinks, trying to fathom this whole fish tank concept, when we noticed that Matty (The Beast) had disappeared. He had not been seen for a while, so we thought he might be getting a lap dance, but then suddenly, we heard people laughing and pointing toward the tank. We looked up, to see Matty in the fish tank, swimming around, wearing one of those pink G-strings with all the girly boys. Needless to say, he looked quite out of place, given that he was around ninety kilograms, white and hairy, compared to the other boys, who were forty-five kilograms, Asian, and…well…certainly didn't fill out the G-string like Matty did. We seriously lost it, for over an hour, laughing at Matty, pulling this kind of stunt.

Matty unleashed in Thailand, was always hilarious. There was one occasion, when Matty returned to the ship at 4am., from a night out. He caught a taxi back to the port and instructed the driver to take him to the cruise ship. When the taxi dropped him off, Matty stumbled up the gangway, quite pissed, before inserting his crew card in the security machine. The machine made a loud buzzing noise and said, "Please try again." Matty fumbled around with his card, before inserting it once more. Again, the card buzzed and said, "Please try again." Matty tried one last time, with the same result, before calling the security guard over to help.

"Hey, you're new," Matty said to the security guard, who he didn't recognize. "When did you start?" he said. The security guard looked at him with a strange look, before grabbing Matty's crew card. The guard looked at Matty's card, looked at Matty and laughed. Matty looked at the guard with a puzzled look, as he tried to stay upright. The security guard then said, "Mate, you're on the wrong fucking ship. This is the Pacific Princess, not the Pacific Sky." It seemed that the taxi dropped him at the wrong ship, but Matty had managed to get through all of the port security and all the way to the wrong ship, without realizing. He swiftly turned around and finally made it back to the right ship, a short time later.

I could honestly tell you stories for hours, of the sort of things that Matty and Morgan got up to in Thailand, but there is not enough paper in the world to print it all.

I recall one funny situation in Pattaya, when I had my best mate's parents, Christine and Graham, visiting me for a few cruises. Graham, Christine, a guest entertainer by the name of Mercedes and I were all in Pattaya for the day. As always, the ladies wanted to go shopping. Graham and I really didn't want to be dragged along, so we went off to do our own thing. We wandered down the streets for a bit and were amazed at the amount of times girls and girly boys would expose themselves, or gesture that they wanted to give us head, right there in broad daylight. We were even grabbed on the crotch on several occasions.

After we'd had enough of this, we found a nice restaurant / bar on the beach. I wanted to explore a little more, but Graham was hungry, so I left him there and headed off. Graham ordered a whole lobster and a large bottle of beer. In Australia, we call them "tallies," but I'm not sure what they are called elsewhere. In short, they are a bottle of beer that is 750ml., so Graham was a very happy chap, with his big beer and even bigger lobster.

After his meal, he reached for his wallet, only to realize that Christine still had it in her handbag. He was unable to pay his bill, so he thought that the logical thing to do, was to order another beer and wait until we arrived back to collect him. After his second beer, he ordered another lobster, then another beer, then another beer and by the time we arrived back, more than three hours after I had initially left him, he was well and truly smashed and barely able to walk, let alone pay the bill. He did manage to explain the situation to us, which we all found highly amusing, except Christine, mostly because of the huge bill that she had to pay on behalf of her husband. I think at final count, Graham had polished off three whole lobsters and nearly four litres of beer. Needless to say, Graham no longer leaves his wallet in Christine's care.

Saga Saga Saga

"If the average age on most cruise ships is 60, then the average age on this one; must have been deceased".

Home yet again.

So, yet another contract had come and gone and once again it has been one of great challenges, but thankfully this time I had returned home with someone very dear to my heart. Klara had spent three weeks onboard with me, as my guest and then went to Australia and stayed with Christine and Graham, until I arrived home a few weeks later. By the time I arrived home, Klara was already searching for a job, so as soon as I got home, we moved straight into my apartment, that I had bought before the last contact and made it our home. The plan, was for me to pursue my own cabaret show that I had developed on board. This meant that I would only be away from Klara, for a few weeks at a time, rather than six months at a time, which had been the case up until that point.

I managed to secure a few dates on board the Pacific Star cruise ship, which sailed out of Australia, doing my own show, so things were looking good for us, to have the life we wanted. We didn't want to spend too much time apart, knowing that this always made relationships difficult. These shorter trips, also meant that Klara could travel, for free, as my guest, whenever I went away. It was great fun being a headline act and over the course of the eight or nine trips that I did, I became very close with the entertainment team on board.

Michael (my old cruise director) was Cruise Director for a short time, as was Chris Nichol (my cruise director from the Tahitian Princess), so they both became great mentors regarding my show, as well. The resident band was only three-piece (piano, bass, and drums). This made it very challenging with my shows, given that swing music is mainly about the brass section (which was nonexistent in this case). We did the best we could and had a great time along the way. The audiences were great and the show was well received. The cast on board were all amazing and my good friend Stella (from the Tahitian Princess) was the lead singer, so we hung out and had a great time also.

With the ever-changing industry, the cruise line began booking less and less vocalists, as headline acts because their resident production singers, had their own cabaret; just like I did when I was a production singer. This meant I either had to take a normal job on land, or perhaps think about heading back to the cruise ships more permanently.

To go back to ships for six months meant one of two things: Either Klara and I would have to spend time apart, or she would have to give up her great job, that she now had and come back to sea with me. This really wasn't something we wanted, because Klara was really enjoying her new job and was about to take over a new salon, that her company was opening up. She was very excited about managing the salon and all of the experience that would come with it.

Klara and I discussed our options and we decided, that I would take up one of the three contracts, that I had been offered the day before. The contract I chose, was with Saga cruises in the UK, which I thought was one I would enjoy. The ship was small, which meant that the theater would also be small; however, the itinerary and the money were amazing, compared to what I had earned previously. We decided that Klara would spend a few months gaining experience as a manager, then apply to join the same ship, that I was heading off too. This way, we would only have a small amount of time apart. I really didn't want to spend any time away from Klara, but after a year on land, I was once again, unfulfilled and yearning to be back at sea.

On the day of my flight to the UK, I sat at the airport with Sue, Klara, and Joanna, who was to be my female singer on this contract, as well as Jo's mother. Jo and I had known each other from a few years earlier, when we were rehearsing for separate ships, at the same time in Sydney. I went to the toilet, just before going through customs and upon my return, I noticed that the girls were all laughing. As I sat down, Jo explained to me, that Klara had only just learnt, that the cruise line we were going to work for, was an "over fifties only" cruise line.

On most cruises, the majority of passengers were over fifty, but on this cruise line, all passengers had to be over fifty to sail with them. If the average age on most cruise ships is sixty, then the average age on this one must have been "deceased." I was not aware of this until then, so I was equally as stunned as Klara was excited. She was extremely happy about this, as she presumed that I would not be tempted to "stray", because of the age of the passengers. My mate Dan from the Tahitian Princess would have loved this ship, though. In his words, "Old chooks mate good soup."

Jo and I knew from the outset, that this contract would be quite different, from the others that either of us had been on before. The passengers were much older, the cruises cost much more than most, and we were doing all our rehearsals on board the ship. Little did I know just how different things would be. We arrived in London and were taken straight to a little town called Gravesend where we would spend the next week taking part in extensive training at the company's expense.

During the week, we completed the same sea survival course, that I had done on my first contract, then a first aid course, followed by a three-day intensive fire-fighting course. We both thoroughly enjoyed the entire week, even though we had concerns as to exactly why we were going through such intensive fire-fighting training. As part of the training, we had to get into full breathing apparatus and firefighting gear and go deep into a simulated engine room, on a "three man left hand search" to fight a real fire, then pull a fake body out. I can totally understand, why every crew member should be able to handle a fire extinguisher, but if a cruise ship is in that much trouble, that they need the two production show singers to do this, then in my opinion, we're totally screwed and should be heading to the life boats.

The week went by quite quick and before we knew it, we were boarding the ship in Dover, England. On the day we arrived there was some debate as to whether or not we would be sailing with the ship, because the company had overbooked the ship and there were no cabins available for both of us. Jo and I sat in the Lido café at the aft of the ship until 5:00 p.m. that day, waiting to find out if we were staying, or going back to Folkestone for a week. Neither of us wanted to go back to Folkestone, because there was nothing there and neither of us had much money, so we wanted to be on the ship where we had little expenses and all meals, etc., paid for.

Just after five, when the ship was supposed to sail, the cruise director told us that we were able to stay but that Jo had to share a cabin with the current female singer. Jo was obviously not very happy about this, given that one of the privileges of being a singer on a cruise ship (as is written in our contracts), is that we never have to share a cabin. Jo was also a diva, but regardless, she was well within her rights, to object. At that point, I thought I would try to help by seeing if Jo felt more comfortable sharing a cabin with me, seeing as we actually knew each other. I have to point out that at that point, I had my own cabin and in no way had to share with anyone, but I felt sorry for Jo and her predicament. Let me tell you, that this will never happen again. It turned out to be one of the biggest regrets in all my time sea. Even more than what happened with Lauren many years earlier.

Throughout the entire week, Jo bitched about every single thing she could think of about the company. She complained that her boyfriend had not been offered a job by the company, so they could be together.

Saga Saga Saga

She bitched about the food, and the shows, and the fact we had to share a cabin. You name it and she had bitched about it. She had even threatened to jump ship several times and to be totally honest, I really wished she would.

When it came time for us to rehearse together, I was of course a little hesitant given the constant foul mood she was in. We did, however, manage to make a start on the first show after a few days, but as soon as it was time for us to debate which way to sing a certain part of the show, Jo once again flipped out and that set the tone for the entire contract. For the next week, I would purposely stay out until I knew she had gone to sleep and would wait until she left for the gym in the mornings to get up.

The other cast members arrived two weeks later, at which time Jo immediately began bitching about me left, right and center to anyone who would listen. She found an ally in Sian from the first day as Sian also loved to complain, and the two of them both comforted each other by reminding each other "how horrible their lives had become." Within days, they had managed to segregate themselves from the rest of the cast and also turn the female cast members against me. Normally, I would bite back at this sort of treatment, but something inside me told me to deal with it in a different way. I decided to ignore it completely, as I knew that it would piss them off much more, than it would, if I lowered myself to their level.

Within a week, Chris (the only other male cast member) came up to me and put his hand on my shoulder and said, "Mate, I don't know how you're not punching the crap out of those two (Jo and Sian). They are a right pair of fucking moles." Chris had sat back and watched this whole situation unfold and noticed that no matter what these girls said about me, or to me, nothing seemed to hit a nerve at all. To be honest, I didn't hear most of what they said anyway, as I was so focused on the shows. I would occasionally hear some of Jo's snide remarks to me, when she thought no one else could hear, but true to my promise to myself, I didn't let it bother me and I especially didn't let her know I even heard it.

C.R.U.I.S.E

The Saga Heart.

As I mentioned before, the passengers on this ship were all fifty, plus, and averaging "deceased." That is, you would be lucky to find a passenger younger than seventy, and we had more wheelchairs and walking sticks than a retirement village. I think we averaged, one death per cruise, during the time I was on the ship. This had nothing to do with the food on board, or the service, or even the way the captain drove. It was simply the age group on board. I should quickly mention at this point that as far as service and food, as well as itinerary are concerned, this company is head and shoulders above any other cruise line in the world. They really do spoil both their passengers and crew alike. This doesn't come cheap, but the passengers get great value for money. The crew ratio is very high (500 passengers to 350 crew) so service is impeccable and the passengers love how spoilt they get.

Given that the passengers were so old on this ship, you would think that the promiscuous behavior, seen on other ships, would not be quite as bad. How wrong you would be for thinking that. Now, before you throw up in the book, thinking that I'm about to tell stories about ninety year old's shagging on deck chairs, let me explain. Just like the food and service, this company was head and shoulders above any other so far as the crew shagging each other rotten. I have honestly never seen anything like it at sea.

I learnt of this, not long after I boarded the ship. I was casually sleeping with Gemma, who was a fill in dancer on board, and she was telling me, that she had slept with nine guys, while she was working for the company. Add me to that list as of the writing of this, so that makes ten. On the following day, I was talking to Jodie (another dancer) and she too started telling me about all of the guys she had slept with from the company. She had a tally of seven; plus, me at the time of writing this book.

Yeah, I have to confess, that I ended up racking up six, during my two contracts with this company, so I am not judging anyone.

The thing I found intriguing, was that most of the names that Gemma and Jodie had mentioned were the same; including mine. Jodie then told me about her friend Yvette, who had racked up quite a sizable tally of the same men; but not including me. Things were starting to seem a little weird, but at the same time, I was now totally curious as to just how incestuous this ship was.

The more I spoke about sex, with crew members on board, (which was the most common topic on there), the more it seemed that everybody was totally open about whom they had slept with. They did not seem in the slightest bit concerned, that they all led back to each other. The only exception to this rule was Pete, the executive Sous Chef from Jamaica. Pete shagged just as many people, but he didn't go around telling anyone; other than me. Pete had a "code", that his fuck buddies had to abide by. He would only sleep with them, if they agreed not to say a word to anyone.

This was for two reasons. One, because he was married and his wife would travel as a passenger sometimes and two, because the chances of other women sleeping with him would be slim, if they knew he was shagging other women. This whole dynamic of who was sleeping with who intrigued me, and I thought it would be interesting to try to piece together some sort of a "family tree" to illustrate this. The only problem, was that it became impossible, because all of the branches on the tree came back on themselves, so I tried a different tact.

I drew a heart shape and put all the male names I had been given, on one side and all of the female names on the other. I then proceeded to draw lines between the people who had slept together. In a very short time, it was totally obvious that in some way everyone had slept with everyone. The heart now looked more like a large city road map than a gentle description of the intimacy people shared, on what was looking like "The Lust Boat."

This reminded me of a television commercial that we had in Australia, in the early 80s when the AIDS virus first came to the general public's attention. The ad showed a closeup of a loving couple in bed together in a white room. The voiceover said, "Next time you go to bed with someone, how many people are you really going to bed with?" The shot panned out, to show the first couple's past sexual partners, in bed together. The camera continued to pan out, to show those partners sexual partners and so on and so on, until the white room had more than 100 couples, in separate beds. The ad implied, that in essence, the original couple had in fact slept with every single one of those people in the room. Scary thought, hey? And that was exactly what I was beginning to think about my current ship. Now this is not to say that it is any worse on a ship than on land, but it is highlighted a lot more, due to the close proximity of everyone.

At the time of compiling this information, I promised both Jodie and Gemma, that I would keep this information to myself. When the original version of this book was printed, I included the full version, with every single person's name, however while re-writing this version, I thought it best, to blur the names, to protect the innocent, and not so innocent. The purpose of displaying this photo, was simply to illustrate, how incestuous cruise ship life can be; especially on that particular ship.

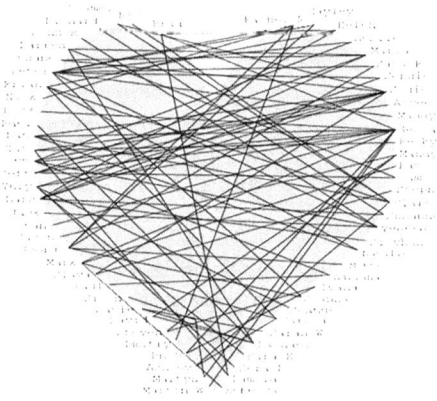

Saga Saga Saga

When it rains, it pours; literally.

Once again, if you read between the lines, I had failed all tests of "being a man," and I was once again bitterly upset at myself and my actions. Jodie and Gemma were both hot, but were both emotionally hung up on other guys, so me getting involved with them, was wrong, on so many levels. Klara was simply perfect in my eyes, but I on the other hand, had acted in a way, that no man should, when in a relationship. On that ship, I was surrounded by so many married people, who were all having extra-marital affairs and while it is no excuse, I got swept up in it too. Klara certainly didn't deserve me doing what I had done.

One morning, in August, 2007, I woke to an unusual ring on my cabin telephone. Normally, when my cabin phone rang, it was a long, continuous ring, like most telephones in the USA. On this occasion, the rings were shorter, which indicated that the call was from outside the ship. Until this day, I had never received an external call on board, so this was a little worrying. I answered it, to find that it was Klara calling from Australia. The line was really bad, and I could only faintly hear her voice. However, I did manage to hear her say, "I'm leaving."

Now, I knew she was not talking about leaving to get milk from the shop. I knew that she meant that she was heading back to Sweden. I told her that I would call her back in a minute, so we could talk properly. I quickly got dressed and ran upstairs to the top deck of the ship and called her from my mobile phone. My mobile was on contract in Australia, and at that point I was in Russia, so I knew that this call would be expensive, but I really didn't care.

I had decided a few nights prior, that I really wanted to make a go of this relationship and give Klara everything that she deserved, so this really wasn't the news I wanted to hear. We spoke for a while, and it became quite clear that she was certain that this was what she wanted and nothing I said, was going to change her mind. About twenty minutes into the conversation, I heard an announcement over the ship's PA system, alerting the crew

C.R.U.I.S.E

of a flood in the spa area, near my cabin. I didn't take any notice of this, as I thought it was too far from my cabin to be an issue.

After just over an hour on the phone trying to convince Klara not to leave, I finally realized I was not going to change her mind. We ended the call, and I made my way back down to my cabin. As I got to the last flight of stairs before my deck, I saw the plumber, who said to me, "Have you seen the state of your cabin?" At that point, I laughed and told him to stop joking around. I proceeded around the corner to my cabin, to see that he was not joking at all. The entire corridor and all the cabins in it, were soaked.

The plumbers had been working on a leaky pipe up the end of the corridor and had the entire ship's water supply shut down. When they turned it all back on, the pipes in the roof exploded, sending hot water gushing all the way through the corridor. Every single cabin was damaged to some extent, but I have to say, that without a word of a lie, mine was by far the worst hit. As I walked into my cabin, there must have been six inches of water across the floor of my cabin and this was more than thirty minutes after it happened. God only knows how deep it was when the pipe first exploded.

The fact that the carpet was wet really didn't bother me too much. It was more the fact that more than a thousand dollars' worth of sheet music for my cabaret show, was under the bed that really got me. A lot of my paperwork in the bottom drawer of the desk was also wet, as were quite a few props for the shows, that I stored under the bed, along with my shoes for the show that night. As I assessed the damage, I heard Sophie yelling and cursing from across the corridor. I went to see how bad her room was, only to find no more than a patch of around one meter of her carpet was slightly damp. I laughed at how hysterical she was at this relatively tiny wet patch, compared to my flood.

The culmination of these events, left me feeling a little like a ship without a rudder, having lost Klara and also my entire collection of sheet music. Klara may be a distant memory now, but the things I learned from my time with her have made me the person I am today. As for my sheet music, thankfully, the company had agreed to replace my sheet music, with big band music, for the up and coming big band cruise, that was a few weeks away. My cruise director Jo Bo was extremely supportive of me and my cabaret, and she was pushing the company to get them to allow me to perform my show as a headline act, during the big band cruise. I was extremely excited at this prospect, and when the sheet music arrived, I was totally pumped and ready to go.

A note about my original damaged sheet music. At the time of the flood, I opened up all the music, dried it out in a spare cabin for a few days and made sure it was all laid flat. More than ten years later, the sheet music is still in great condition, so I now have my entire collection in formats from six-piece, all the way up to eighteen-piece. Talk about a score; pardon the pun!

In search of the ultimate love.

The next cruise rolled around very quickly and on the afternoon, that we left Southampton headed for the USA and Canada, I attended the welcome drinks that Jo Bo had. Just in case you're a little confused, let me explain that Jo Bo is not the same Jo as the singer, that I was having trouble with. We had three Jos on the ship. This was confusing even for us, and they all had a surname starting with the letter "B" also, but I will refer to this Jo as "Jo Bo" to save confusion.

I was at Jo Bo's drinks, when this attractive blonde girl walked in. She had a certain style about her and a real sweetness about her also. A short while after, I learnt that her name was Sarah, and she was a soprano singer, who was on as a headline act, to perform her own show. Sarah had starred in various West End shows such as Evita, Phantom of the Opera, and Les Misérables. Because I was from Australia, I had no idea who she was. I just knew that she must be extremely good at what she did, to have starred in those musicals. Sarah and I hit it off straight away and seemed to have good chemistry between us. At the end of the party, we went separate ways and didn't actually see each other for a few nights. We had horrendous weather going across the Atlantic Ocean, for four days. It seemed that Sarah was not that great in rough weather and was quite ill for the whole time and barely came out of her cabin.

On the night we left Greenland, headed for Canada, Sarah performed her show in almost impossible conditions. The ship was pitching all night and was also listing at a disturbing angle from a howling wind, that was blowing right across the bow of the ship and thus causing it to list badly. Despite this, Sarah produced an amazing show and wowed the audience. Her voice was everything you would expect from a star of London's West End. This woman was a truly incredible singer. During her show, the weather was so rough, that several passengers fell out of their seats. For more than an hour after the show, myself, Jo Bo, and a few of the gentleman dance hosts assisted passengers back to their cabins. We also assisted several passengers to the medical center to be treated by the doctor for cuts and bruises. It really was quite a hideous night in that regard.

Once we managed to get everyone safely back to their cabins, or down to the doctor's, Jo Bo and I went for a drink in her cabin. All the bars were closed due to the weather, and besides, Jo Bo had a huge amount or alcohol in her cabin all the time. We had a few drinks and just relaxed. I have to admit, I found it a little difficult to relax, because Jo Bo's cabin was situated right at the front of the ship and in big seas, you felt the waves twice as bad as anywhere else on the ship.

Jo Bo and I were always close, so much so, that people often thought that we had slept together at some stage; even though this was not the case. We got along like brother and sister. We had a laugh together and we both told it like it was; no bullshit. Looking back, it was amazing that Jo Bo and I ended up as friends, because our very first ever meeting, was less than pleasant. It was at 8:00 a.m. one morning, when my cabin door flew open and Jo Bo stood in the doorway screaming, "Get out of bed, you little fucker, and get your lazy ass up to rehearsals."

Jo Bo had a way with words and we both laugh about this all the time as I certainly deserved it on this occasion. I had not turned up to an early morning rehearsal, because Jodie and Rachael (dance captain) were acting like total wenches, the night before, so I thought, *fuck 'em, I'm not turning up*. Once Jo Bo learned of what the girls had done (no point in wasting paper going into it here) her and I instantly got on like a house on fire and never had a cross word at each other for the remainder of the contract. We still laugh at that initial meeting to this day.

So back to the current story, Jo Bo and I were getting a little inebriated, when things became a little tense in her cabin. Not tense, as in we were angry at each other, but tense, like there was a sudden chemistry between us. I adored Jo Bo, and I knew she felt the same about me, so for us to take it further, we would both have to have felt right about it, as it might have jeopardized the friendship we had. So, there we were and things were at the point, where something might happen. I wasn't feeling too great though, with all the movement of the ship, so when Jo Bo asked if I wanted to stay the night, I told her that I couldn't.

Jo Bo thought I was flatly knocking her back; which was simply not the case. I mean, she was cute and funny and stylish and basically everything most men would die to have in a woman. She is the type of woman, who would be your lover and best friend; which isn't that common. On any other night, I probably would have jumped at the opportunity, but I was seriously not feeling well. I knew that if I stayed, I'd be spending more time in the bathroom, than her bed, because you really felt the movement in her cabin. I really don't know how the cruise directors live in that cabin when it's rough. It really was hideous. I don't get sea sick, but this cabin was making me feel like absolute crap.

I tried to explain to Jo Bo, that it was only because I was not feeling well that I declined her offer, but she didn't believe me. She got the shits with me that night as she thought I didn't find her attractive. I often wonder what would have happened if Jo Bo and I did sleep together that night, but as soon as the following night came along, I knew that some things are just meant to be and that everything in life happens for reason.

The following day, the weather was much better. We were still heading down to Canada from Greenland, but the seas were much calmer. I met up with Sarah and the comedian on board, for a drink in the bar after his show. Jo Bo mentioned that she was having drinks in her cabin again, so Sarah and I went to Sarah's cabin on the way to Jo Bo's, so Sarah could change quickly, into something more comfortable. Once Sarah was changed, we made our way to Jo Bo's cabin and not more than ten paces along, as we walked side by side down the narrow corridor, our fingers brushed each other. It was like there was an electric field between us. It felt like a really small electric shock, as we touched.

Neither of us said anything, but I know Sarah also felt it. We were at Jo Bo's for a while and I was sat beside Sarah on the lounge, when for no apparent reason, our hands felt like they were drawn together and suddenly we were holding hands. As neither of us was quite sure how this happened, we adjusted the pillow that was resting on our laps, to cover our hands, so that the others couldn't see. We sat there like two school kids for a while, giggling and not quite understanding how we came to be holding hands, when we barely knew each other.

We finally excused ourselves and went to the lido café at around 1:00 a.m. for a coffee. On the way, Sarah said that she wanted to show me this amazing cabin she had until the night before. She had been moved, but still had the key. She wanted to show me how awesome it was. The moment we walked inside the cabin, we were instantly drawn to each other and before we knew it we were caught up in what can only be described as an amazing night of passion. For so many reasons this situation seamed wrong, but at the same time it felt so perfectly right. It only felt wrong, because we had only just met. Despite this, it somehow felt, like we'd known each other for years.

It was so refreshing to meet a woman who was not only talented and beautiful, but who had a similar zest for life, as I did and was actually prepared to put it all on the line, for the chance of finding what most people search their whole lives for; true love. The conversations over the next few days, flowed so effortlessly and everything was so perfectly blissful. We discussed our dreams in all areas of our lives, and they all seemed to somehow fit perfectly together. Even though, it was only a few days, since we had met, I was totally head over heels for her. Within days, we had discussed how we could be together and made plans to work together. Meeting each other, had literally turned our worlds upside down.

The remainder of the week was simply amazing, and we were both buzzing around the ship, like a pair of love sick teenagers. The social host on board, June, described our meeting as being like watching fireworks go off. June actually captured the moment Sarah and I had our first dance together, in a photo. Looking back on that photo, always reminds me of those fireworks, that everyone saw. I said goodbye to Sarah in Quebec a week later, knowing what I wanted, but not sure if it would be possible, or if what I was feeling was truly the real deal. The more distance the ship put between us though, the closer we seemed to get and our connection seemed to be so much stronger for having this distance between us.

The drowsy chaperone.

The cruise continued toward the U.S.A., and the night before we arrived in New York I was standing out on the front of the Promenade deck, looking up at the most amazing night sky. The night sky looked incredible, so I thought that I should ask for some guidance, about my situation with Sarah. I wanted to know if what Sarah and I had, was real so I asked for a "sign." I looked up into the night sky and said, "Give me a clue if this is real." I continued to enjoy the stunning evening as we sailed along, before retiring to my cabin for the evening.

We arrived in New York the following afternoon after the most amazing sail in, that I have ever witnessed. They say that the best "sail ins" around the world, are Sydney in Australia and New York. Having done both, I have to agree. It was spectacular sailing right past the Statue of Liberty and along Manhattan Island. As soon as the ship was cleared by customs, I made my way into Broadway to see a show. I had been planning to see "Jersey Boys" that night, but when I got to the box office, I somehow felt compelled to have a look at what else was showing. I went to the box office for "Mama Mia" and again I was not drawn to see it. I walked down the street a little and saw a flashing sign for "The Drowsy Chaperone," a smaller production right on Times Square. I had heard about this show from Michael, who was a fellow crew member, a few days earlier. He didn't give me much detail about the show, but he said that it was a great show and a "must see," so I took his advice and bought a ticket.

I took my seats and was then moved down to better seats by the usher, before the show started. *Bonus*, I thought, especially seeing as I'd only paid twenty-six dollars for the ticket. The show began, and I instantly got my "sign" that I had asked for. For those of you who have not seen "The Drowsy Chaperone," it's a musical inside a musical, about a famous female Broadway actress who was about to give it all up, to marry a guy, that she met on a cruise ship. Hello! There's my fucking sign. I got chills down my back as I thought about it.

As soon as the show finished, I rang Sarah and told her about the whole "sign" thing and the show. She was as amazed as I was and we were both certain that we had a very exciting future ahead of us. Sarah and I spoke almost every day, and she was planning to come and see me in Southampton when the ship returned a few weeks later. I found myself totally distracted for the rest of the cruise while also being totally inspired both personally and professionally. Having seen Sarah perform so brilliantly on stage, made me realize, that I had become a little complacent and slack in my own performance. From the time she got off the ship, I found myself much more dedicated to my performance and also to perfecting my craft. I had so much more energy on stage, and I was trying new things and felt like I had lifted my game to the next level.

Big band time.

I had an amazing opportunity coming up, to work with my first big band and I was totally pumped for it. My cabaret show consisted of all the classic swing hits from Frank Sinatra, Dean Martin, Bobby Darin, etc., so to do this kind of show with a big band, was really where it was at. We had a group of older jazz musicians board the ship in New York, for the return trip across the Atlantic. These guys would be in addition to our six-piece band that we had on board. This would make up a fourteen-piece band. To look at these guys, you would be excused for wondering if they could play a note, let alone be as brilliant as they turned out to be. They must have all been at least seventy years old, but let me tell you, I have never worked with a finer bunch of musicians, in my life.

I'll get to the show in a minute, but I have to say that I'm so glad I didn't do any research on any of them before the show, because if I did, I would not have been able to perform, for being in awe of not only their ability, but also their experience and impressive resumes. I did a search on Google for all of them after the show and what I discovered was mind blowing. They had all worked with the likes of Frank Sinatra, Dean Martin, Sammy Davis Jr., Liza Minnelli, Ella Fitzgerald, Tony Bennett, and Tom Jones; just to name a few.

The lineup I had for this show would be the sort of line up that a singer, of any calibre would dream about. Needless to say, I was blown away by them, both on and off stage. For those of you who know jazz and are familiar with some old names of the UK scene, I had Tony Fisher playing lead trumpet, Duncan Lemont playing lead tenor sax (the same as he did on Frank Sinatra's "One for my baby" single), Bill Geldard on lead trombone, Colin Bryant on tenor, clarinet virtuoso Kenny Martyn and Roy Willox on Alto sax. Add to this line up Brian Dee who was Michael Parkinson's Musical Director and the resident band and you've got one hell of a line up.

We all arrived at the rehearsal in the afternoon and as soon as the band let fly with the opening four bars, both Jo Bo and I knew, that this was going to be special night. The ship had never had such a big band on board, so the difference in sound, was incredible. We've yet to confirm this one hundred percent, but it is believed that this was the first ever big band on any cruise ship, so therefore, with me being the first artist to use the band on this particular cruise, then I would be the first artist to work with a big band on a cruise ship, anywhere in the world. This had me feeling extremely proud, not to mention very thankful, for the flood several weeks earlier, that led to me having big band sheet music and thus the opportunity to do this. See how everything in life happens for a reason?

C. R. U. I. S. E

From those first four bars of rehearsals, I felt that I had bitten off more than I could chew, with this massive lineup. It really was such a different "animal" (as Kenny Martin said), going from a six-piece band, to a fourteen-piece band. It is such a huge difference in sound, feel, and dynamic. Thankfully, with the calibre of musicians behind me, they instantly took care of any glitches that were in the sheet music or arrangements, which allowed me to concentrate solely on singing.

These guys were so amazing to watch. They all knew their role and were all able to direct or sit back if needed. They all did so, with such precision, that everything fell totally into place and allowed my nerves to disappear. Showtime came that night and my nerves had found their way back, simply because of the occasion. I was about to perform with the biggest band I had ever worked with, while also working with some of the greatest jazz musicians the UK and the world, had produced. During the rehearsal, I felt a great sense of leadership from all of them. It was like each and every one of them wanted to help me realize a dream. It was like they were "passing the baton" so to speak, to the next generation of performers, who would hopefully carry this genre on for many more years. I wanted to be as brilliant as I knew they would be, so the pressure really was on.

Jo Bo gave me a fantastic introduction and with that, the big band struck up and away we went. It truly was such a special night for everyone in the room. Jo Bo was so proud of me and of this whole event, Kenny Martin was wrapped that he had managed to pull this whole jazz night together and the audience and I thoroughly enjoyed an amazing night of music. The beauty of working with this genre and this caliber of musician, was that I too got to enjoy the show, during the instrumental breaks. I think the audience saw the excitement and energy in me, from the moment I came out on stage, and we all went with it, for the entire forty-five minutes. Roy, the production manager, recorded the show and edited a great promotional DVD for me, which I absolutely love and now use to promote myself all over the world.

Not the Poseidon Adventure.

The remainder of the contract flew, and before I knew it, I was on the gangway in Southampton, leaving the ship, but preparing to fly to Alicante in Spain to join Sarah, who was on board the company's other ship as Headline Act. The interesting thing about my trip to Alicante, was that I had no idea where I was flying to, until I arrived at the airport. Saga Cruises, has mystery cruises, where the passengers book for certain dates, but have no idea, where the ship is sailing to. It's a great concept and one that is very popular with the passengers and crew.

It is very secretive, as to where the ship is going. Only the captain and a select few department heads know, otherwise, word would get out and it would spoil the surprise. When I left Southampton, the cruise I was joining to see Sarah, was a mystery cruise, so the company was not telling me, where they were flying me, in case I let slip to someone, and word got out. I only found out, when I received my boarding pass.

I arrived in Alicante later that afternoon and saw Sarah for the first time in over a month. The moment we saw each other again, we knew we'd made the right decision to be together and to move in together. We had the most amazing week on board, but on our final sea day on board, we were lying in bed at about 8:00 a.m. when the captain made an announcement, that he was closing the Lido Café at the back of the ship, due to rough seas. The captain advised all passengers to go down to the dining room, which was situated in the middle of the ship one deck lower. This was simply so that the elderly passengers could be waited on, rather than having them walking around the buffet in such rough weather.

Not fifteen minutes later, Sarah and I were beginning to go back to sleep, when the ship began to list to the port side. At first, I thought nothing of it, as several waves earlier in the morning, had caused the ship to list in such a way. Before too long though, I realized that this wave was not like the others. The wave came from the ships starboard side aft and caused the ship to continue to list very heavily, for what seemed like an eternity. It may have only been for a matter of twenty seconds, but it certainly felt like much longer, that the ship was listing at somewhere around forty degrees.

Sarah held on tightly to me and was visibly shaken, as the plant on the table and all of the contents of the side tables and benches in the cabin, slid right off the end and onto the floor. Things were smashing as they hit the floor and this sound, echoed in the corridors outside as well. The ship eventually corrected, but not before the wave had done considerable damage. A few seconds later, the captain made an announcement over the ship's P.A system, asking all crew members to go to the dining room immediately.

Even though I was no longer crew (I was there as Sarah's guest), the sea farer in me, jumped out of bed, got dressed, and felt obliged to assist, in any way I could. Sarah didn't want me to leave, as she was worried that another similar wave may hit the ship while I was gone. I reassured her that everything was alright, before hurrying down to the dining room. Upon arriving in the dining room, I was totally blown away by the destruction that the wave had caused. Anyone seeing this scene would have been excused for thinking that they were on the set of *The Poseidon Adventure* and not in the dining room of an over-fifties cruise ship.

On first impression you would be excused for thinking that there was loss of life, for there were so many people lying motionless on the floor, amongst the mess of overturned tables, broken crockery, and food scraps. One by one, people made their way back to their feet, as the hundreds of crew members began arriving to assist, in both the clean-up and the patching up of passengers. Jo Bo, who had left my old ship and was now contracted to this ship, looked at me and said, "What are you doing here? You're a guest." "I know," I said, "but once a seaman, always a seaman." She smiled, as we continued to clean up the mess. It's an unwritten law with those who are at sea, that no matter what, you always help a fellow sailor. Whether it be on a cruise ship, or a small boat, if someone is in trouble, you jump in and lend a hand.

As we assisted injured passengers off the floor, wheel chairs began arriving to assist any injured passengers down to the medical center on board, so that the doctor could attend to them and their minor injuries. It took almost an hour for the crew to have the dining room back to its original state, and thankfully the weather returned to a more comfortable state shortly afterwards, and we had a more relaxed final day at sea before arriving in Southampton.

A new life.

The following day, Sarah and I drove from Southampton to Harpenden, just north of London, where we would begin our new life together. Her place was a beautiful apartment in a quiet street in such a gorgeous little typical English village. Everything about it, was quaint and romantic. Because it was nearly Christmas time, the main street was lined with the usual Christmas decorations and lights and there was a very friendly, warm feeling about it. One of our first jobs when arriving at Sarah's place was to decorate the apartment for Christmas. Like a couple of ten-year-old kids, we set about making the place look more "Christmassy" than a department store, and let me tell you, we succeeded. Having lived in Australia all my life, I had never had a cold Christmas, so I was very excited at the prospect of this totally different celebration with Sarah and her family.

Sarah was quite busy with gigs during that first week, so I was left to my own devices, as I settled into my new surroundings. Unfortunately, something seemed to happen during the next two weeks, and suddenly, Sarah and I were not as blissfully in love, as we had first thought. Sarah was quite an independent woman, so having someone suddenly in her life, after being single for a while, seemed to unsettle her. Add to this the fact that her ex-boyfriend's belongings were still in her apartment, and he was still quite a big part of her life, and things started to turn a little pear shaped. On a few occasions, I wondered if Sarah had completely moved on from her last relationship, as she had made several comments, that made me wonder, if she still had feelings for her ex.

We ended up in London one night, when Sarah had a work Christmas party to attend; that she said partners were not allowed to go to. I trusted her and instead of sitting at home alone, decided to meet a friend of mine for a drink, while Sarah attended her party. We agreed to meet at 11:00 p.m. out the front of the venue she was at and stay at her friend's place that night.

At 11:00 p.m. (as agreed), I arrived at the venue and sent Sarah a text, to let her know I was downstairs and ready to go. I received a reply from her saying that she was saying goodbye to everyone and would be down in five minutes. The night was bitterly cold, and I think it was possibly the coldest I have ever been in my entire life. After twenty minutes, with no sign of Sarah, I once again removed my warm gloves from my frozen hands and sent her another text. She said she was on her way down and would only be a minute. Another forty-five minutes later, I texted her again, at which point she said that she wouldn't be long. Given that I had been waiting in the bitter cold for more than an hour, I decided to talk to security and see if I could go up and see Sarah quickly.

I managed to convince the security guy that I was not staying, and that I was simply collecting my girlfriend, so he let me in. I made my way upstairs to the function room where Sarah was, and as I opened the door, I saw Sarah with her back to me, talking to a man, who I knew was her ex. I had seen pictures of him, so I knew what he looked like. I guess he knew who I was, too, because as soon as he saw me, his face must have shown enough shock, for Sarah to slowly turn around, with a look of "Oh no" at who might be behind her.

Her ex disappeared to the bar, to allow us to sort things out, but as soon as Sarah opened her mouth, I knew it was over. She was extremely drunk and had an attitude, like that of a commoner and not the well-brought-up girl that Sarah was. She refused to leave and did not seem at all interested in me or us, so given that it was glaringly obvious that she wanted to get back with her ex; I left.

The problem I now faced, was that it was after midnight, all the trains had stopped for the night, and I had no idea how to get back to Sarah's, because we were supposed to be staying at her friend's place. I hailed a taxi and spent the next hour and a half trying to explain where Sarah lived.

Saga Saga Saga

He was a London cab driver, who never ventured outside of the greater London area. During the trek, I called Jo Bo, who was also home off the ship and between us, we somehow directed the driver back to Sarah's place, which was over fifty miles from London. Two hours and £180 later, I was home, but quite distressed about all that had occurred that night.

I really don't quite know what caused this to happen, but perhaps me being unsure of my new environment and looking for work on land, combined with Sarah having unresolved issues with her ex-boyfriend, certainly didn't help. It was disappointing in my opinion that at the first sign of trouble, Sarah threw her hands in the air and gave up on us. I spent the next two days trying to contact Sarah, as she did not come home the following day. When I finally did get a hold of her, she demanded that I return home to Australia.

I've always believed, that everything happens for a reason, and sure enough, within two hours of her telling me to leave, that reason presented itself. That afternoon, I received a job offer on a large cruise ship with Princess Cruises again. I had always wanted to do a large ship, and this was starting rehearsals in only a few weeks.

Within forty-eight hours, I was back home in Australia, soaking up copious amounts of sun and alcohol with family and friends. My dream of a white Christmas was yet again unachievable, but I was now surrounded by loved ones and that was exactly what I needed at that time. I had two weeks at home before I was due to fly out to Florida to start rehearsals, so I made the most of it by catching up with everyone who I had not seen in eight months. The one thing about returning home, that wasn't too pleasant, was the fact that I was returning to my apartment, where Klara and I had lived, even though she was no longer there. By that stage, I had rented it out, but I still wanted to see the apartment, just to get a grip of the fact that Klara was no longer there. The tenant was great, by allowing me to do an inspection and even though it felt weird going back there, I was then able to truly move on.

Where to next?

"Travel - it's the only thing you can buy, that enriches your life."

Looks like we made it (or did we?)

From the time I started working on cruise ships, I had always dreamed of working on one of the huge ships, that look like floating hotels (or as captains of small ships call them, "Ice Bergs"). Some people hate the really large ships, but for an entertainer, they really are where it's at. The theatres on board, are just like the big theatres on land, with all the bells and whistles. They are usually three decks high, with seating on three levels. They have ten-piece orchestras for the shows, and all the moving flies, hydraulic platforms, moving sets, pyrotechnics and even revolving platforms required, to dazzle the audience. Casts onboard the bigger ships are anywhere up to twenty-two people, and they really are spectacular shows to say the least. These days, there are even full-blown Broadway versions of musicals, such as Cats, Hairspray, Grease and Chicago.

So, there I was on the plane, only two weeks after having everything

Where to next?

that I thought was right, come crashing down around me. Instead, I was about to embark on something I had actually dreamed of for years. I really was starting to believe in fate at this stage, but somehow this new-found belief was about to be tested.

I touched down in Florida, a few days after New Year's Day and was met by Eric, the son of the producer. Eric took me to a little motel in Cocoa, Florida, where the cast would be staying, for the duration of rehearsals. Because the company couldn't get me an earlier flight, I was arriving a few days after the other singers. I met Le Michael who was one of the singer/dancers and the following morning, he took me down to the rehearsal studio, which was a five-minute walk away. When we arrived, I met my female lead singer Nicole and also Sarah the female singer/dancer, as well as our musical director, Amy.

We got straight into it by singing through a few of the shows and over the course of the next few days, we had completed all five shows, so far as knowing what parts each of us was singing. This in itself, was different, because, on all of my previous ships, it was just myself and a female singer, who sang live. The rest of the vocals, that the audience heard in the shows, were pre-recorded. Even though I was still the lead, I also had two more voices, to blend and harmonize with, throughout the shows. The singer / dancers, had one or two solo numbers, throughout the shows, while the leads, were changing, but other than that, it was mostly in full-cast numbers, that they sang with us. For the rest of the time, they were hired more for their dance ability, than their singing.

A few days later, the dancers all arrived. They gave the singers a few days head start on the dancers, so that we had a fair knowledge of the songs before we started to add choreography to them. I was thankful, that one of the shows, that we were learning, was "Tribute", which I had performed, on the Pacific Sky, so that released a bit of the pressure, knowing that I only really had to learn four shows.

On first impressions, everyone seemed really nice. Most of the dancers were American with only me and three British dancers, making up the cast of fourteen. It was very exciting being in a bigger cast and also working

C. R. U. I. S. E

with Americans, as I had not done so over my previous five contracts. We spent the first evening getting to know each other and then headed down to the studio for a cast meeting, with the directors and producers. As we were walking to the studio, I started chatting with Tamzin (a British dancer). As we chatted, she mentioned she had worked for the same budget cruise line that my ex, Lauren had worked for, after she caused all sorts of trouble for me and P&O. I told you the cruise industry was a small world.

I mentioned Lauren's name to Tamzin, and her tone automatically changed. At first, I thought, *oh great. What on Earth has Lauren said about me?* But to my surprise, Tamzin actually said she couldn't stand Lauren. They had shared a cabin together, for the entire contract and while they got along at first, Tamzin very quickly disagreed with Lauren's morals. I asked what she meant by this. Tamzin explained, that Lauren was having sex with several guys on board the ship, even though she had a boyfriend back in Scotland. I said, "Was his name Barry?" To which she replied, "Yes." Suddenly, so many things that had bothered me and caused me to feel guilt, over what had happened years ago between Lauren and I, vanished.

I have noticed with ships, that almost everyone who has worked on one, has at one time or another, been unfaithful to their partner back home, or has engaged in random casual sex. The thing I found funny, was how each of these people, including myself, from time to time, were so quick to judge everyone else, despite the fact that they are doing the same thing. You always hear people on ships say, "Oh, I feel so sorry for that person's wife (or husband) who is at home, while they are fucking around with the entire ship." If you were to stereotype this, you might say that the worst culprits, were the Italian officers. They always seem to have a girlfriend or two on board and also a wife back home.

We are all so quick to judge them for their behavior, yet we fail to see the other side of the equation. Now while this might not sit well with everyone's morals, allow me to throw another thought into the mix. While these men (or women) are being unfaithful at sea, how are we to know whether or not, their partner back home is not engaging in sex

Where to next?

with either the pool cleaner, or local butcher or gardener. All while their partner at sea, is sending huge amounts of money home to them, so that these services can be taken care of on their behalf. All while they live this extravagant lifestyle. I'm just saying, that we are all so quick to judge the men and women who work at sea for this kind of behavior, while forgetting that on the other side of the coin, is possibly someone acting in an equally distrusting manner.

Over the course of the next week or so, my new cast and I began to bond, as we slowly worked our way through learning the five production shows. Out of all the casts I had worked with, I found that this one, was the one that I felt most comfortable with. It was certainly a pleasant change from all the issues I had been dealing with from my previous cast with Jo and Sian. There was one particular female dancer who I was getting along well with. Her name was Caitlin and she was twenty-one. She was a little quirky and a little plain looking, but she seemed very sweet; if not a tad peculiar. I was a little concerned that she was very much along the lines of Lauren, Sarah or Jodie, so far as she was still very hung up on her ex-boyfriend. That this seemed to be a trend that I was attracting more frequently.

Despite these thoughts, Caitlin seemed keen and before we knew it we were sneaking around behind the rest of the cast's backs being intimate. We decided to keep things quiet, at least until we got on board the ship, or until we had decided that this was something that was more than just sex. Personally, I was more concerned with her ex constantly calling and texting her at all hours of the morning and her talking about him 24/7. A sign, perhaps; yes. Hindsight would be a wonderful thing, if it was only in foresight.

In front of everyone else, we'd just act like friends, but once everyone had gone to bed, I would go over to Caitlin's room and we'd be together. This arrangement seemed to be working for both of us, until Caitlin's ex started calling and texting even more often and really upsetting her on a daily basis. This obviously put somewhat of a strain on us and subsequently we were beginning to fight.

C.R.U.I.S.E

I suddenly found Caitlin to be very "hot and cold" in regards to us. If I'm being honest I too had a lot of doubts, given the "ex" situation and was probably chopping and changing my mind also. Either way it led to us having a huge argument late one night on the phone; even though we were staying in the same motel. After cooling down from the fight, I thought I'd go over to talk to Caitlin, to at least resolve things, so that we could be friends. I called her room, to ask if I could come over to chat. She said she didn't want to talk, but after a few minutes on the phone, she agreed that I could come over.

I went over to her room, and as I arrived, her roommate Nikki said to me, "Caitlin told you that she didn't want to see you," which I thought was strange, given that I'd just gotten off the phone to her and she had asked me to come over. I told Nikki that it really was none of her business and that it was something that Caitlin and I were going to discuss.

I went to Caitlin's room and we discussed things, and by the end of the discussion, I felt that everything was fine and that we would continue being friends. As I mentioned a moment ago, as far as the cast were concerned nothing was going on with Caitlin and I so as far as they were concerned the situation between Caitlin and I, was that we were friends. They simply thought, that because we were always hanging out together, that it was a one-way situation. Caitlin must have denied that anything was going on with us, when the other girls asked, so they thought that I was just chasing her. They had no idea of the actual truth; and probably still don't. This was fine, and I had no problem with it, until it came back and bit me, harder than I've ever been bitten before.

I had the following morning off from rehearsals and was relaxing by the pool, when I got a call from Dan at the office. He asked if I could come into the studio. I knew that something wasn't right; however, I didn't realize the magnitude of the problem. It seemed that once I had left Caitlin's room the night before, the other girls had gone to see her, to discuss the situation about her and I, and they were all concerned that in their eyes, I was hanging around Caitlin too much and pestering her. If this discussion had taken place any other day, then I'm certain that Caitlin

Where to next?

would have told them not to worry, but given the latest incident, between Caitlin and I, she of course told them that nothing had happened between us and that she didn't want to talk to me anymore.

With that, the other girls took it upon themselves to call the office and say they thought I was harassing Caitlin. The directors sat down with Caitlin to discuss the matter with her and asked her what (if anything) had happened between her and I. Caitlin flatly denied any intimate involvement with me, so given what the other girls had claimed, it appeared to the directors, that I had indeed engaged in unwanted harassment.

The problem the directors had with this, was that they had a similar situation occur recently, on the same ship so they were very cautious in the way they dealt with this current situation. The directors sat down with me and explained the situation, and to my absolute horror, they explained that Caitlin was claiming I had been harassing her. I gave a detailed account of what had really happened between Caitlin and I, including the fact that we had been having sex, every night, for more than two weeks.

In view of my version of events, the directors explained that if this was the case, then there would be no reason for any further discussions to take place and that things would continue as before. I then explained to them that regardless of the outcome of this situation, I would not be socializing with Caitlin in any way, for fear of this type of manipulation happening again.

It seemed that yet again, I had failed to read the signs, so far as letting a woman into my life, who had some serious issues and insecurities. In hindsight, (ten years later), I think it is more of an age thing. I take responsibility, for the fact, that I became involved with younger women, who were less than developed, emotionally. This, more than likely, led to all of the before-mentioned, dramas, over several contracts. Each of them, were aged between nineteen and twenty-one, so I have no doubt that this was the case.

The directors went and spoke to Caitlin and explained to her that my job was actually on the line, if what she was saying was correct, and that they would have to find a replacement singer, with only two days left, before the cast was due to join the ship. They informed Caitlin of my version of events and asked her once again to be totally honest with them. I think at this time, Caitlin basically shit herself and thought that if she was to admit the truth at this point, that it would be her job that would be on the line, instead of mine. Caitlyn once again, denied that anything sexual had happened between us.

When the directors returned, I was once again stunned to learn that Caitlin was still denying that anything had happened between us. As none of the cast was aware of it, I was not able to prove in any way, that anything had actually happened. The only way, was for DNA testing to be done on Caitlin's sheets, which would still have my DNA on them from, the night before last, when we last had sex. I know this sounds kind of sick, but hey, it was the only proof there was, other than mine or Caitlin's word (which at this point was hers against mine). Unfortunately, the directors were unwilling to pursue that avenue and decided to send me home.

To this day, I didn't say a bad word to any of the cast as I left. I simply went back to the motel, packed my things, and went to the airport, knowing that once again "everything was exactly how it should be." Unless the cast ever reads this, they will never know the truth behind this matter, and to be honest, that doesn't really bother me too much. I know I conducted myself in a proper manner, and I can hold my head high, knowing that I did the right thing. Caitlin, on the other hand, has something called karma coming her way, no doubt.

At that point, I was quite surprised that I wasn't totally livid and ready to take legal action against Caitlin or the company, for unfair dismissal. I rang Claudia, who lived in Florida, and explained the situation to her. She was angrier than I was and was convinced that I should take legal action against both Caitlin for defamation and also the entertainment company, for wrongful dismissal. Claudia was advising me of my legal rights and even giving me contacts of lawyers who specialized in this type of law. For some reason, I felt that I did not need to fight this outcome, but rather accept, that the good Lord wanted me somewhere else, and hence the reason for this occurring.

Where to next?

Not a failure but rather a lesson learned.

When I landed back home, I had to re-look at what I was going to do for the next six months. I had no contract lined up, because I had told the other cruise lines that I was unavailable for six months. This meant that it would be at least a few months, before another contract would come up. Within a few months though, I was offered another contract with Saga Cruises. It was on the same ship as the previous year, but with a different cast and a few different shows. I arrived on board a few weeks later and slotted into an existing cast.

The male singer that took over from me, had extended beyond the dates of the rest of the cast, so he was the only one leaving, at that time. It was a totally new challenge, coming into a cast that were already established and quite close. I have to say, that they didn't exactly welcome me with open arms, but I was not too fussed by this. I had a goal to start writing this book and also finish writing the movie script, that I was working on during that contract as well.

Part of the problem with the cast not accepting me at first, was that one of the female dancers, was screwing the previous male singer, even though he had a girlfriend on land. His onboard fling, Pam, instantly took a disliking to me, for taking away her "bed buddy." The other reason for them not accepting me at first, may have been that I had not let them in; just as they had not let me in. By that I mean, that I'm not one of these performers who needs to constantly be around people. In my younger years, I always had to be surrounded by people and with people, otherwise I would feel lonely or lost. These days, I love my own company and more often than not, prefer to sit alone or do things on my own, because my life has always been in the spotlight. Even though I love being around people, sometimes, it's nice to just be by yourself.

Eventually though, something clicked, and for the most part, the cast and I had an amazing contract together. It all happened on my birthday, when they kind of had to be nice to me and I relaxed and showed them my true personality. We had a great night and I was very thankful for the

C.R.U.I.S.E

time we had, as well as the love they showed me. Birthdays on board can be kind of sad sometimes, but just like Christmas onboard, your "surrogate family" fills the void left by loved ones back home.

We had a great time on my birthday and ever since that night, we seemed to get along better than any cast I had worked with, in seven contracts at sea. When you are in a cast at sea, you really do have to love each other like brothers and sisters, because they are all you have. We agree and disagree, love and loath each other, but I can honestly say that I always respected their opinion and appreciated their different (or same) points of view. I seriously lost count of all the times that we got totally pissed and stumbled back to our cabins, banging against the walls and falling flat on our faces or tumbling down stairs like ragdolls.

I remember so fondly, the night we were in New York, on the same Jazz Cruise, that I had been on the year before. I was out on the town in New York and was on my way home at about three in the morning. I had been to Hooters for dinner, various sports bars and I was coming out of Larry Flint's Hustler strip club, when I heard a car horn honking and two girls screaming out the window.

I was about to yell out, "Shut up you drunk bitches," when I realized that it was two of my cast members; Krystal and Nikki. I looked at them as their taxi pulled up and said, "shut up you drunk bitches," anyway. They opened the taxi door and told me to get in. We drove back to the ship and as we got out of the cab, Krystal, fell over on the pavement. I helped her back up, only for her to fall over as she took her next step.

Even though it was our night off, we weren't supposed to be too drunk. Crew are allowed to have a few drinks, but it is expected, that if there is an emergency, then you would still be able to conduct your duties, so far as mustering passengers, or anything else. Krystal, was not able to walk, let alone, perform any duty, so Nikki and I put our arms around her, like we were all being overly affectionate, walking back to the ship.

We managed to get through the terminal and as we approached the gangway, leading onto the ship, I said to Krystal, "you have twenty steps to take, to get past security, then we're good". We walked onto the ship and

Where to next?

past the security guard standing at the entrance, before heading for the nearest staircase, to head down to our cabins. As we took one step down, I lost my grip on Krystal and she went tumbling down the flight of stairs, ending up in a ball, up against the partition wall.

As Nikki and I ran down to help, Krystal began laughing, so we knew she was ok. We thought that the noise, might have alerted the security guard, so I quickly picked Krystal up and carried her down the stairs. As we got to the bottom of the three flights of stairs, I had to negotiate narrow corridors, to get to their cabin. Each step that I took down the corridor, led to either Krystal's head of feet banging against the adjacent walls. We got to their cabin, Nikki opened the door and I fall forward with Krystal, onto her bed.

The following morning, I went around to see how the girls were. As I walked into their cabin, I saw Krystal lying in bed, looking worse for wear. I asked her how she was feeling. She said, "I feel ok, except I've got a really bad headache, and bruises all over my head and body." Nikki and I laughed, as we remembered the events of the night before.

The girls in that cast, (Nikki, Krystal, Helena, Victoria and Pam), used to call me "Dirty Daddy" because I was ten years older than most of them and was always making dirty or cheeky remarks either to them or with them. Even though we had such a close bond, I was not in any way intimate with any of them. I'd dare say, that they wouldn't be interested, but even if they were, I think I had finally learnt my lesson, with shagging cast members; after Lauren, Charlotte, Kara, Gemma, Jodie and Caitlin.

The girls would put shit on me, at any opportunity and I would do the same, but rest assured, that when any of them were hungry, they'd come running to "Dirty Daddy", because I could order free room service at any time. Only the two singers had this privilege, so I was their best friend, when they were hungry at two in the morning. I only had one rule in doing this for them and that was, that they had to bring £2 as a tip for the crew member who delivered it.

I always tipped the crew £2, every single time they delivered something, no matter how small it was. They were always so happy to receive this and never once denied me any request that I had. Throughout my time at sea, I always treated the crew with respect; which was more than some entertainers or other officers did. Because of this, for the duration of my time at sea, I was always treated like a king, whether it be by getting extra prawns on the buffet, or being given a brand-new mattress, or having my cabin renovated.

It's amazing how far being polite and respectful can get you in life. On a few contracts I had female singers who were rude, arrogant and just nasty to crew, talking down to them and basically treating the crew like shit. Subsequently, they never got jack shit from the crew, while I got whatever I wanted and this pissed the female singers off no end. All they had to do was to be nice and show respect and they too could get whatever they wanted. My mother's motto in life was, "Do unto others, as you would have them do unto you."

As for Nikki, Victoria, Helena and Krystal, I miss them more than any other dancers and have so many fond memories of that contract. On the day I said goodbye to them I was truly devastated about possibly never seeing those four girls again. They had become such a huge part of my life, and although we got off to the roughest of starts, we ended up being the closest I had felt with any cast. This is not discounting Carola (my female singer) or Catalin and Pam (the adagio dancers) but these four girls, really were special to me.

I walked off the ship, that cold November day, in Southampton, with no idea where I was going next. For the first time in eight years, I had no idea if I would return to ships, nor did I have anything lined up. I was at the top of my game so far as my performances and I was certainly sort after in the industry, but for some reason, the only thing I was focused on, was going home.

My new life (after ships – well kind of)

Once I returned home and had decided that I wanted to settle down, away from ships, I was faced with the unenviable task, of finding a way to make

Where to next?

money. I had money saved, but only enough to last a few months. I didn't waste my money at sea, nor did I sit in my cabin all contract. I explored the ports of call that I visited and I saw so much of the world; without pissing all of my money away. So, with that, I knew I had to find some sort of work within a few months, in order to survive. Besides, if I was going to settle down and meet someone, I had to have a job, or no one would date me; well not the type of women I desired anyway.

Having been paid huge amounts of money, for very little work on board ships, I was hesitant to take just any job. I could have done a few gigs on land, but let's face it, after you've been paid up to $1,000 per hour of work, to be paid $300 for 4-5 hours singing in front of fifty diners in a restaurant, or a dozen drunk patrons in a pub, just doesn't cut it. The music scene on the Gold Coast isn't exactly very good, so the few entertainers who do work here, work very hard, for very little reward. I am not saying that I was above this kind of work, but …. Ok, that's exactly what I am saying.

I sat down and thought about what I loved to do and what I was skilled at. I did not want to go back to the hospitality industry and singing in pubs wasn't an option. Then I realized, that I loved to travel and with over four-hundred destinations under my belt, I thought I'd be able to sell travel. After all, when you book a holiday, don't you want an expert to help you, who has been there? Well, I could certainly tick off a few destinations, so I began enquiring as to how I could make this transition.

I rang a few travel companies, but the first question each of them asked was, "Do you have experience as a travel agent, or any travel qualifications." As an entertainer, I am used to selling myself, so of course I tried to duck the main question, by explaining that I had visited over four-hundred places around the world. While each company was polite, they advised me that I would need to get qualifications, such as a diploma or degree, to get a job as a travel agent.

One lady did say however, that with my travel experience, Flight Centre (Australia's largest travel agency brand), may be willing to train me. I immediately searched for how to apply with Flight Centre. I re-wrote my resume and included on the final page, a list of every single destination, that I had been to.

A couple of days later, to my surprise, I received a call from the human resources department at Flight Centre. The lady chuckled as she explained to me that never in her nine years working for the company, had anyone A): been to so many places or B): included them in their resume. She was so impressed that she thought I would be worth an interview. Long story short, I got the job and after three intensive weeks of training, I was assigned to open a brand-new store.

The day before our store was to open, Flight Centre had one of their massive travel expos. Our small team of four, went along to drum up business for our new store. As I walked into the expo hall, with my boss and team, a tall lady briskly walked over and said, "you must be the 'cruise-boy' I have heard about." Good news travels fast, I thought to myself. "Um I guess," I said. She introduced herself as Joelle and explained that she was the national manager for the company's cruise brand. She had read about my experience at sea and said that she wanted me in the cruise brand, within six months,

Her plans almost came true, as I moved over to the brand as assistant manager within twelve months in the company.

Throughout the seven years, after leaving ships, I was a very successful consultant, selling over $3 Million in travel every year. This was certainly not because of my brilliant skills with computers and the seriously difficult systems that travel agents use. It was simply a case of my "no bullshit" honest approach to selling holidays and cruises. I was known in the company as someone who told a lot of stories when talking to clients. While many sales people train others to tell stories to create sales, I stumbled upon this method through my love of travel and relaying my excitement of the destinations, that the clients were about to travel to.

It seems that I painted such vivid pictures, that my clients felt compelled to book and experience these feelings themselves. This is the thing about travel, it's the only thing you can buy that enriches your life. I know firsthand that this really is the case. As I look at my office desk, I see

Where to next?

twenty-five photo albums, each with two-hundred photos from all over the world in them.

Yes, I am one of these people who still print photos. This is for two reasons. Firstly, I have had computers and hard drives crash, where I lost everything, so as well as having a digital back up of all my photos, I also keep hard copies. Secondly, it's nice to pick an album now and then and flick through the pages. It is also easier, if you have friends over to look at various albums, rather than crowd around a computer, or a mobile device, to see pictures.

Pictures and memories are why people travel. As a consultant, I was very good at painting pictures, so that clients could imagine themselves on that beach, or ship. As many people say, when you love what you do, you will more than likely do it very well. I love to travel and I love to assist others to travel. I may not sell travel directly these days, but I still inspire others to travel, whether it be through my stories, books or training travel agents, to sell better to their clients.

One of the perks of working in the travel industry is the travel benefits. Unfortunately, the days of plentiful free travel for agents is long gone, but none the less, there are still opportunities. One common myth is that travel agents get free travel. In the old days, yes, but not anymore. Travel agents save a lot on travel because they know when to book and they see what's on special every day, through marketing information that is sent to them. As a whole though, free travel is rare.

One thing that still exists to some extent, are travel agent famils. A famil is simply short for "familiarization". This is where a company such as APT river cruising or Rocky Mountaineer, choose a select group of agents and take them on an all-expenses paid trip, so that the agents can experience the product firsthand. Remember what I said about painting pictures? Well this is what the supplier is doing. They know that once the agent returns home with an incredible experience and the excitement of the trip, they will be much better equipped to sell the product.

The way the agents are usually chosen, comes down to their sales record with that particluar product. The top ten or twenty consultants get first choice. If they decline, it is offered to the next ones in order. In most cases, even though the main portion of the trip is paid for by the supplier, the agent is sometimes left to pay for flights or pay a set fee to attend. My company that I moved to after starting in the industry, had a budget for famils, so any time we were offered one, the manager would allocate funds to pick up any additional costs, so that the trip was completely free for us. I was fortunate during my time there, to be offered three incredible famils.

The first was to Oman, in the middle east. While this wasn't on my bucket list of destinations and to be honest, I had not actually heard of it, before being offered the spot, I must say that it is one of the most incredible destinations in the world. The scenery is spectacular, the culture is amazing and the people are so beautiful. Forget any preconceived stereotypes or thoughts about Oman or the middle-east, it is such an awesome place and one that I highly recommend.

My second famil, was on the APT river cruise from Amsterdam to Budapest. As I mentioned earlier, there is a misconception that river cruising is for old people. While this may be partly true, the demographic and the type of passengers on board, is far from old. This "all-inclusive" style of travel is so stress-free and the scenery along the entire trip is breathtaking. While the ships are small and have minimal facilities, compared to ocean liners, the fact you're tripping around every day, makes up for it. I honestly didn't spend a single dollar (other than on cheap souvenirs) on the entire journey. A river cruise is more of a cultural experience than most ocean cruises, so I highly recommend trying it at least once in your life.

My final famil, was probably my favourite and is on most people's bucket lists. It was to Canada to experience the Rocky Mountaineer rail journey. The Rocky Mountaineer is usually an ad-on for most people when they do an Alaskan cruise itinerary. You may be thinking, "Why would anyone want to sit on a train for two full days." Well as anyone who has experienced it will profess, it is an incredible experience. I must add here, that it you are going to spend the money to do the journey, then please, spend the extra and do it in "gold-leaf" class.

The carriages in Gold-leaf, have completely glass roofs, enabling you

Where to next?

to see the sheer magnitude of the Rocky Mountains as you travel along. The seats are more luxurious and you also have a separate dining area on board to, enjoy upgraded meals. Oh, and they ply you with as much free alcohol as you like too. Yes, it costs more than Red-leaf, but like I said, travel is the one thing you can buy, that enriches your life, so why not take home extraordinary memories and not just good ones?

To say that the scenery onboard the Rocky Mountaineer was breathtaking, is an understatement. Everywhere you look is stunning.

A Couple of Random Stories

Celebrations at sea.

Being away from friends and loved ones for months at a time, can be hard, but as I have said, your fellow crew members, and in particular, cast members, become like your family. Captain Rivera from the Pacific Sky used to always refer to the ship as "your home away from home" and it was true. The ship was your home and the crew became your family members. Just like family, you may fight, but they usually had your back as well.

During my time at sea, I happened to be on board for three birthdays. While it was hard being away from family, my cast mates mate me feel special, as was the case with every cast member on their birthday. There would be the usual birthday cake, prepared by the galley, some presents and more often than not, a lot of drinking.

After my first two birthdays on ships, I was beginning to think that I should not celebrate them anymore, because they had both lead to complete chaos. On my very first contract, we had a few sneaky drinks for my birthday (because it was a dry ship), and all was well, until one of the new cast members Tim, had a little too much to drink.

A Couple of Random Stories

After we had all finished drinking and had trotted off to bed, Tim was clearly not ready for bed and was in fact very hungry. He found himself in the crew mess in search of some food at three o'clock in the morning. After hours, there really wasn't must food to be found in the crew mess, other than a few slices of stale bread and a couple of small tubs of yoghurt.

Now, Tim was a pretty well-mannered young guy and certainly not aggressive, but according to the security report handed to the Captain later that morning, Tim was last seen standing on top of one of the tables in the crew mess, yelling at the top of his voice, while throwing tubs of yoghurt all around the crew mess as well as pouring them all over himself.

While the above actions may not have been a dismissible offence, the fact that he blew well over the allowable limit of alcohol; which was zero, was grounds for dismissal. Unfortunately, this meant that Tim was disembarked later that day and we were one cast member down until a replacement could be found. Thankfully, Keiron who had only recently gone home, was available and slotted back into the shows within a week.

My next birthday at sea, was on the Tahitian Princess a few years later. I'd like to say that myself and my fellow cast members were more mature that time around, but the record books suggest otherwise. We had spent the night drinking in the crew bar and in town in Papeete, then proceeded to one of the dancer's cabins to continue drinking and partying. Because we all lived in cabins which were in passenger areas, security came knocking, after a passenger had made a complaint about the excessive noise.

This was no big deal, but we needed to tone things down a little. Myself and Dan, the cocktail pianist, thought it would be a great idea to go down to the promenade deck and climb up to the fast rescue craft to retrieve the "man overboard dummy" which was located inside the fast rescue craft.

To give you an idea, this dummy was the same height and weight as an average person. It was made from pillow stuffing and material and was used to simulate water rescues during crew training. Somehow the dummy was soaking wet, so carrying it was actually quite difficult. Dan and I managed to get it down from the rescue craft, though the passenger areas and up a flight of stairs to the dancer's cabin.

C.R.U.I.S.E

All hell broke loose when everyone saw what we had brought back and Dan and I were as proud as a domestic cat, bringing its owner a dead mouse. We messed around with the soaking wet dummy, before returning it to its place of origin. Soon after, everyone dispersed and went to bed; or so we thought.

Apparently, Josh and Ashley (dancers), both went looking for more to drink. They managed to find someone in crew areas with alcohol and preceded to drink there until god knows what time. At the time, Sheldon and Ashley were sharing a cabin and Sheldon had gone to bed, like the rest of us, at a relatively normal hour.

A few hours later, however, according to Sheldon, Ashley returned to the cabin, stinking of alcohol and cigarette smoke. Ashley slumped into bed and remained there, passed out for a few minutes. A short while later, Ashley got up out of bed, walked over to the cabinet below the television, opened the door and began pissing in the cupboard. While this was disturbing in itself, what was even more upsetting for Sheldon, was that this cupboard was where all of his clothes and uniforms were neatly folded and stored.

Sheldon sat bolt upright in his bed, realizing what Ashley was doing and shouted, "Ash, what the fuck are you doing?" Ashley grunted, zipped up his pants and fell back into his bed, a few feet away. The following morning, Sheldon cleaned up the mess and had his cabin steward take his clothes away for my cleaned.

At three o'clock in the afternoon, after several attempts to contact Ashley in his cabin and after Ashley had missed two of his duties earlier in the day, Chris the cruise director, went to Ash's cabin with security to check on him. As they entered the cabin, Ashley was still passed out in bed. Chris woke Ash up and after trying to conduct a semi-coherent conversation with Ash, Security breathalyzed him. At three the following afternoon, you would have thought that most of the alcohol would have been out of Ash's system; but no. He was well and truly over the 0.8 level, that was acceptable for crew onboard.

Subsequently, Ashley was disembarked the following day in Papeete

A Couple of Random Stories

and flown home to Australia; at his own expense. Once again, my birthday curse had struck and once again, the cast and I had to re-block shows with one person missing. This time, we had no easy replacement for the long term. Thankfully one of the dancers from the previous cast was able to fly out and fill in for a few weeks, but it still meant more rehearsing to block him into the shows and then more rehearsals when his full-time replacement arrived onboard four weeks later.

Joel, who ended up replacing Ash in the long term was awesome and fitted in really well. He was an awesome dancer and an even better bloke. Even though Joel was gay, you would have sworn he was straight, given his mannerisms. On many occasions, Joel and I would wonder around the ship and he would say to me, "Hey, have a look at the tits on her," or "Wow. She is a milf," to which on each occasion, I would be in shock at his "straight" comments. Joel himself referred to himself as the "straightest gay man alive."

Even though I was beginning to think that my birthdays on board were a curse, I soon realized that disembarkations can happen at any time. On board the Pacific Sky, we had not even started performing for the passengers, when we were faced with a similar situation.

It was what I had referred to previously as "hell week", where we spent the best part of midnight to six o'clock in the morning, while passengers slept, rehearsing and blocking in the new shows. What little time we had free, was usually spent sleeping, so god only knows how the following incident even happened.

It was day eight, of fourteen, during an extended hell week and we were all exhausted so our director, Julie sent us all to bed early; at 2am. Julie could see the exhaustion on our faces and she was growing ever frustrated at the silly errors we were making running the shows, so she decided to send us to bed to rest up, with a view of tackling it hard the following day.

The previous cast had left the ship the day before, so we were all settled into our crew cabins, so the thought of our first night's sleep in our own bed, was attractive. Our first show was in two nights time, so a good sleep was crucial to ensuring that our first show was a success. When the rest of us went to bed, one of the dancers, Eugene, must have been still buzzing from the five red bull drinks, he had consumed earlier in the night. Instead of going to bed, Eugene went up to the nightclub to have a look around.

While in the club, he met a young lady who took a liking to him and proceeded to go back to his cabin with him. Now, while taking a passenger back to a crew cabin on most ships is not allowed, in many instances back in those days, a blind eye was often turned, when it came to this type of indiscretion. In this case, it was not possible to turn such a blind eye.

As it turned out, the young lady had only recently turned eighteen, so her protective parents, were still quite wary of their daughter's actions; and rightly so of course. When their daughter had not returned to their cabin at 4am., her parents contacted the pursers desk and subsequently security, in order to locate their missing daughter. Because the ship is contained at sea, a person can't go missing, unless it is overboard, so within minutes, this seemingly innocent incident, had turned into a full-scale search for the missing girl.

Most passengers had gone to bed, so the ship passenger areas were empty. With this being the case, it was pretty obvious that the girl was not out and about. I remember being woken up with a P.A announcement, which blasted into our crew cabins, not that long after I had finally gotten to sleep. Announcements never go into crew cabins on ships, unless it is a crew drill, or a major emergency.

The Captain asked if anyone had seen this girl and if so, to contact the bridge immediately. At this stage, it was feared that she may have fallen overboard. This event occurred only a few years after Diane Brimble had been found dead in a passenger cabin, so the cruise line was taking all precautions with regards to this matter.

This announcement was repeated a few minutes later, before bridge officers and security staff, went from cabin to cabin, searching every single crew cabin, trying to locate the missing girl. During the cabin searches, they finally discovered the girl, in Eugene's cabin. Security returned the girl to her parents. The parents were grateful that their daughter was fine and while they were very disappointed with her actions, they made it clear to the Captain, that they did not want to see Eugene face serious disciplinary action.

Unfortunately for Eugene, Captain Rivera was very "by the book" and Eugene was sent home a few days later. Once again, there the cast was, one dancer down, before our first show. This time, we were premiering two new shows, so there was no one who knew the shows, apart from our cast. This meant that a new dancer had to learn the shows on his own in Sydney, they fly to join the ship four weeks later, at which time, we start blocking him to the shows again.

Thankfully, this was the last time, myself or any of my casts had to deal with a disembarkation, which I was very thankful for.

That's so not "Disney."

Of the hundreds of cruise ships around the world, four of the most unique, are the Disney ships. Most people in Australia don't even know that the Disney ships exist, but in America they are well known and very popular, especially with families, of course. Now we all know that Disney has a reputation as being a very wholesome and family orientated company and to work for them, you must be of a certain personality. Most people in the entertainment industry joke when someone is over the top, by saying that they are "Disney," meaning that they are very camp or O.T.T (over the top).

There is nothing wrong with this and Disney has built a marvelous reputation throughout the world by having their staff live by those core values that the company created many years ago. You will never find a Disney crew member, on land or at sea, unhappy or anything less than vibrant and enthusiastic while on duty; whether in the public eye or behind the scenes. That is just the Disney culture and that is what makes Disney such a special brand. All of their characters, theme parks and movies typify the pure Disney values.

It is precisely those values, that make this next story even funnier. I have to mention at this point, that I was not at sea on a Disney ship, nor have I met anyone who was on board a Disney ship when this happened, so I have to stress, that even though I have the following information from reliable sources, I cannot confirm or deny that the following events actually did occur. Either way, it is piss funny, if it did happen.

On Disney ships, the Disney characters such as Donald Duck and Mickey Mouse feature heavily in their production shows on board. It was one cruise a few years ago, when a large group of the entertainers on board one of the Disney ships, had a huge party backstage. They all ended up pretty pissed, when one of the performers grabbed the Mickey Mouse suit head and began playing around with it. One by one the drunk entertainers, all grabbed suit heads, from the various Disney characters costumes and put them on. Before too long everyone had character heads on and they were having a harmless laugh, out of sight from any passengers.

A short while after, one of the female cast members, with her character head on, pulled down the pants of one of the male cast members and began masturbating him. This seemed to trigger a chain reaction between all the party goers and before too long, a full-scale orgy had broken out backstage. One smart, or perhaps, not so smart, cast member decided to take photos of this entire escapade. The crew members didn't want to be identified so they all put back on their character heads. So now you had photos of Mickey fucking Pluto, Minney getting fucked from behind, against the wall, by Tigger, Donald taking turns at poking half of the seven dwarfs (I'm sure Sleazy had to be there). Yes, apparently, he was "fucking dopey" as well as "fucking happy" too. All of which while Goofey was fucking Pooh bear in the corner.

This went on for quite a while, and at the end of it all, everyone put the character heads back where they belong and no one knew that anything had occurred. That was until the photos were found by a high-ranking officer and given to the Disney head office.

As you can imagine, they were none too impressed with this kind of behavior, as it certainly did not sit amongst the before mentioned Disney values. The Disney executives wanted to punish all of those who were involved in this incident, however, due to the elaborate costumes, no one could be identified, so Disney sacked the entire entertainment team in one fell swoop. I have to say that I would have loved to seen the looks on the Disney executives faces, when they saw the photos. I would bet that every single one of them would have had quite a chuckle, before dealing with the matter in the way that they did.

Learn to ride the waves

One of the biggest fears, that first time cruisers have, is whether or not they will end up being sea-sick. I too had reservations about this before going to sea, despite having grown up on boats. It's the age-old question of "what makes people sea-sick." I am not a doctor, but even the medical professionals disagree on this one most of the time. From my experience, I am of the opinion, that the sea-sickness is basically caused, when the fluid between our ears, is reacting in a different way, than what the signals are, that our eyes are sending to our brain.

In other words. When you're in an enclosed room, such as a cabin at sea, your eyes are sending the brain signals that the room is not moving. At the same time, the fluid between your ears, is telling your brain conflicting stories, and this is what makes us sea-sick. I know I've kind of dumbed it down, but it's the best way for people to understand, so they then know how to fix it. At the end of the day, most people who are sea-sick, don't care about the science behind it, they just want it to stop.

This imbalance, can be reduced through medication, but the simplest way, from my experience, is to have these signals matching. Throughout my time at sea, I spent a lot of time, sailing through some horrendous conditions. The Bay of Biscay, where I spent my first two years, is notoriously rough, almost every day. I have sailed across the Atlantic four times, and that too is known to always be dreadful. On each occasion that I felt slightly off, while in rough seas, the first thing I would do, was to go out on deck and get fresh air.

The fresh air itself, was good for me, but it was the correlation of me seeing the same thing, as what the fluid between my ears was telling my brain, that alleviated the feeling of being nauseous. One of the hardest

C.R.U.I.S.E

things to do on a cruise ship, is walk, when the seas are rough. When you're on the inside of the ship, walking around, you are never quite sure of the next exact movement that the ship will take. When you're on deck, you can see which way the ship is going to lean, pitch or roll. Your body can then prepare and adjust accordingly. This is surprisingly helpful, if you can feel sea-sickness coming on.

While I would never tell this to someone, who is throwing up over the railing of a ship, sea-sickness, is mostly in the head; both literally and figuratively. The other thing I did notice though, was that when the seas were really rough, the passengers that were managing the best, were the ones who were the most drunk. Perhaps, these two opposing forces of stumbling, counter-balanced each other.

I first started writing this book, on my last contract in 2008. It was during our thirty-day cruise from Southampton to New York and back, when I sat down and began. It was the perfect opportunity, because I had four shows to perform in thirty days, so that gave me twenty-six days off, to focus on it. I locked myself away in my cabin, for days at a time, nutting out the early stages of the book. As we approached New York, the ship was headed for a hurricane, so the captain, decided to change course, so that we didn't sail right into it.

Even though we steered clear of the most dangerous part of the hurricane, we still encountered some pretty hideous sized waves. For the entire day, our small 23,000 tonne ship, battled waves in excess of eight metres. All of the passengers were in bed and all of the ships facilities were closed. No one was in passenger areas and the ship looked like a ghost town. After doing a few hours work on this book, I was getting bored with being in my cabin, so I decided to have a look around, upstairs. I looked on my tv monitor and saw on the ships camera at the front of the ship, that the seas were huge.

I grabbed my camera, my life jacket and a small piece of rope, that I had in my cabin and headed up to the top deck. As I approached the door leading out onto deck, I saw a sign on the door, saying, "no access" and a rope across the door, to prevent passengers from going outside. I paused for a moment, looked around and thought, "fuck it," before opening the door and going outside.

Opening the door in itself, was a task, because the wind was so strong, that the door felt like it was sealed shut. I managed to get it open and once outside, I realized why I wasn't supposed to be there. The wind was howling and the spray from the waves was lashing me, as it deflected off the bow of the ship. I crouched down, out of the wind, long enough to put my life jacket on, then crawled over to the railing. Once at the railing, I tied the rope around the railing, and around myself, ensuring that I was securely attached to the ship; no matter what.

Once secure, I stood and removed the lens cap of my camera. For the next minute or so, I managed to take some photos of the ship ploughing through the huge seas. The sight was incredible and the photos, even more so. Even though, I was dicing with death and possible sacking, for disobeying safety rules, it was one hell of an adrenalin rush.

I made my way back inside and headed to the back of the ship, to a much safer vantage point for photos. I made my way to deck five and out onto the mooring deck, where all of the ropes were stored for when the ship docks. From there, I could see all the way forward, along the side of the ship, as well as out along the horizon and all the way behind the ship too. As I stood there, the waves were so high, that they were rolling past me, well above eye level. This was five decks, up, so they would have been above eight metres still.

As I looked forward to see what was coming, I noticed that an absolute monster of a wave, was headed our way. This wave looked much larger than the already huge waves we were experiencing. My eyes must have lit up like a deer in headlights, as my gut sank. I quickly turned and ran towards the massive winches, that held the large ropes. I grabbed the loose end of one of the ropes and wrapped it around me several times. As I did this, I could feel the ship's bow moving upwards, as it went over the monster wave.

Because of the size of this wave, when the ship finally went over the top of it, the bow then plunged into the trough in between that wave and the next, as the stern of the ship headed upwards, in a way that I had never experienced before. I may have imagined it, but I could have sworn, that I heard the ship's propellers leave the water, for a second or two, as the ship nose-dived into the next wave. The ship shuttered and shook as this happened.

As the ship came back to a more normal (but still unstable) leveling, I unwrapped myself from the rope and scurried inside. I walked along deck five, from the aft to the front, where my cabin was located. As I reached a stairwell, I saw Captain Rentell, coming down the stairs. He stopped and looked at me, not sure of what to make of me wearing my life jacket and carrying a camera and said, "did you get a good photo?" I nodded and asked him, "How big do you think that one was?" "At least twelve metres," he replied. I am pretty sure I looked like I had seen a ghost after that wave.

He laughed at the sight of me, as he went on his way, inspecting the ship, to make sure there were no serious issues. The interesting thing about this, is that because we had not done a show in a few days, and our next show was not for three more days, if something happened to me and I ended up overboard, there is every chance, that no one would have realized for several days.

My cast, knew that I was working on my book and they were used to not seeing me for a few days at a time, so they would not have battered an eyelid, if I was not seen. Only a few hours later, the ship began our approach into New York. By the time, we arrived, the sun was shining and the waves had calmed. It was a stunning arrival and even more stunning turnaround, in such a short amount of time. Talk about it "always being darkest, before the dawn."

Take your medicine orally.

This has to be one of the worst stories I had ever witnessed, during my time on ships. It's a story that I had to include in this book, simply because it would not have happened on land. It was on my second contract on Saga cruises, when we were experiencing quite a few cases of Norovirus on

A Couple of Random Stories

board. Let me explain very quickly what Norovirus is and how it works. Norovirus causes the intestinal flu. People infected with a Norovirus, generally experience stomach cramps, diarrhea, vomiting, and slight fever. Coming into contact with hands or food, that was prepared by hands that are contaminated with molecules of infected stool, can cause outbreaks. Sometimes exposure to raw sewage, may also cause outbreaks of Norovirus. Most commonly however, an outbreak begins with a person who is infected preparing food for others, without thoroughly washing the hands.

For example, on a cruise ship, a person who has not washed his hands and then cut fruit for a large fruit salad, could infect a large numbers of people. Incubation for the illness is usually about one to two days. This means that people exposed to Norovirus, get sick quite rapidly after exposure. Norovirus is not a disease that is contained to only cruise ships. You can contract it on land as well, but on land it is more likely to only affect a few people in each case, whereas on a ship, it is much more easily spread.

For example, on a ship, all of the passengers and crew usually use the hand rails when moving around the ship, to keep their balance if the ship is moving about at all. If one of those people has the virus, touches the rail, then the virus can easily be transferred across to the next person who uses the rail. If they then go to the buffet and eat without washing their hands, then they are more than likely going to contract the virus. There are so many other simple ways to do so as well and it is for these reasons that all ships have hand sanitizer in all food areas. Crew are constantly reminding passengers to sanitize their hands before entering eating areas.

Now, on a normal ship, where the average age of passengers might be fifty, this sort of outbreak can usually be contained quite easily, with the right procedures by passengers and crew. However, on this ship, the average age was eighty, so for starters, the passenger's immune systems were not the best, making them more susceptible to such viruses. There have been many cases of Noro on cruise ships and a few highly publicised ones where the ship had to return to port, in order to fix the problem.

In this particular case, once the virus began to spread, it did so very rapidly, so much so, that within forty-eight hours of the first known case on board, more than 140 cases had been reported. With only 580 passengers and 416 crew members on board, this was quite a concern for the captain and the company. The crew worked tirelessly, cleaning, scrubbing, and disinfecting all parts of the ship, both day and night, in an attempt to get the situation under control. Although the number of outbreaks was not increasing, it was not decreasing either. When the ship returned to Southampton, all of the cabins, corridors and internal spaces on board were heavily fumigated.

The ship headed off on the very next cruise and once again, things began to flare up. What appeared to happen, was that while all of the infected passengers left the ship and the ship was fumigated, a few infected crew members were still on board. This meant, that the virus had not been completely contained. Again, on the next cruise, the number of people infected reached 100 and there were real concerns that the ship would have to return to port, earlier than expected, so that something major could be done to ensure that the problem didn't continue.

It was a beautiful day in Rome and one of our cruise staff, Adam, was on tour with a group of passengers for the day. Quite often crew are requested to go on tour and escort the group around with the local tour guides. The crew member acts as a familiar face, or ship's representative, should anything arise on the tour. The tour went reasonably well, apart from one passenger complaining of a fever and diarrhea. The group arrived back at the ship, at which time Adam informed the ship of the passenger's illness and the ships nurses came to the gangway to assist the passenger and put him into quarantine, until he was better.

The passenger in question, was around about the age of ninety and was not the fittest gentleman either. He struggled to walk at the best of times (as did most of our passengers actually) so Adam was assisting the man up the gangway. On the way up the very short gangway, the man tripped and fell forward onto his hands. As he did, he must have exerted too much energy and actually shit himself, while falling forward. Now while this gentleman was more than likely very embarrassed, I think that Adam was even more embarrassed, as he was directly behind the gentleman. When the passenger crapped himself, some parts of the passenger's "movement" flew from his short shorts and one small particular particle made its way into Adam's mouth.

I really have no idea, how on Earth this could have happened, but to be honest, after hearing this story from Adam, I was not going to ask, as I was already feeling sick myself. Everyone present, was stunned by this occurrence and straight away, the nurses assisted the man to the medical center and took Adam to his cabin, where he was quarantined for forty-eight hours, as a precaution.

As it turned out, Adam did contract the virus and was stuck in his cabin for four days, while he recovered. Talk about taking one for the team! The cruise finished a few days later and when the ship arrived in Southampton, a massive swat team from England, came on board to try to sort the problem of the virus still being on board. Every single pillow, mattress, sheet, and towel on board, was thrown out and new ones were brought on. Every cabin and public area, had its carpet cleaned, walls wiped and was fumigated. Every book in the library was wiped with disinfectant or removed and every single part of the ship was totally fumigated, so that a repeat of this would not occur.

That particular day, was the day that I disembarked the ship, so I am not too sure if this procedure actually worked, but I did chat to a few crew that were still on board, a few weeks later and they said that there didn't seem to be any more problems so it must have. Adam on the other hand has never recovered from this incident or lived it down with the crew.

Polynesian traditions.

One of the nicest things about cruising, is how you get to experience different cultures. In Tahiti, I was able to see and experience their culture on a daily basis, for six months. As I mentioned earlier, the way they do things is very different to us. One tradition that many people adopt from Polynesia is the wearing of a flower on your hair, or ear. This happens, all around the world, but may people don't know the meaning behind this tradition.

C.R.U.I.S.E

Whenever I see a lady wearing a flower in her hair, I ask her if she knows the meaning of where she is wearing it. Each placement of the flower, gives a different signal to the opposite sex. Of course, many years ago, Polynesians didn't have rings, so this was the way to communicate, whether, or not, you were married or single.

According to Polynesian tradition, if the flower is worn above the left ear, that means that you are in love, or married. The reason for this, is simple. The left ear, is closest to the heart. If a Polynesian woman was wearing a flower in her left ear, then men would know that they could not approach her, as such, because she was taken.

If a woman wears the flower in her right ear, that means that she is single. A man noticing this, could talk to her in the interests of becoming her partner as such. If on the other hand, the woman wears the flower at the back, in the middle, this indicates, that she is taken, but still up for fun; if you know what I mean.

The other interesting tradition that I learnt in Tahiti was that it is tradition, that if there is no girl born into a family, then the first-born male, must assume the role of the woman of the house. This means that he does all of the cooking, cleaning and duties, that would have been considered normal for a woman in those days. I only found this out, after seeing many men in Tahiti wearing dresses. This was well before cross-dressing, or transgender people were seen in mainstream, so I was curious as to why the men wore dresses.

I asked a local and they explained this tradition to me. The male was still a man, but as the first-born, he assumed the role of the female, which included wearing the dress. If you go back far enough, it was also tradition, that the first-born male would be sacrificed to the Gods. I am not sure about you, but if I was born a boy in Tahiti, in the old days, I would be praying for a sister.

A Couple of Random Stories

Piano! What piano?

One great story that I witnessed on board ships, involved a group of drunken entertainers. It was late one night and the piano bar had long closed, but a half a dozen crew were still drinking at the bar. Everyone was pretty pissed and things were starting to quiet right down, when Ed, the piano player, decided to pick things up a bit. He went back around to the piano and started playing some up-tempo numbers. Before too long, everyone was dancing and singing again. Ed was a great piano player and had a stack of sequences to accompany him.

He programmed his sequencer and started belting out "Shake your tail feather" from The Blues Brothers and as the music kicked in, everyone starting dancing. Three female crew members got up on top of the piano as Ed played and were dancing around full out, when all of a sudden, the ship hit a wave and the three girls and the piano came crashing down onto the floor. Thankfully Ed was standing up while playing at the time, otherwise his legs would have been crushed, as the piano fell. Everyone stood in total shock, starring at the mess of polished wood and keys from the piano, lying on the floor. Ed looked in disbelief for a moment, before kneeling down and continuing to play the song (to everyone's pleasure and amusement). Once the song finished, we all stood around trying to work out what to do and how to explain what happened to the piano.

By that stage, it was about 2:00 a.m. and security was due to do their rounds at any moment, so we either needed to clear out, or try to do something about the wreckage on the floor, that was once a beautiful baby grand piano. Ed came up with the idea to simply get rid of the evidence. At first, his idea was laughed at, but before long, everyone had a piece of the piano and was headed for the back door, which lead out onto the deck. Ed, me, and a few others, grabbed the body of the piano and also headed outside. We struggled with this bloody heavy thing, all the way out to the back deck. We managed to lift it up onto the railing, before letting it drop into the water and sink to the bottom of the Pacific Ocean.

The following morning all of the department heads were asking crew, if they knew what had happened to the piano, but to this day, no one ever knew what happened, because no one who was there, was ever going to let that secret out.

A world of choices.

When people think of cruising, they think of the Love Boat, or your standard cruise ship, that ranges from 25,000 GRT - Gross Registered Tonne (500 passengers) up to 120,000 GRT (2,500 passengers), that sail to the Caribbean or Alaska. These days though, there are so many different sizes of ships, varieties of itineraries, and types of vessels, that are still cruises.

After finishing work on cruise ships, I spent many years as a cruise consultant, selling cruises. During that time, I was lucky enough to travel on different types of cruises, all of which, further fueled my obsession with cruising in general.

Most people think that river cruising is for old people. Let me tell you, while there are passengers, who are older than the "twenty-something" crowd on a Caribbean cruise, the passengers on river cruises, are certainly not old farts. When I sailed from Amsterdam to Budapest, the crowd on board, were in the forties and above, but they were as full of energy, as any cruise ship passengers, I had seen. Every year, the demographic on river cruises, is getting lower and lower, as more people realize the incredible value and unique opportunities, that river cruising offers.

Just like an ocean cruise, more often than not, you wake up in a different port, or country, every day. The difference with river cruising though, is that while you're sailing from one port to the next, you can sit on the deck and watch people go about their daily lives, on the shore, only fifty metres away. It is fascinating to experience the river systems of Europe or Asia in this way. For the most part, river cruising is all-inclusive as well.

On this cruise, our flights were taken care of, as were the transfers. We had exclusive tickets to a stunning private performance by Vienna's best opera singers and musicians and we had our choice of several shore tours each day, in port. I am certainly not saying that I prefer river cruising,

A Couple of Random Stories

over ocean cruising. All I am saying, is, don't discount river cruising, as a must do adventure. If you've sailed to Alaska, The Caribbean, the Baltic and South Pacific, then maybe it's time you tried river cruising.

Another great option, that is different to traditional ocean cruising, is small ship cruising. One example that I truly loved, was the Blue Lagoon Cruises itinerary that I went on. The ship left from Denarau, in Fiji and sailed up into the Yasawa Islands, north of the mainland. I mentioned Nanuya La Lai, in my favourite destinations, earlier in the book. This was one of the stops that we had on the seven-night cruise.

The thing I loved about this cruise, was that the ship was small and cozy, so you got to know every single crew member, very well. The captain of the vessel, also doubled as the nightly entertainment, with his guitar. He also drove the small boats into shore, each day, so it was a very personal experience. The ship carried eighty passengers and each of the ports, were incredible.

We visited remote islands, and visited local villages. We experienced their local cultures, and dined with their families on some nights. Along with my favourite place in the world; Nanuya Lai Lai, we also visited "Naviti Island", which is where Tom Hanks filmed some of Castaway. We spent the day at "Sacred Island", which was so beautiful and so remote. Because there were so few passengers, it felt like I was alone on every island. It was the most relaxing cruise, I have ever had, and one that I recommend very highly.

On the completely opposite end of the scale, there are the new "Oasis Class" ships, that Royal Caribbean have launched in the last decade. The Oasis, Allure, Harmony and Symphony of the seas, have revolutionized the way we cruise. When the Oasis of the seas was launched in December 2009, it broke the mold of how ships were built and what could be done on board. The ship was more than 70,000 GRT larger than the biggest ship previously built and carried 45% more passengers, than ever before.

This was the ship I began describing in the introduction of this book. In the months leading up to my cruise on the Oasis of the seas in December 2017, I struggled to get my head around the concept of a ship that was as large as the Oasis. For me, the largest ship I had ever set foot on, was the Emerald Princess, when I visited my old Cruise Director, Stevie C, for the day, when he and the ship were in Brisbane. This ship was only 113,000 GRT and even though it was a very large ship, it was pretty small, compared to the Oasis class ships, so I was really struggling to grasp what I was about to witness.

The twelve months I spent waiting, from the time I booked, until the day I boarded, initially dragged on, but as the cruise drew closer, time flew, until I was finally waking up in Orlando, the day of the cruise and preparing to board this beautiful lady. In the preceding six months, I had watched the Oasis come into Port Canaveral via webcam, and as I wasn't able to sleep the night before, because of excitement, I once again watched her sail into port. This time though, I was watching her from only an hour away.

I got dressed, packed my bags, checked out of my hotel and drove down to port Canaveral. Along the way, I was still finding it hard to believe that I was about to experience this incredible vessel firsthand. As I drove over a large arching bridge, coming into Port Canaveral, I got my first glimpse of this beautiful ship. "Holy fuck." I said out loud, as I spotted the ship in the distance. "That is fucking huge." I said.

The ship towered over all of the buildings nearby. I drove to the port and dropped my bags off, before walking around to the back of the pier for a closer look. I am quite partial to a substantial ass, but let me say, that the Oasis has the biggest ass I've ever seen. It's a mighty fine-looking ass too, I must add. To give you an idea, most cruise ships have a beam (Width) of around thirty-six metres. The Oasis and her sister ships, have a beam of forty-eight metres. That's as wide as an Olympic swimming pool is long and more than ten metres wider than any other ship in the world. She is also more than three-hundred and sixty metres long, which is the length of three and a half football fields.

To see pictures of this ship, you really can't fathom just how big she is. I mean, for a photographer to fit the entire ship in a picture, they need to be so far back that the actual size of the ship doesn't seem that big. In person

A Couple of Random Stories

though, let me tell you, she is fucking massive. Only when you stand on the pier and look up at this ship, do you fully grasp the sheer size of her.

The concept of "neighbourhoods", ice-skating, hi-diving, flow riders, ziplines and a Central Park with 12,000 live plants, were game changers, when Royal Caribbean designed the Oasis class ships. When building a ship that carries 6,500 passengers and 3,200 crew, the potential for crowding issues, is a real concern. The ship designers came up with a brilliant design of which passenger flow is as smooth as a ship a tenth of her size.

The distinct neighbourhoods that the Oasis class ships have, mean that passengers are dispersed better than any other ship in the world. Throughout the seven days that I spent on board, not once, did I feel like there were any more than one-thousand passengers on board, let alone more than six-thousand.

So, there I was more than seventeen years after first boarding the Pride of Bilbao, sitting in awe of the most incredible cruise ship afloat. I had come full-circle and I was enjoying cruising more than that first day in 2001. I felt like I was twenty-eight again (Or even younger) as I was literally running all over the ship, like a child. I was seriously losing my shit, as I tried to do everything the ship had to offer in under an hour.

The concept that I actually had a full week to do everything didn't dawn on me. Thankfully, I had pre-written a plan as to how I would get around to doing everything on board, so once I settled with a cocktail at the "adults-only" area at the front of the ship, I took a breath and just took in the moment. Besides the flow-riders, ziplines and aqua-theatre I mentioned earlier, the Oasis has a huge area called "Central Park" in the middle of the ship. Because Oasis is eighteen metres wider than any other ship, it is actually hollow almost the entire length of the ship.

By that, I mean that you can stand on the top pool deck, on either side and look down six decks, at balcony cabins and a forested area with more than 12,000 live plants. Personally, this was the highlight of the ship. To come up with this concept, Royal Caribbean had to break all the rules of ship building. Strolling through Central Park at night was incredible. There

C.R.U.I.S.E

are high-end restaurants along the path, bench seats, plants all around and even fake cricket noises, to create even more ambiance.

As you look up, you can see several hundred balcony cabins, of which one was mine, which have this awesome view. The floating bar that starts on deck seven where Central Park is, lowers down, as passengers sip their cocktails, until it arrives two decks below on Promenade deck, which is the main hub for bars and shops. This in itself is an engineering masterpiece, but just one of the many mind-blowing features the Oasis class ships possess. From the massive casino and gym, that is bigger than most on land, to the ice-skating rink and twenty-four glass elevators, there is wonderment everywhere you look.

To give you some background, I had previously booked and paid for this cruise twice in the preceding three years, but due to events mostly beyond my control, I had to cancel both attempts; including one, the day before departure. This was the main reason for my over-excitement and child-like mental state on the day of embarkation. I was not only struggling with the concept of how big this ship was, but also with the realization, that I was actually finally here, experiencing my dream holiday.

The reason for me mentioning this ship and my experience, is simply because I want anyone who reads this book, to experience this cruise ship for themselves. The other reason, is because this ship and its sister ships, are like no other cruise ships anywhere in the world. Forget everything you knew about cruising, when it comes to the Oasis class ships. These ships are in a different stratosphere and have to be experienced, to be believed. I don't care if you hate cruising, prefer small ships, or have cruised all over the world, unless you have cruised on one of these ships, you have missed out on a mind-blowing and life-changing experience.

From 2001 when I first went to sea, until now in early 2018, life has changed and so has the cruise industry. The technological advancements, and the competitive nature of the cruise industry, has meant that the cruise lines have lifted their game, in order to attract new passengers and keep past passengers returning for more. Even though I had sailed more than one-millions miles at sea on cruise ships, the three-thousand miles I sailed onboard the Oasis of the seas, in the western Caribbean, was by far the most incredible.

To be honest, I didn't give a shit about the islands we visited; Haiti, Jamaica and Cozumel. Even though they were all awesome, it was the ship that captivated me the most. Trying to eat in all of the twenty-four restaurants, drink in the eleven bars, watch the Broadway musical, the ice-skating show, aqua theatre show, comedy show and headliner show, plus try the zipline, flow-rider, the four pools and eight hot-tubs, while still finding time for shopping on board, was downright exhausting. If you're sailing with a partner or family, achieving all of this is impossible. I however, was travelling solo, so I did manage to do all of this and still find time to relax. For most, to see everything these ships have to offer, you may want to book two consecutive cruises, or come back for another cruise at a later date. Either way, you must add this fleet of ships to your bucket list of must-do's in life.

Conclusion

"Luck is simply the crossroad, where opportunity meets persistence".

WHEN I FIRST went out to sea in 2001, I had very little idea of what to expect. Back then, I was in my twenties and now I am in my forties. So much has changed in the cruising industry, but one thing that has not changed a bit, is my love of cruising. I went to sea, hoping to find love. As you have witnessed throughout the book, when it came to women, love had eluded me. What I didn't realise though, was that the love that I was searching for, was right in front of me all along. It was there every day, in every port, every sea day and in every single moment that I spent at sea. Cruising, was in fact my first love and the thing that I adore, more than anything in the world.

To this day, seventeen years and more than 1 million miles after I first went to sea and more than thirty years after watching the final episode of the Love boat, I am still as fascinated by cruising as I was all those years ago. Just the sight of a cruise ship in my home port of Brisbane, or footage of a cruise ship on a TV show, sends me into a giddy spin, like that of a child, who just met his childhood hero; such as He-Man.

Conclusion

The industry, the people, the places and the lifestyle had me hooked all those years ago and I am certain that I will continue to be hooked and completely obsessed with all things cruising, until the day I die. I left ships in late 2008, when I was at the top of my game. When I retired, I could have chosen whatever ship I wanted to work on, and I was at the peak of my craft. I was being paid ridiculous amounts of money, to travel the world, doing what I love. So why did I walk away from it? Even now, I am still not sure of the answer myself.

At the time, I had this idea of leaving ships, while I was still young enough to meet and marry the woman of my dreams. I didn't feel like cruise ships were going to provide me with the same opportunities in that regard, as being on land would. The plan was to settle down, have a family and never go back to sea. That was the plan, but like a drug addict, I was not happy, unless I was able to get my fix and in this case, my drug was the ocean and ships. If I knew then, what I know now, I would have stayed at sea, for at least another ten years.

Ever since leaving ships, I have stayed close to the industry. With my 400 destinations, that I had travelled to on ships, I was extremely successful as a cruise consultant, selling $3 million worth of sales every year for seven years. Even though, I was on land and making good money, I was not fulfilled. The only time that I was truly happy, was when I was offered a free cruise through work, or I booked a cruise, as a holiday. During those years, I was able to experience ships as a passenger, but I wasn't sure it was the same. I found myself wandering the ship's corridors, looking into crew areas, wishing I could go exploring. I knew that behind those doors, lay a labyrinth of corridors and alleyways, that held so many secrets and tales, but as a passenger, they were off limits.

Working in the travel industry as a consultant was great, but in order to go cruising, I had to endure working 9-5 in an office, typing on a computer, answering calls, booking flights, and dealing with airlines and other wholesalers. Don't get me wrong, I enjoyed the experience and the perks were great, but the job itself, was a means to an end. The end, was to be at sea. For a while, I owned my own cruise ship agency, that hired entertainers for cruise ships. That was cool and kept me in the loop, but I still wasn't out at sea. My passion was helping people experience cruise ship life, so I still do that, but not for money; for the love of it. Whenever I am on a cruise, I always make friends with the entertainers and share my industry contacts and advice with them, so they can further their careers.

It wasn't until I stated looking outside the usual means of earning money, working for a company, that I discovered what I love, while still remaining close to cruising. I began writing this book as a way to relay my unique journey and to hopefully inspire others to explore the cruise ship industry as a passenger or crew member. I also came up with the crazy idea to turn those acronyms of C.R.U.I.S.E into a funky clothing label. I am currently growing the brand, with a few cheeky variations of this book's title.

They are:

"Can't Rest Until I've snogged Everybody"
"Can't Rest Until I've Shagged Everything"
"Can't Really Understand Italians Speaking English"
"Can't Rest Until I've Sailed Everywhere"

And the kid's version:

"Can't Rest Until I've Smashed Everything"

I realized that these would be a hit, when I saw many people on embarkation day, wearing matching cruise shirts or quirky shirts as a group. I had never thought about creating a label, but the opportunity presented itself, so I took it and ran with it. Along with the book, the clothing label and assisting entertainers to get cruise ship jobs, my other passion is writing. I have always wanted to share the cruise industry with those unaware of its intricacies, so the idea of having a story made into a feature-length film, excites and inspires me.

It's been forty years since the "Love Boat" was on television, so I think the world is ready for a romantic comedy based on a cruise ship. I think

Conclusion

that due to the Love Boat's huge success in the seventies and eighties, most writers and production companies, were hesitant to take on such a project, but now, I think the landscape has changed and hence why I am pursuing this. Keep your eyes and ears open for a hilarious romantic comedy on the silver screen in the near future.

My mission for all of these ventures is very simple. I want to share this incredible world of cruising, with as many people as possible, so that even those who may never get to experience cruise ship life first hand, can understand, experience, and fully appreciate what it's like to live at sea. My vision has always been to "open up" the cruise industry in the same way that the movie "Cocktail" did for bartenders, by explaining in detail all the unbelievable elements, that make it the unique world that it is.

I know that the only way to truly experience this incredible world is by actually being a part of it; however, I do hope that through reading this book or watching the subsequent movies, that you will have a much clearer understanding, of life as a crew member on cruise ships and indeed realize how special and fortunate each and every person who has ever worked on a cruise ship really is.

I've met some fantastic people, dated some amazing women and have experienced pleasures, heartaches and destinations that most people could never imagine. From the moment that I set foot on my first cruise ship, I realized that this was an amazing world and in fact, another totally different world, from that which most of us live. I was certain from day one, that the lifestyle that I was experiencing, living on cruise ships, was one that others on land, did not fully understand. I always felt that someone needed to try to bring the essence of cruising to the rest of the world, by way of a book or even a movie.

This other world, doesn't have mythical creatures of Martians living on it, but rather regular human beings like you and I. Human beings, that rather than living and working in what most would refer to as a "normal life," they choose to explore, not only the world, but themselves, along the way. Travelling the world allows you to experience other cultures, see how other people live and really appreciate what you have in your own country and how lucky you really are. As I've said a few times, "Travel is the only thing you can buy, that enriches your life."

I would like to thank every single person that I have met on board the ships that I have travelled on. Every single one of them, have played an important role, in my life and subsequently, this book. I would like to conclude, by thanking you for allowing me to share this story with you. I hope that by reading this book, you have either been inspired to go and work on a cruise ship, or at the very least, that you go and book a cruise and get a taste of this incredible lifestyle.

Where is my next cruise adventure? Well, now that I've experienced the world's largest cruise ship, later this year (2018), I am off to try the world's most technologically advanced ship; the Ovation if the seas. This is one of Royal Caribbean's "Quantum Class" ships. While they are slightly smaller than the Oasis class ships, they boast some mind-blowing features, never before seen at sea. Things such as bumper cars, indoor skydiving and the "NorthStar" observation tower which has 360 degree views, that rises to 300 feet above sea level, towering over the ship as it sails along. The ship also features the first ever bionic bar, where all of your drinks are made by robots and a wristband that does everything from paying for purchases, to opening your cabin door.

With Norwegian Cruise Line building a ship which will have a 1,000 feet go-cart track on the top deck, who knows what else we will see on cruise ships in the future. After my cruise on Ovation, my only real goals, so far as cruising are, an Alaskan cruise and a 104-day world cruise, on the Queen Mary II. By that stage, who knows. Maybe my obsession with cruising may have waned; although I doubt it.

To conclude, I'd like to leave you with this thought:

Just like the ocean, life can throw you into turmoil in an instant and turn you upside down. It can in one moment, be calm and peaceful and within an instant, seem like the next wave that hits you, will sink you. The biggest similarity though, is that if we can learn to ride the peaks and troughs of life's ocean, while always keeping yourself focused on the land

Conclusion

ahead, then there is total certainty that you will eventually find your destination. It is not the direction of the wind that determines your destiny, but rather the direction of your sails.

It is often said that every single person has a story, or a book in them —Thank you for allowing me to share mine with you.

J. D Moorea

www.ingramcontent.com/pod-product-compliance
Lightning Source LLC
Chambersburg PA
CBHW050629300426
44112CB00012B/1719